Of Virgins and Martyrs

THEMES IN GLOBAL SOCIAL CHANGE

Christopher Chase-Dunn, *Series Editor*

Consulting Editors
Janet Lippman Abu-Lughod
Giovanni Arrighi
Jonathan Friedman
Keith Griffin

OF VIRGINS AND MARTYRS

Women and Sexuality in Global Conflict

DAVID JACOBSON

The Johns Hopkins University Press

Baltimore

© 2013 The Johns Hopkins University Press
All rights reserved. Published 2013
Printed in the United States of America on acid-free paper
2 4 6 8 9 7 5 3 1

The Johns Hopkins University Press
2715 North Charles Street
Baltimore, Maryland 21218-4363
www.press.jhu.edu

Library of Congress Cataloging-in-Publication Data
Jacobson, David, 1959–
Of virgins and martyrs : women and sexuality in global conflict /
David Jacobson.
p. cm. — (Themes in global social change)
Includes bibliographical references and index.
ISBN 978-1-4214-0753-1 (hdbk. : alk. paper) — ISBN 978-1-4214-0754-8
(pbk. : alk. paper) — ISBN 978-1-4214-0828-6 (electronic) — ISBN 1-4214-0753-1
(hdbk. : alk. paper) — ISBN 1-4214-0754-X (pbk. : alk. paper) —
ISBN 1-4214-0828-7 (electronic)
1. Sex role—History. 2. Women—Sexual behavior—History.
3. Women—Identity—History. 4. War and society—History. I. Title.
HQ1075.J34   2013
305.409—dc23
2012013954

A catalog record for this book is available from the British Library.

Special discounts are available for bulk purchases of this book. For more information,
please contact Special Sales at 410-516-6936 or specialsales@press.jhu.edu.

The Johns Hopkins University Press uses environmentally friendly book
materials, including recycled text paper that is composed of at least 30 percent
post-consumer waste, whenever possible.

For my friends, Lori and Gina
my sisters, Ruth and Lisa
my bomme, *Virginia and Emma*
and in memory of my mother, Dina

Plates appear following page 21.

Of Virgins and Martyrs

Introduction

When the HMS *Dolphin*, exploring the South Pacific under the command of Samuel Wallis, came across Tahiti in 1767, the Tahitians had never before seen Europeans. Suspicious of these exotic intruders, they were at first hostile. As the *London Magazine* reported it, the islanders sent two parties by canoe, one with women who distracted the sailors "by exposing their beauties to their view, whilst the men from [their] canoes threw great quantities of stones." A few of the English sailors were hurt, but the Tahitians were soon beaten off after the seamen sent forth volleys of small arms fire. The Tahitians, shocked by this awesome power, were obliged to "retire in great confusion." The islanders then sued for peace, bringing gifts of cloth and food. In time, Tahitian women even made themselves sexually available to the sailors.[1] The encounter with Tahiti has captivated the West ever since.

Women and sex are enduring motifs more generally in war and conflict. The allusions are sometimes romantic but much more often brutal. War itself, tellingly, is often portrayed as an act of sexual violence—as in the Rape of Nanking, where hundreds of thousands of Chinese were brutalized and killed by soldiers of the Imperial Japanese Army in 1937.[2] In present times we are confronted by the seemingly universal constant of rape, in staggering numbers, from the former Yugoslavia to Somalia.[3] But something distinctly different animates the role of women in global conflict today.

Women's place and status in society, the way women dress, and women's sexuality has extraordinary play in the world today, not simply as the ambience and background of violent struggles but as the *casus belli*, an incendiary of the violence itself. Surveys show that women's status and sexuality—as well as sexuality issues in general (for example, gay rights)—are the basis of the widest divisions between the public opinions of the West and the Muslim world more broadly.

If the tendency in the West is toward an expansive and liberal view of women, their role in society, and their sexual freedoms, so is the tendency in the Islamic universe toward a more conservative direction.

Yet if we dig deeper, we find that traditional (and especially tribal) patriarchy, the rule of men—and not Islam as such—tends to be in the mold of vitriolic hostility to women's rights. Islam's relationship to patriarchy is ambivalent except for its embrace by militant Islamists who have projected patriarchal values globally.[4] Islamist patriarchy—a political Islam distinct from the broader Muslim community as such—is a core expression of a deeper global fissure. This is the first global struggle over the nature of the self; and in that struggle, gender and sexuality, so crucial to people's understanding of themselves and their cultures, lie at the very center. A critical issue is "self-possession," or who owns and control's one's body, especially when it comes to women: is it the individual herself or the community, through enforced practices of honor, virginity, veiling, and marriage?

Women are now at the heart of the world's most dangerous quarrel.

The Global Village

Why the role of women is so prominent in this conflict, and what that means for different paths the conflict will take, is the central question of this book. To treat this question as a side issue only compounds the dangers lurking in the underlying rift that divides the West from a significant part of the Muslim world.

Why is the issue of women's sexuality so, literally, inflammatory? Why do the protagonists think in such vastly different ways about the importance of virginity? Why did the West historically shift away from such extreme patriarchy? How does the embrace of the global economy and of global media change the role of women—and what are the political implications?

When we look at specific eruptions of religiously motivated violence, it is as if a tribal culture of honor and patriarchy has been writ global—noticeably, where men's honor is defined through the degrading of women. Terrorists exulted at the promise of female victims—or "slags," slang for promiscuous women—outside the London nightclub they planned to bomb in 2006.[5] Jihadists are captivated by the promise of seventy-two virgins in the afterlife for acts of "martyrdom."

Consider Mohammed Atta, the leader of the attacks on 9/11, who left behind a will, written in 1996. He forbade women to attend his funeral or visit his grave at any time thereafter. "I don't want a pregnant woman . . . to come and say good-bye to me," he wrote, "because I don't approve of it." He also instructed that the person who washed his body "must wear gloves on his hands so he won't touch my genitals."[6]

Atta was following the spirit of Sayyid Qutb, a core ideological figure in modern Islamic fundamentalism, who complained of oversexed American women. One of these women, drunk and semi-naked—so he claimed—tried to seduce him during a boat crossing of the Atlantic when he visited America in 1948. He later told his biographer that her spymasters at Langley had sent her. But, he said, the encounter failed to overcome his resolve to protect his identity as an Egyptian and a Muslim.[7] Qutb later wrote that the

> American girl is well acquainted with her body's seductive capacity. She knows it
> lies in the face, and in expressive eyes, and thirsty lips. She knows seductiveness
> lies in the round breasts, the full buttocks, and in the shapely thighs, sleek legs and
> she shows all this and does not hide it. She knows it lies in clothes: in bright colors
> that awaken primal sensations, and in designs that reveal the temptations of the
> body and in American girls these are sometimes live, screaming temptations! Then
> she adds to all this the fetching laugh, the naked looks, and the bold moves, and
> she does not ignore this for one moment or forget it![8]

We are exposing ourselves to injury if we do not delve into the role of women's status and sexuality in global conflict. Understanding this issue is a critical window into the major challenges of our time. How will parts of immigrant communities that are informed by honor codes be assimilated into Western societies? How can women's rights be promoted when such efforts in severely patriarchal environments have generated repressive responses? Most importantly, can we tease apart what is Islamic from what is distinctive to honor-based societies (which precede Islam by thousands of years)?

By addressing these questions we can reveal the varied expressions of Islam. Many of those expressions are detached from the severe, biblical-like patriarchy with historical roots in the greater Middle East, from Afghanistan and Pakistan to Yemen and Somalia and across North Africa.[9] We may thus be able to find ways of softening the gnawing quarrel between many in the Islamic world and the West.[10]

Sex and Violence

In global conflicts of the past, the combatant parties shared a rough symmetry in their conception of the place of women. The French and the Germans were not far apart on the issue in, say, the nineteenth century, as they battled each other in the Franco-Prussian war. Not so today. Women's status and sexuality are central markers of the conflict itself.

The world's present clash brings women and sexuality to the foreground in a unique way. At heart, it is a struggle over the woman's body represented by two opposing paradigms: *honor* and *interest*. In an honor society, patriarchal and tribal traditions dictate that a woman's body belongs to and serves the community. An interest-based society privileges self-determination, the sovereignty of the individual over her body, and ownership of one's own capital, be it economic, cultural, or social.

Globalization—economically, culturally, and politically—is felt as the swift imposition on honor societies of the interest-based values of the West. It comes with an impressive expansion of options for women. Women are making tremendous strides (given the opportunity) in both education and the job market. Women are catching up and even surpassing men in many parts of the world. This newfound autonomy of women is expressed in areas from marriage (and divorce) to fashion.

What we see in the current turbulence within patriarchal communities is a broader backlash against these cultural violations inflicted by globalization. Interest is trespassing on honor, and honor is resisting with a blunt ferocity. As we will see, this clash between honor and interest inexorably takes on further oppositions that reverberate around the globe: community against self; patriarchy against modernity; tribalism against the nation-state; justice against freedom.

Readers may assume that this clash is an Islamic phenomenon, but it is a broader patriarchal reaction, varying in degrees of severity. As we will discover, however, radical Islamist ideologies tend to be nurtured in tribal patriarchal environments. Furthermore, these Islamist movements build on a backlash that would otherwise be local and familial, and make it ideological and global. Islamist movements have mostly had their origins where tribal patriarchy is well rooted, notably in the greater Middle East.

In contrast, Indonesia, which is the largest Muslim country in the world, though patriarchal, does not share the severity of Middle Eastern tribal patriarchy. Its Islamist movement is mostly rooted in Middle Eastern sources and is proportionately limited in size. Islamist political parties have won far greater support in elections in Arab countries, following the Arab Spring that began in late 2010, than they have in Indonesia.

To demonstrate the dynamics surrounding women's status and sexuality requires different methods and even the development of new tools to reveal underlying trends—something we will do in this book.

Discoveries

With these issues and questions in mind, I ask the reader to join me on not one but four explorations. One involves a journey to a form of society that is essentially biblical in structure yet is pervasive to this day, especially in the Middle East and North Africa. These are honor societies, where gender and sex are the primary social indicators of status, where honor lies in a man's fighting prowess, including the protection of "his" women, and where a woman's honor lies in guarding her chastity before marriage and in begetting children for her husband, should she marry.

A second journey starts in sixteenth-century Western Europe, notably in countries like the Netherlands. Gradually, a women's body became her own property, to be used in capitalist terms, to sell her labor, and to flaunt her erotic beauty. Being able to choose one's marriage partner, to wear artful clothes, and even to divorce—all accompanied this gradual change toward self-determination for women. This moment is, in other words, the genesis of the world most of us now experience.

The third exploration regards a hugely significant aspect of globalization, especially in the last fifty years: namely, that it has, on the whole, advantaged women—economically and even politically. The emergence of global markets, the growing importance of the service sector, and the accompanying diffusion of women's rights—all processes that are part of globalization—have forced many regions to open their economies to women. Women now outpace men in education in many areas of the world. Micro-loans are often limited to women because they have proven to be more reliable than men in repaying them. Even in the United States, the global recession that began in 2008 affected mostly men: No matter their age or education, unemployment rose significantly faster for men than for women.[11]

But as globalization has accelerated in recent decades, breaking across the last bastions of national and local autonomy, it has provoked a nasty and often violent backlash that threatens women across the globe. Globalization creates tensions in patriarchal, honor-based societies where women traditionally have a decidedly inferior status. In patriarchal societies, the gender distinction is the pivot around which many communities are built. Women are often spatially segregated to the home and enter public life only with the accompaniment of men. Cultural practices of gender discrimination cut throughout the human life cycle, from birth to marriage and beyond.

As globalization challenges patriarchal customs—through demand for women in the labor market, the diffusion of women's rights, and the supposedly provocative images of women, for example—men (and even women) resist this felt violation of honor. The violent response is directed internally against women seen to cross the bounds of tradition, and externally at the (real or perceived) Western agents and symbols of globalization. Opposition to women joining the labor market has been most fierce and most effective in the Middle East and in North Africa.

What, then, is our fourth exploration? As markets globalize, diffusing Western images and beliefs, so immigrants expand their footprint in the West, especially in Europe. Among Muslim immigrant communities, only a subsection is Islamist and fundamentalist. But it is a significant part. The status of women has become an important cause of fissure as a consequence. In a palpable sense, Europe is the ground zero of the conflicts regarding patriarchal practices. Here the conflict is not mediated over distant lands—literally mediated, through global media— but is a direct experience of communities living in close proximity.

Travels Abroad

Ghana is a wonderfully vibrant and sensual society, and, as travelers from Western countries often observe, it is literally full of color. Women do much of the work here, especially in the rural areas. They have traditionally been viewed as distinctly unequal to men. That view is changing, however, and there is an increasing awareness of women's rights. One sign of this is the growing rate of divorce, often initiated by women. Women are recognized as a critical force in economic development.

Relations are good across tribal lines and between the Christian majority and the Muslim minority at this time. Ghanaians have an optimism not seen in most of Africa. Civic-minded signs exhort the populace to confront social ills: "Have Fun but Think About AIDS!" or "Control Your Lust—HIV-AIDS." One billboard in particular catches the traveler's eye. Showing smiling women and clearly directed at women, it calls out in big letters, "Make the change that's good for you. It's your life."[12] A similar sentiment is conveyed on a bumper sticker in my native country, South Africa—part of the agitprop against the abuse of women—that says, simply, "Young Women Break the Silence."

It's your life. It's my body. In the West, and in growing parts of the world such as Ghana or South Africa, this notion is so intrinsic to who we are that we don't even think about it anymore. It's your life is also an economic credo—called capitalism. "It's your life" could be a political slogan. You decide, you vote, you think for yourself: democracy. The assumptions underlying "It's your life" are so self-evident to those in the West that they are considered a natural condition.

For much of history, however, and to this day in substantial parts of the world, the social imperative of communities has been the individual's readiness to make sacrifices for the community, the church, the *Ummah* (the global Muslim community), the proletariat, or the nation. The assumption that it's my life stems from a remarkable shift in history that gradually began to emerge half a millennium ago: a shift from the onus on individuals to sacrifice themselves for their communities in a variety of ways, to individual independence.

That shift is rooted in the idea of self-control, in all of its paradoxical meanings—first and foremost that we control ourselves, and that we *own* ourselves, in body and mind. Beyond that is the related meaning—now our common understanding of self-control—that we must discipline ourselves, not act on impulse or on the passions of the moment. "It's your life" means both, and both elements are important to understand. But for most of human history, in most civilizations—as well as for much of the world today—communal fiat has reigned. This is demonstrably not limited to Muslims by any means. And when community and family are privileged over the individual, it is women who pay a particular price.

Globalization has made universal the idea that individuals have the right to self-determination (at least in principle), both economically and culturally. State-directed economic planning and socialist models have, for now, largely been pushed aside. An increasing reliance on the role of the individual in production and development has brought women to the forefront in many parts of the world because they are critical to that development. This generates cultural and political ripples that buffet traditional boundaries of social control. Simultaneously, for some societies fundamentalism replaces communism as a bulwark against capitalism. (On occasion, notably in Europe, we do see cases of "red-green" alliances, though "green" in this case represents Muslim groups rather than environmentalists.)

Deep changes in technology, economies, and politics have always created violent social and cultural upheaval. Groups jockey for position, and in any new political, economic, and social configuration some will win and others will lose. In the Reformation, the aristocracy sought to draw power away from kings. Henry VIII used the Reformation to break away from Rome and the Catholic Church so he could remarry. The middle classes benefited from the French Revolution; the aristocrats lost their heads. Globalization now generates challenges to the traditional status of women precisely in those cultures in which gender has relegated them to a passive and inferior position. Unlike countries, tribes, or ethnic groups, women and men are not likely to go to war in any sustained way with each other. This creates an interesting and rather combustible mix.

Globalization may have yet to scrub away the structures of state, nation, tribe, and religion, but it has eroded the ability of those structures to isolate people from currents that have inexorably grown over the centuries—notably the increasing sovereignty of the individual over his (and later her) body and mind. Present-day political and human rights movements champion this sovereignty of the individual. Economic development theories, however varied, now all substantiate the notion that individual empowerment is key—even if government regulation becomes salient in the wake of global recession.

In the social, economic, and political flows and eddies that now lap over traditional bulwarks, a basic, even primordial, struggle has arisen. This is the first global quarrel over the nature of the self and over the most fundamental quality that defines our self-understanding: our gender and sexuality.

Territory, national self-determination, tribal expansion, treasure—the goals of wars past—are secondary now to this global struggle over the fundamentals of the self. Is the individual at the center of the world, or is it her family, community, nation, or Ummah? Religion may not necessarily prove to be the core issue. Islam has come to play a central role in our time, and there are a number of factors that have come together to bring Islam to the fore. But this religion is far from the exception historically when it comes to the patriarchal treatment of women.

The Adventure of the Self

When we own ourselves—when we are sovereign over our bodies—we *make* ourselves (in contrast to community fiat in effect making us). We seek to define ourselves—through consumerism, careerism, fashion, travel, and various modes of self-presentation—to the world at large and to ourselves. There is in varying ways a preoccupation with the subjective sense of self. In desired sexuality, we find the most immediate (unmediated) and visceral sense of self, body, and expression. Life is an *adventure of the self* rather than, foremost, a scripted set of duties to family and community.[13]

The "adventurous self" is thus deeply subversive of traditional patriarchy, especially when it comes to women. Since the very foundation of human conduct is implicated in this sense of the self, in traditional environments such a development permeates every pore of the social body, from relations between women and men to issues of government. Every human moment becomes a possible battleground, from family relationships to popular culture.

Take a popular cultural artifact like the Barbie doll. Once derided as simply a prop for domesticating young girls, Barbie soon developed a mind of her own. She has many careers, from veterinarian, firefighter, ballerina, or army paratrooper to ambassador for world peace. Her wardrobe is extensive. She drinks cocktails and flaunts her impossible figure in a bikini. She drives her sports car with her boyfriend Ken at her side. Little girls (and sometimes boys) can dress her as they wish and guide her adventurous self—and their own imagination of their futures.

Barbie is also cosmopolitan and in demand across the world. In that context she can also be subversive and dangerous (as odd this may sound to many ears). As Barbie globalized, she generated a backlash. The Iranian government responded to Barbie with their own doll in the mid-1990s (just one example of alternative, more traditional dolls). "Sara" wore a conservative *chador* (an outer garment that exposes only the face), while her "brother," Dara, wore a long coat and the turban of a mullah, or cleric. Sara and Dara's designer, Majid Ghaderi, said, "Barbie is an American woman who never wants to get pregnant and have babies. She never wants to look old, and this contradicts our culture." Ghaderi, also a director of a government institute, further suggested that "Barbie is like a Trojan Horse. Inside it, it carries its Western cultural influences, such as makeup and indecent clothes. Once it enters our society, it dumps these influences on our children." Not only was Barbie's presentation problematic, but she also had a boyfriend, Ken: a clear no-go. Sara fulfilled traditional expectations. A palette of careers, let alone public exposure in a bikini with an alcoholic drink at hand, was outside her purview.[14]

Such tensions around women's presentation are not absent within the West. The "SlutWalk" protest marches that started in Toronto, Canada, in 2011 as a result of a Toronto police officer saying that "women should avoid dressing like sluts in order not to be victimized" is one example. SlutWalk protests, consisting of women often purposely dressed in skimpy or supposedly provocative dress, went international. A SlutWalk movement even emerged in India. The protest declared that women should be able to dress as they wish and that dress is no basis for explaining away sexual assault or rape.[15]

Still, the tensions around women's status and sexuality in countries like Pakistan or Iran, or in highly patriarchal sectors of immigrant communities, supersede in orders of magnitude the tensions that generated the SlutWalk movement. Those tensions, from Pakistan to Iran, are more extensive, often expressed in physical aggression, and significantly inform the violent rhetoric and actions of militant movements.

That geographic expanse, with the Middle East at its core, stands out globally regarding the problematic status of women and women's sexuality. But this is an interdenominational phenomenon. Severe patriarchy is significant not just among the Muslim majorities in the region but across religious lines, including conservative Christians, Druze, and, in Israel, Orthodox Jews.

On the global stage, "the personal is political" is a statement now true to a degree that the feminists who coined that phrase could never have imagined.

The Invention of Sex

The English poet Philip Larkin's droll observation that "sex was invented in 1963 / a little bit too late for me" could perhaps be phrased in a somewhat more accurate fashion: in or about 1963, virginity disappeared—or at least the social valuation of virginity was in free-fall in Western countries. But in an oblique, even unwitting way, Larkin was on to something: the loosening of externally imposed fetters.

The iconic Virginia Woolf, who made stream-of-consciousness fashionable in literature, made an earlier, more far-reaching claim that "on or about December 1910 human character changed," with a turning inward to the experience of the self, or inner-character.[16] We could go back further still to the birth of Protestantism, which led in some circumstances to an unbinding of the individual. In a way, the great Christian mystic Jacob Boehme had anticipated Woolf around the year 1600 in his call, "O great and holy God, I pray thee, set open my inwardness to me; that I may rightly know what I am; and open in me what was shut up in Adam."[17]

The turn toward individuality was not only directed to an inner self as such. Adam Smith set the cornerstone of the modern global economy in *Wealth of Nations* in 1776, resting on the notion of the rational, self-driven, self-enriching individual. And the declarations of individual human rights that went along with the American and French revolutions in the eighteenth century were, critically, writ global in 1948, in the Universal Declaration of Human Rights. The basis of all of these profound acts was the creation—or at least the discovery—of the individual as, in principle, an autonomous being.

Here and there, then and now, accompanied by a good degree of violence, we observe growing claims of self-possession, or the self-ownership, of body and mind. Watershed dates fixed to particular years notwithstanding, this is a transformation that develops in fits and starts, with breathtaking implications for religion, politics, culture, and economics. We tend today to stress the economic aspect and the commodification of modern global life. From workers to consumers, possession has a distinctly materialist tone. But the shift to a notion that the individual is his or, more dramatically, her own proprietor, is far beyond the material. It is a recasting of first principles, of the very grounding of what it means to be human.

Individualism, loosely speaking, has been around in various ways for a long time. But communal forms—of nation and state, class and clan, caste and religion—have until recent history superseded it. At different times and places, nationalism or tribal affiliation, economic class, feudal rank or caste, to name principle examples, were the crucibles of the self, of identity, and of human categorization. Individuals were indelibly molded by the confluence of such inexorable political, economic, and social forces. Crucible is in fact a fitting term, meaning, metaphorically, a test by fire of affiliation, identity, and commitment. If the individual has been subsumed historically for the most part by transcendent demands of nation, class, or even religion, then in the hyper-globalization of the last two to three decades, the control of one's own self—*self-control,* in a variety of senses—is fast becoming the underlying crucible of our current age. This test puts women closest to the flame.

In how many cultures, in language and practice, were women literally owned by their husbands? In this light, the idea of a woman imbued with rights, self-determination, and economic freedom is a remarkable global revolution. At base this is a freedom that is expressed through the body. And in a very real way this is fundamentally about the expression of the freedom of movement, work, and, notably, of femininity and sexuality. From art to fashion to the striking advertisements in modern women's magazines, this freedom of movement and of sexual expression is forthright.

This public demonstration of freedom coupled with issues of sexuality explains why clothing, of all things, generates such deep political conflict. The *burqa* sends a collective shiver through many, even though wearing those clothes might in fact be an individual's choice. The burqa conceals the body and muffles personal expression in contrast to the way women are portrayed and express themselves in much of the world today—publicly (rather than sequestered), individually (not uniformly), colorfully, fashionably, authoritatively, and with unabashed eroticism.

In the West—and now in other parts of the world—we are increasingly our own proprietors, and traditional control has waned. Whom we marry is a good illustration. Religion and nationality are becoming less significant factors in choosing our partners. Even race is less compelling—along with the convention that partners should be of the opposite sex.

Space has been opening for expression of individual self-possession for five hundred years. In Europe these spaces were first available to the economically privileged, for control over property was believed to be essential for the exercise of individual rights. But the physical space of ownership soon moved to a more abstract level. Space for others grew, albeit slowly—first for men, for whites, for other races; and finally for women. As rights expanded, people claimed increasing proprietary control over their very selves in body and thought, bolstering the buffer between outside forces and individual authority.

The idea of an autonomous, self-reflective individual had revolutionary consequences for economics—"I" can now sell my bodily labor or intellect and buy that of others. I have power to shape and influence the body politic. An enormous literature describes such economic and political developments, but far less discussed is the profound impact this liberation had on private life and on marriage and sex—from the "sexless sex" of medieval church doctrine to the idea of romance and marriage by a choice calculated upon any number of romantic and instrumental considerations.

The increasing sovereignty of the individual would prove to be of special significance for women, who historically were (and are) least likely to determine their "freedom of movement" in a literal sense. In fact, the historical significance of the bodily control of women and their sexuality is a window to social form and conflict that has not been very well explored—surprisingly, given the flowering of women's studies in recent decades.

We are well aware of the war and conflict that have ensued from capitalist and democratic revolutions, but we have yet to comprehend in any coherent or systemic way the ripple effects of the unbinding of the woman through the literal and figurative freeing of her body. We understand how *homo economicus* or *homo politicus* can be a cause of war: We declare wars for democracy or suggest that wars are fought for treasure. But we have a harder time, curiously, understanding how the literal body and all that it represents can generate such bloodshed. In fact, it becomes the *ultimate ideological cause* behind such debasements of humanity, from honor killings to war, that we witness in the world today.[18]

Thinking about the Body

The historical shift to an emphasis on the mind and subjectivity is captured in Descartes' now-familiar maxim in the seventeenth century: "I think, therefore I am." In the popular rendition of this maxim, we are our minds, and our bodies are the convenient containers, as it were.[19] But the irony is that the increasing stress on the "mind" has led us to understate the importance of feelings, emotions, and desires (or *eros*) in our understanding of social and political life. The mind suggests "thinking" and calculation, whereas the body is about feeling, emotion, movement, space, beauty, attraction, and repulsion. The mind conjures the rational; the body, the non-rational or even irrational.

This is important to keep in mind when we consider "the body" so centrally, and who is in control of the body—as well as, above all, women and their bodies. Political scientists and sociologists are inclined to emphasize the world of thinking rather than the world of feeling and consequently to consider human behavior to be more rational than it is. We must be all the more wary when we take up a topic such women's status and sexuality and questions of bodily control in circumstances of conflict. We have to be aware of the *visceral* (literally, of the body) responses—from communities as well as individuals—engendered by contesting a woman's position, her dress, and even her affection.

The question of the body has been much debated and studied by philosophers and neuroscientists in terms of what has been called the mind-body problem. Regardless of what side one may take in that debate, it is clear from accumulated research in neuroscience and biology that much of our meaning arises from ties to bodily life. In other words, underlying concepts, propositions, and sentences are sensorimotor processes, emotions, and bodily qualities that make meaning possible. Even "thought-out" meaning is abstracted from the prior "feeling" of shape, form, quantity, movement in space and time, and other essentially "felt" qualities. Thus even thought is ultimately rooted in feeling. I feel "closed in." She felt that she faced an "uphill" battle. He felt "unconstrained" to express himself.[20]

This play of our body in shaping our very comprehension of life around us is a point made by cognitive scientists. But less remarked upon is how our body is also viscerally felt in our experience of community. What we view as our "natural" community (be it tribal, national, or religious) is also *felt* as a body. It is felt even as an extension of our own body. We think of the nation as a body politic. We talk of "self-government." France is embodied in the image of a woman, Marianne (once officially represented by Brigitte Bardot). The maternal imagery of women has been integral to the "birth" of many nations.

The sense of communal embodiment is not only national. The church, for believers, reflects the body of Christ. A *hadith* (a saying of the Prophet Muhammad or his companions) talks of the global Muslim community, the Ummah, as a body. The hadith suggests that believers will feel "pain" for the suffering of other parts of the spiritual body, the Ummah. The body's encounter with the world thus not only shapes the language of everyday life but also our cognition of social existence. The sympathy of and for family and community is a bodily experience. The same principles of a shared sense of self apply to other bodies, spiritual or political.[21]

It is curious to see how much the body has been ignored, or positively rejected, at the right and left poles of scholarship. At one end we have the view of "supernumerary body": humans are calculating beings defined by their minds. The body needs to "perform"—walks, talks, and is generally healthy—but in essence it plays a supportive role to the "mind."[22]

But at the other end of the spectrum are the approaches to the body of those who come closest to celebrity status among academics, Michel Foucault and Judith Butler. In this view, the body itself, and especially the idea of dual sexes, is a social construction. This goes beyond social norms about how a man or woman should act or the social approbation of certain sexual mores. Rather, it is the rejection of the idea of "sex" (female and male) itself or, at least, of the binary division of sexes.[23] The delineation of sex derives from customs that reflect the power relations embedded in social interaction. In an essay that was itself something of a cause célèbre, the philosopher Martha Nussbaum deconstructed this claim, targeting Judith Butler:

> [It] is much too simple to say that power is all that the body is. We might have had the bodies of birds or dinosaurs or lions, but we do not; and this reality shapes our choices. Culture can shape and reshape some aspects of our bodily existence, but it does not shape all the aspects of it. "In the man burdened by hunger and thirst," as Sextus Empiricus observed long ago, "it is impossible to produce by argument the conviction that he is not so burdened."[24]

We may perhaps ignore this role of the body in an analysis of, say, party politics, or in the coffeehouse repartee of aspirant intellectuals. But it would be foolhardy to do so in the emotionally and aesthetically heightened world of sex and gender and of women and their role in politics, families, and communities.

Unraveling an Enigma: A Map for the Way Ahead

The prominence of gender and sexuality in global rifts is an extraordinary phenomenon. To decipher this enigma demands a certain amount of detective work, carefully unwinding different threads of the issue. We need to turn to different sources of evidence: historical narratives; the personal journeys of iconic characters; religious and political doctrines; language and its changes; fashion and media; economic and opinion data; statistical analysis; and legal developments.

In this book I do all this and more, including developing a statistical tool (the Tribal Patriarchy Index) to bring to the surface the extent and influence of patriarchy on religiously motivated violence and how patriarchy interacts, in sometimes counterintuitive ways, with religion. I also analyze the results of a survey of Muslim communities I directed in 2011 across three continents.

This book covers a broad canvas in space and time, geography, and history. Thus a sketch showing the way ahead is essential.

The chapters are divided into four parts. Part I contrasts the distinct approaches to the body in the history relevant to our story—namely, in the greater Middle East from the biblical period and in Western Europe. In these approaches we can see how notions of honor and interest evolved. Note that a rigorous patriarchy cut across these regions of the world—and historically across much of the terrestrial surface.

I begin by illustrating this patriarchal pattern through a biblical story, that of David and Bathsheba, which has much sociological resonance to this day. Communal fiat is central, in the (frequently guilty) consciences of both women and men. But women, seen as the source of cultural as well as maternal reproduction, are under especially stringent patriarchal command.

The puzzle of Western Europe is why and how it shifts away from the stern patriarchy of Medieval Europe. The story of Catherine of Siena is used to illustrate this patriarchy. But from roughly the sixteenth and seventeenth centuries we see a gradual, patchwork change in Europe. The Dutch stand out in this early period and are illustrative of the change. Dutch women for their time were remarkably at ease with sexual matters and even ran their own businesses; they were free in ways well beyond much of the world even today. More broadly, we begin to see changes in art, marriage, divorce, attitudes to personal violence, and dress that intimate the dramatic changes ahead. In short, men and, more gradually, women attain a growing sovereignty over themselves and their bodies. This is associated with an increasing accentuation of self-interest.

The first part concludes by observing the rise of Islam in Arabia in the seventh century, in a region where tribal patriarchy is at its apogee. Critical to our story is understanding how Islam both intersected, *and* was in tension with, the preexisting tribal patriarchy of the region. Islamist movements today seek to regain the "purity" of an Arabian tribal past (if in a new global form).

While Part I sets the stage for our contemporary global drama, Part II reveals the impact of recent globalization, in economic and cultural terms, on women. Globalization is a much more gendered and sexualized process than most people imagine; it also deeply challenging to patriarchal societies.

In recent decades economic globalization has entered a new phase, with fundamental implications for women. Colonization in the years after World War II came to an end, but this gave way to a globalization that generated a worldwide production process. In chapter 4 we learn about the ways women are, on the whole, advantaged in the labor market and play a more significant role in national economies. This enlarged role in the formal economy is associated with expanding women's rights.

Multinational corporations and export-oriented industries generate a greater demand for women's labor. This is not uniform: The Middle East and North Africa prove more resistant to absorbing women into the labor market compared to other parts of the developing world (even while the education of women still expands in the region). Countries filter these changes in different ways, often reproducing a gendered division of labor by a different route. Nonetheless, on the global stage women on the whole have developed a greater income-generating role, and along with that, greater autonomy. In this light, in chapter 4 we take a closer look at Indonesia, the largest Muslim country but one where the militant Islamists have been (relatively) held at bay.

The significance of these changes is in the ways in which they have reshaped the status of women in much of the world by effecting greater individual sovereignty over their bodies. This has remarkable impact on areas from work and fashion to marriage patterns. Even prostitution, though more often than not part of the unsightly corners of our cities, can occasionally reflect a shifting use of sexuality by independent women (and men). This is illustrated in a brief foray to Cuba in chapter 4.

These changes are profound not only in terms of women's financial capital, education, or even rights. Rather, they signal a re-orientation in the sense of self.

Fashion and the growing accent on beauty and aesthetics are often treated as trivial, but in fact reflect a fundamental societal change in parts of the world that have been traditional. They illustrate a change in the very sense of self, from the dutiful self defined through honor and custom, to a sense of self-discovery and self-realization. This includes a growing emphasis on erotic capital as well. In chapter 5 we explore the play and dynamics of erotic capital and fashion.

In Part III, in chapters 6 and 7, we turn to the backlash. I address how and why the changing place of women in a globalizing world generates such a vociferous response among Islamist groups. Indeed, the issue of women's status is a central defining characteristic of these groups. In this part, I bring out the importance of tribal patriarchy in this dynamic of Islamist resistance.

Since no prior statistical gauge of tribalism was available, I developed the Tribal Patriarchy Index. This tool allows us to appraise the impact of tribal patriarchy on religiously motivated violence and its geographic variation. We can also parse the distinct role of tribal patriarchy and Islam as factors (or not) in driving religiously motivated violence, and its export to the West.

In Muslim countries where tribal patriarchy is not especially high, like Indonesia, Islamist militancy has relatively limited support. Islamist militancy grows most readily, in general, when tribal patriarchy is strongly institutionalized in Muslim countries (or in diasporic communities with origins in such societies). In other words, the most severe problems arise, in terms of Islamist militancy, in areas of marked tribal patriarchy. This is the case across the greater Middle East, from Afghanistan and Pakistan through to North Africa—and in immigrant communities with roots in these areas. Through the Tribal Patriarchy Index, I clarify the role of tribal patriarchy, the circumstance in which Islamist militancy evolves, and how this militancy extends through parts of some diasporic communities. This also helps to explain some of the tribe-like qualities in militant Islamist networks.

In chapter 7, I sketch out ideological developments and the importance of the image of women in Islamist militancy. To do so I focus on key figures. Bodies, not just of women but also of those proclaimed as martyrs, loom large in the writings of the militant scholars. The thread of honor and bodily sacrifice is written, as an aphorism of one scholar has it, with ink and blood.

Part IV examines the give-and-take of globalization. As markets and media globalize, diffusing Western images and beliefs, so immigrant communities have expanded their footprint in the West, especially in Europe. The status of women has become a remarkably important cause of fissure with the "host" societies as a consequence of communities living in close proximity. In this fourth part, I pull apart what are essentially three separate challenges that are often conflated in the public mind.

One challenge is *multiculturalism*. Compromising women's control over their bodies, and thus over their status and sexuality, is the line the vast majority in the West are not willing to cross. The mediation of these issues can be seen in the courts, and it is in such cases that we see illuminated the basic tensions at work: they are battles over defining the woman's body and its control.

The second challenge is the *social and economic dilemmas* of the poorer immigrant neighborhoods, some of which have periodically erupted in unrest. We find second-generation Muslim males pooling disproportionately at the bottom of the social ladder. Second-generation immigrant Muslim women are making great strides in education. But that progress falters at the university level and in labor market participation—though that faltering is more accentuated in the United Kingdom than in France (the two countries of primary interest). However, contrary to received wisdom, poverty as such is not the key driver of radicalism.

The third challenge is that of *radical Islam*. Drawing on a commissioned survey and on analysis of Islamists convicted under terrorism laws, I sketch a profile of those who slip into radicalism or even terrorism. I focus on France and Britain because they provide us a lens into two very different responses to patriarchy and to religion. The new and existing data converge on a number of revealing findings. One is that the French republican model, with its stress on assimilation, works better than British multiculturalism, with respect to Muslim women's progress and to national integration in the respective countries.

In the Conclusion, I consider the broader global implications of an astonishing historical turn in the extraordinary progress of women. Yet that turn is not universally felt across the world. This brings us back to the region of much concern, the Middle East, and teasing out the promises and disappointments of the Arab Spring, which was, at its birth, at first celebrated. However, subsequent events revealed for a global audience the fracture lines in Middle Eastern tectonics—from the status of women, to tribalism, and to the social roots of Islamists.

Two final comments for the reader before embarking on our journey. First, conflict over woman's status can range from family arguments, to honor killings, to organized political violence. So in using the term *conflict* in this book, I range across organized resistance, violent and nonviolent, to opposition to a woman's untraditional conduct at the level of family. However, I do cover at greater length the sharper edge of conflict, that is, the political violence. This is not to suggest such violence is representative of conflict around gender, but that violence does reflect broader structural and social strains in these patriarchal communities.[25]

Last, I have endeavored to make the text as accessible as possible to the interested general reader, while (I trust) not sacrificing the rigor of argument and supporting evidence. Readers will find expanded information in the notes, some of which will be of interest primarily to specialists.

PART I

HISTORICAL TRAJECTORIES OF THE MIDDLE EAST AND EUROPE

Here we explore the historical staging of our contemporary dramas over women's sexuality and status. We learn of the biblical roots of patriarchy in the Middle East and Europe, of the turn of some European women (as well as men) toward "self control" after the Protestant Reformation, and of the rise of Islam among the tribes of Arabia.

PLATE 1. Tahiti, 1767. This rendition of the HMS *Dolphin*'s arrival in Tahiti reads, "The natives of Otaheite [Tahiti] attacking Captain Wallis, the first discoverer of that island." The deployment of women rapidly became a way of translating cultures—for combat or mediation. The Tahitian women exposed "their beauties" to the sailors of HMS *Dolphin,* distracting the British sailors from an impending attack. Eventually, after the defeated Tahitians sued for peace, the women engaged the sailors in a more amorous fashion. Not for the first time or for the last, women's sexuality was mutually understood—and negotiated. Artist unknown. Watercolor. 33 × 41 cm. National Library of Australia, Sydney.

PLATE 2. David spies a seductive Bathsheba on her rooftop in Jerusalem. In this portrayal David struggles with the fateful decision he is about to make. In the biblical and tribal milieu, his moral failure is not just personal but also social and public. The House of David and his people suffer the consequences of David's transgressions. *David Sees Bath-Sheba Bathing*, by James Tissot. 1836–1902. Oil on canvas. Jewish Museum, New York.

PLATE 3. St. Catherine of Siena. The value of virginity before marriage cut across cultures historically, and in some cases virginity has been held as more honorable than marriage itself. An iconic figure of the Catholic Church, Saint Catherine of Siena, born in 1347, promised her virginity to Christ at the age of seven. She warned, "We are letting the Word of God be smothered by the inordinate affections and desires of the world." *St. Catherine of Siena*, sixteenth-seventeenth century, by an unknown artist. Oil on copper. Brooklyn Museum, Frank L. Babbott Fund, Frank Sherman Benson Fund, Carl H. de Silver Fund, A. Augustus Healy Fund, Caroline A. L. Pratt Fund, Charles Stewart Smith Memorial Fund, and the Ella C. Woodward Memorial Fund, New York.

PLATE 4. Titian's *Venus of Urbino*. This masterpiece, painted in 1538, exhibits a sharp
turn in the approach to the body in Western art. For the medieval church, in art as in
life, to be naked was to show shame. Here, in contrast, Venus radiates self-assurance
and self-possession. She displays an open readiness to employ her beauty to her own
advantage. The painting has been imitated and reinterpreted by other artists through
the centuries, from Velasquez to Manet. *Venus of Urbino*, by Titan. 1538. Oil on canvas.
Galleria degli Uffizi, Florence, Italy.

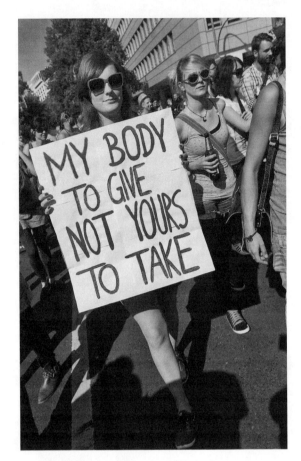

PLATE 5. A "SlutWalk" protest in Berlin in 2011. The worldwide protests were yet another marker in the turn, not just to the right to "own" one's body (especially for women), but also to display one's "erotic capital." Getty Images News. Sean Gallup.

PLATE 6. Dara and Sara: The Iranian answer to Ken and Barbie. Unlike Barbie and her boyfriend Ken, Dara and Sara are brother and sister and are much more modestly dressed. The Iranian designer of Dara and Sara disparaged Barbie as "a Trojan Horse of corrupt, Western values." Sara, in turn, fulfills traditional roles and eschews the numerous careers and revealing outfits of Barbie. 2011. KanoonParvaresh, Tehran.

PLATE 7. Fulla: Another riposte to Barbie. In contrast
to the Iranian Sara, Fulla has Arab origins, but
she shares Sara's "Muslim values," according to the
description of the proprietary company. Fulla, who
has fans across the Muslim world, rejects "lewd"
clothes; her primary dress is an abaya. She takes on
traditionally acceptable professions like doctor and
teacher. She does, self-consciously, compete with the
MTV generation in the "Singing Fulla" but does so
with a "pure heart." Permission granted via flickr.com,
September 26, 2011.

Chador   Abaya   Niqab

Burqa   Hijab

PLATE 8. Muslim dress can vary across the world, shaped by different cultural currents. The niqab, for example, is mostly seen in the Arab world, Afghanistan, and Pakistan. The chador is more common among Iranian women. Illustration adapted by Leslie Trinkle, from "From Scarves to Full Coverings, Variations on a Veil," The Wall Street Journal (online), March 12, 2011.

PLATE 9. Individualizing tradition. With affluence and exposure to different global fashions, many women display Muslim dress in increasingly individualized styles. Fashionability is expressed through consumerism (such as using rich fabrics, color, brand names, and conspicuous display). A model displays the creation of Malaysian designer Tom Abang Saufi during the Islamic Fashion Festival in Jakarta, Indonesia, on May 25, 2009. AFP / Getty Images. Romeo Gacad.

....

CHAPTER ONE

The Honor of Virgins

The Biblical Roots of Patriarchy

And it happened at eventide that David arose from his bed and walked about on the roof of the king's house, and he saw from the roof a woman bathing, and the woman was very beautiful. And David sent and enquired after the woman, and the one he sent said, "Why, this is Bathsheba daughter of Eliam and wife of Uriah the Hittite." And David sent messengers and fetched her and she came to him and he lay with her, she having just cleansed herself of her impurity, and she returned to her house. (2 Samuel 11:2-4)

So begins the story of David and Bathsheba, a story of adultery and murder (plate 2). It is in the violations of norms that we learn of the boundaries of communities. And in the story of David and Bathsheba we learn of the workings of tribal patriarchy—of the interplay of virginity, honor, and vengeance. The extent to which the norms of this epic story, which tells of a society that existed 3,000 years ago, are still in play in the Middle East today is remarkable. Of numerous civilizations that have made their way through the Middle East, this tribal society has remained. It has formed the interlopers and helped to shape religions, including Islam, in varying ways.

Patriarchy in one form or another has been historically almost universal. But it has taken on diverse social configurations. Whereas biblical and Middle Eastern society is mostly tribal in its foundations, medieval Christianity is based on an agricultural society, organized feudally. In principle, the Church is separate from worldly, temporal, and political authority. The Church also celebrates a monastic ideal of the spirit over the flesh. Through the story of Catherine of Siena, we will draw out the Church's approach to the body in this chapter as well. But whereas the biblical form of patriarchy has remained remarkably durable in the greater Middle East, medieval Christianity collapsed, setting off a revolution in the approach to the body, an approach that informs the modern and globalizing world.

Virgins, Warriors, and Honor

David is the greatest of great figures: the ancestor of Jesus in Christianity, and the ancestor of the future Messiah of the Jews. Yet he is a deeply flawed character. David brings back Uriah from the war front and seeks to lure him into relations with the now-pregnant Bathsheba in order to disguise his adultery. But Uriah, thinking of his men at the front, demurs. David then arranges for Uriah's death in combat. Uriah, who is of foreign origins, is a self-sacrificing soldier of Israel. The Israelite king, in contrast, betrays and kills him.

The biblical scholar and translator Robert Alter describes the story of David as "probably the greatest single narrative representation in antiquity of a human life evolving by slow stages through time, shaped and altered by the pressures of political life, public institutions, family, the impulses of body and spirit, [and] the eventual sad decay of the flesh."[1] From David rising out of his bed to walk on the roof, to his son Amnon lying on his bed—pretending to be sick, calling his sister Tamar to tend to him in a ruse to rape her—sex weaves through the biblical epic.

This human story, however, hides what is essentially a description of *relations* that are the warp and woof of the nation; for in breaking those communal commitments, the fabric of the nation is itself torn. The characters are individuals, but the moral thread is found in the larger community. Personal failings of the flesh, acts of impulse, lead to widespread political disarray and turmoil. Issues of the body and overcoming or failing to overcome physical and material wants and desires are intricately part of the integrity of the nation—both in the sense of "righteousness" and of "wholeness." In many traditional societies they are one and the same.

In the biblical society of David the sin is, in other words, social and public, not personal and private. David had failed not only Bathsheba and Uriah but also his entire kingdom and people. The consequences are felt by a family and nation rent asunder as a result. To act out of personal impulse—herein lies the moral failure. To sacrifice for the larger good—herein lies moral worth and honor. It is the performance that matters, not an individual's internal musings or motivations. (In Psalm 51, the psalmist has David beseeching God to "blot out my transgressions," and the psalm ends, "Then shalt thou be pleased with the sacrifices of righteousness . . .") This biblical depiction is not only of historical or theological interest but is a pervasive sociological and political phenomenon in much of the world—notably, in the Middle East and North Africa.

For the biblical woman, honor and purity lie in her virginity prior to marriage. Amnon "fell sick over" his beautiful sister Tamar, *"for she was a virgin* and it seemed beyond Amnon to do anything to her." The rape of Tamar is portrayed as brutal, stripped of any emotional affinity. Tamar pleads with Amnon, "Don't, my brother, don't abuse me, for *it should not be done thus in Israel."* Tamar's plea appeals to communal proscriptions, not to Amnon's sense of personal ethics. But Amnon "overpowered her and abused her and bedded her" and then ordered her to go. Tamar responds, "Don't!—this wrong is greater than the other you did me, to send me away now" (2 Samuel 13). The modern reader may be puzzled, as Alter notes, as to why being sent away is worse than the rape itself. It is due to the pariah status heaped on "dishonored" women in biblical (and many contemporary) milieus. The one remedy for such women was marriage with the rapist—a dubious honor, but one that prevented the victim from being cast out from the community.[2]

In the biblical form of society, the woman is a marker of family boundaries, a symbol of the community, and as such, she is under the control of men—fathers, husbands, and brothers.[3] Even rape and adultery are understood, in this context, as one man's violation of another man's possession, or possible possession, of a woman. Rape in this regard is comprehended as a subset of adultery, not an abuse of the woman herself. Consent or consensual relations are not, tellingly, the issue. Nor is it the bodily integrity or autonomy of the woman. Rather, what is operating here is the social structure—and its integrity (literally and morally)—regarding scripted relations among men and women, families, those in positions of influence and their inferiors, and the propagation of family, tribe, and nation.

Virginity itself thus reflected the imperatives of the larger society, promising society's continuity through marriage and children. The woman's consent, her agency, is immaterial since her purposes transcended herself, so to speak. Prohibitions against a woman going out in public unaccompanied—to this very day in, notably, much of the greater Middle East and North Africa—were ways of her family ensuring her honor. A bride's virginity, publicly made evident through bloody sheets from the wedding night, for example, also indicated that her father's household was stable.

For men, the face is outward, public, as the women's is domestic, private. But the sense of shared bodily sacrifice involves both women and men. In women, the sacrifice is to family and community, including sexual abstinence until marriage and then physical sacrifice through childbirth. In men, the expressions of sacrifice are more martial, through protecting family honor or in warfare. Manhood in such contexts implies the readiness to engage violently and can be literally written into the language.

Case in point: the letter "zayin" in modern Hebrew script (ז), which looks something like a dagger, both means weapon and is slang for penis. Biblical invocations talk of taking away the enemy's masculinity or taunt the enemy soldiers by referring to them as women. Then as now, war is clearly gendered, in that overwhelmingly men are the combatants, and the language of sex (let alone actual sexual violence) is used in the "rape" of cities. Even God threatens Jerusalem thus: "Shall not sorrows take thee, as a woman in travail? . . . For the greatness of thine iniquity are thy skirts discovered, *and* thy heels made bare" (Jeremiah 13:22).[4] For men, as for women, their honor (or dishonor) is always on display.

For both men and women, their sacrifice is to something larger than themselves, from family to nation. It is a theme that runs across peoples and through history. How can one forget, for example, the piercing words of the World War I poet, Rupert Brooke, who, foreseeing his own death, consoles himself with the words, "If I should die, think only this of me; / That there's some corner of a foreign field / That is for ever England."[5]

In biblical life, and for a great sweep of humanity to the present day, the family and community are essential to survival. The modern citizen of a functioning state, in contrast, can get on reasonably well without family or an immediate community.[6] That citizen shares a national community that is indirect and mediated: he or she does not know the vast majority of his or her fellow citizens. Not so in traditional societies. On the personal level, in the biblical milieu (or for that matter in the Middle Ages, or tribal and village societies), the social world is mostly direct and visceral.

The texture and contrast of day and night, man and woman, good and bad, and inferiors and superiors are deeply felt. The family's role is preeminent. Marriage stems from and is arranged through kin relations. Life is a finely grained set of dependencies.[7] What defines the individual and the rhythm of his or her life is communally demarcated; well-being, in that context, rests on reputation, and reputation rests in honor.

The individual is, likewise, valued on the basis of his or her commitment to, and sacrifice for, the community. The individual's integrity is in fulfilling the wholeness of the community, in following scripted relations. To fail is to suffer humiliation and shame. Your honor lies in fulfilling your social obligations. Rather than being "true to yourself," you are true to the community. Telling the truth, for example, may be less important than maintaining the tenor of communal relations and your family's honor.

For women, historically, honor has above all been sexually defined, through chastity and virginity if unmarried. Women are culturally and literally the source of a community's continuity—hence the importance of women, and their sexuality, in the community's imagination. Acting on individual self-interest is corrupting and reaches its lowest point in wanton sexual desire, independent of social frameworks or norms—the very antithesis of honor. Sacrificing oneself to family and community expresses the "sacred." Indeed, the Latin roots of the word *sacrifice* are associated with the sacred. Selfishness conjures up the world of the profane.

I distinguish honor in stark terms. Yet in the Bible we find sensuous, evocative passages, above all in the Song of Songs:

> Behold, thou art fair, my love; behold, thou art fair; thou hast doves' eyes within thy locks: thy hair is as a flock of goats that appear from Mount Gilead . . .
>
> Thy lips are like a thread of scarlet, and thy speech is comely: thy temples are like a piece of a pomegranate within thy locks.
>
> Thy neck is like the tower of David . . .
>
> Thy two breasts are like two young roes that are twins, which feed among the lilies . . .
>
> Thou art all fair, my love; there is no spot in thee . . .
>
> Thou hast ravished my heart, my sister, my spouse; thou hast ravished my heart with one of thine eyes, with one chain of thy neck.
>
> How fair is thy love, my sister, my spouse! how much better is thy love than wine! and the smell of thine ointments than all spices!
>
> Thy lips, O my spouse, drop as the honeycomb: honey and milk are under thy tongue . . .
>
> Awake, O north wind; and come, thou south; blow upon my garden, that the spices thereof may flow out. Let my beloved come into his garden, and eat his pleasant fruits . . .
>
> I rose up to open to my beloved; and my hands dropped with myrrh, and my fingers with sweet smelling myrrh, upon the handles of the lock . . .
>
> I am my beloved's, and my beloved is mine . . .
>
> —Song of Songs (Song of Solomon) 4–6

The erotic is not rejected as such in the Hebrew tradition, if expressed within the bounds of family and tradition. As we shall see, the opposition between body and spirit and the rejection of sensuality even within marriage is much more sharply expressed in, for example, the medieval Catholic Church. Yet, in more or less nuanced terms, if the struggle of the modern self is for truthfulness and for the authenticity of oneself, in honor societies the struggle is between the desires of the body and the demands of honor. Indeed, it is telling that the biblical heroes—David, above all—are fallible, drawn astray in David's case by the beauty of a woman. But as a consequence, David brings almost endless pain on his nation as well as on himself. The biblical story resonates as literature, even for the non-believer, precisely because of its nuanced and often tragic depiction of the human condition.

Honor, sacrifice, reputation—it is remarkable how much these come down to transcending the body. The body is singular; the self, one's identity, is viewed as relational (as a daughter, father, cousin, kinsman). Chastity is a commitment to future marriage, family, and social reproduction. Conversely, the *victims* of rape are dishonored, having lost their "purity."

The forms that patriarchy takes are critical, not just in the moment but for the future dynamics of societies. Middle Eastern tribal patriarchy forms the background for the rise of Islam (a story we will turn to later). Subsequently, both complementarities and oppositions between different forms of Islam and tribal patriarchy continue throughout the Middle East to this day.

In significant parts of the contemporary greater Middle East, as the anthropologist Unni Wikan writes of Sohar in Oman, women's lives in many cases still "unfold in the homes and in the adjacent narrow lanes and back streets":

> Market, mosques and all main thoroughfares are off-limits, except where the latter cannot be avoided. . . . But then the woman is required to make herself as nearly invisible as possible, by donning a black, sacklike cloth cloak reaching from the top of the head to the ankles . . . and by screening her face by a mask. . . . Each [woman] should keep to her own home and to those of her very close neighbors, altogether some five to ten houses. . . . Epitomizing women's seclusion and the narrow horizon of their world is their own reference to these wards and villages as "my country" . . . a usage the men find bemusing.[8]

Women in this environment go beyond "this country" only with the permission of the menfolk. The men are said to be physically and intellectually superior. Women are said to have "animal" spirits. They are expected to show absolute obedience to their men, and they have the status of minors throughout their lives. Their obedience and their keeping to these narrow social and geographic confines are deemed essential to the honor of their men. Socially, the time of David is not that distant.[9]

In Europe of the Middle Ages, patriarchy took on forms distinct from the Middle East of the same period—but with clear commonalities around issues of virginity and of self-sacrifice for the larger community. But in the European case, this proved to be the setting for a revolutionary change in the attitude to the self and the body.

The Profession of Virginity

Kill, kill your own will . . . mortify your body, and do not so pamper it in delicate ways. Despise yourself, and have in regard neither rank nor riches, for virtue is the only thing that makes us gentlefolk, and the riches of this life are the worst of poverty when possessed with inordinate love apart from God. . . . Limit your intercourse, dearest and most beloved Sister, to Christ crucified; set your affection and desire on following Him by the way of shame and true humility, in gentleness, binding you to the Lamb with the bands of charity. (Saint Catherine of Siena in a letter to Monna Colomba of Lucca)[10]

The importance attributed to virginity in global history is extraordinary— as is the rapid decline in its value from the mid-twentieth century in the West. Why has the value of virginity resonated so compellingly, historically, across traditions? The virgin is the "outward and visible sign of continuity, integration and unity," writes the scholar William Shullenberger, "the emblem and human center of the moral and regenerative energies of the world." Virginity is the "point where the temporal realities of bodily existence intersect with the spiritual possibilities of the eternal." It guarantees to the unmarried woman her value, socially. Her sexual purity becomes "a dangerous focal point of male fantasy, desire, and competition."[11] The destiny of families and nations is interwoven with the deeply personal struggles of women and men. Virginity is the nexus between this world and the next, personal honor and dishonor, communal "regeneration" and collapse. The "focal point" of virginity celebrates women yet cloisters and controls them at the same time.

What is telling is how the approach to the body also reveals an "economy" (regarding our material world, and the distribution and consumption of resources) and a "politics" (regarding power and what constitutes legitimate authority). The approach to the body is expressed in different ways across religions and ideologies.

Yet the denial of the body, for example, generates curious parallels on matters sexual or economic among those otherwise separated by vast swaths of time and space.[12]

In Christianity the guiding imagery of bodily sacrifice is central, the nexus between the here-and-now and the eternal, between flesh and godliness. It is personified in the Virgin Mary and above all in Jesus. In Saint Catherine's words, "Christ crucified alone was the Lamb who with love unsearchable sacrificed His Body, making Him our Purification and Healing, our Food and Raiment, and the Bed where we can rest. He had no regard to love of self nor fleshly joy, but abased Himself in pain, enduring shames and insults, seeking the honor of the Father and our salvation."[13] The desire to almost literally transcend the body and the accompanying stress on virginity, celibacy, and, in marriage, "sexless sex," are pushed with a blunt intensity in the Middle Ages.[14]

Saint Catherine of Siena is an iconic figure, radiating the medieval Catholic ambience (plate 3). Born in Siena in 1347, she lived just thirty-three years but left an indelible impression on the Church. The youngest of a very large family, she saw "visions" from her earliest childhood, and later would talk of celestial visitations and conversations with Christ. At the age of seven she promised her virginity to Christ; at sixteen she took the habit of the Dominican Tertiaries. She tended to the poor and sick, especially those with "repulsive" diseases. In 1370, she sensed a divine command to leave her "cell" and enter public life to heal the wars then ravaging her land. She sought to unite the Christian princes, to join in Pope Gregory XI's designs for a crusade against the infidels. She died in 1380 after a period of extreme pain and agony of three months, which she bore with "exultation and delight."

Her letters, addressed to popes and princes, to ordinary individuals and family members, provided a contemporary exposition on the spiritual condition—in practice and in aspiration—of Christendom. A common thread is self-sacrifice, expressed through an asceticism with sexual, economic, and political implications. Mortification of one's flesh reflects a rejection of the world as it is, it was believed, a desire to be imbued with the ineffable, the otherworldly. "We are letting the Word of God be smothered by the inordinate affections and desires of the world," she wrote, "and are walking in the way of its luxuries and pleasures, studying to please our fellow-beings rather than our Creator."[15]

Catherine repented to her last days, so it was said, bitterly and with tears, for having let an older sister dress her prettily, as a young girl, and blanch her hair. She had delighted in beautiful things, she told a confessor, and forever after felt mortified by that knowledge.[16] The dangers of self-regard could only be overcome, she said, by "holy hatred of one's self."[17] These themes also reflected Church doctrine and social institutions, notably in marriage and the family.

Catherine was echoing, and championing, disgust with the body and a sharp division between the flesh and the spirit. A certain ambiguity was inevitably introduced, however, with the knowledge that the body was the temple of the soul. The body was ephemeral, corrupt, prone to temptation, carnal, inevitably to become dust; yet it had to be restrained and channeled with an eye to the Resurrection on Judgment Day. Disease and infection were fleshly evidence of the susceptibility of the body and a realization of its weakness and corruption.

But the soul could be revealed through its "dwelling place," through complexion or skin color or, in exceptional cases, the ability to endure a burning iron or immersion in water. Monastic orders pursued mastery over the body through vows of silence or, more radically, by mortifying the body through inviting vermin and parasites into their clothing.[18] Extreme holiness demanded neglect of the flesh, as attention to the body distracted from matters of the spirit. Orifices had to be especially guarded, as they were openings for corruption.

Medieval Chastity

In medieval storytelling, a woman's body is the mirror image of Adam's, the sexual organs the same but internalized, introverted, more private, more suspect. The woman was naturally more exposed, more open, more corruptible, and hence she had to be more carefully guarded and watched. By nature she had to be secluded, her chastity protected by a man. A man's honor was dependent on containing this danger of a woman's body, so perilous for being so alluring. A woman was always *in* danger while simultaneously a *source* of danger. She was Venus, a promise of intimacy and an intimation of Hell—a fatal attraction we are revisiting in our present global moment.

Nakedness itself was a mark of exile, nudity a taboo. Punishments sometimes involved the disrobing of the apparent criminal—the act of stripping metaphorically wiping away his or her identity. Clothing almost literally made the person, as the "last wrapping" of social life. Church moralists regarded bathing and grooming (as well as "pampering" and make-up) with suspicion, though they were still valued by the upper ranks. Clothing was a complex marking of status and place in society. Sex differences were underscored through dress—but emphatically not sexuality. Women—respectable women, at least—hid their hair, since hair radiated such compelling, erotic power.[19]

Not only nuns and monks but everyday couples could achieve a "chaste" life in the marital bed, even if they had sexual relations. For the Church, "marital chastity" concerned moderating sexual urges—and of course confining them within the bounds of matrimony. Subordination of women was essential, because the "wanton" sexuality of women had to be controlled to ensure the legitimacy of any offspring. Couples, the Church moralists held, should approach intercourse with "sober calculation," and with reason, not passion.[20]

St. Clement of Alexandria, who unified Christian belief with Greek philosophy up to his death in about 215, set the standard when he warned, "Our ideal is not to experience desire at all. . . . A man who marries for the sake of begetting children must practice continence so that it is not desire he feels for his wife . . . that he may beget children with a chaste and controlled will."[21] St. Jerome—who translated the Bible into Latin from its respective Hebrew and Greek in the late fourth and early fifth centuries—taught that "the wise man should love his wife with cool discretion, not with hot desire." Procreation, not pleasure, was the object.

Such an approach characterizes the New Testament. Paul wrote in his first letter to the Corinthians, "If . . . you do marry, there is nothing wrong in it; and if a virgin marries, she has done no wrong. But those who marry will have pain and grief in this bodily life. . . . The unmarried man cares for the Lord's business; his aim is to please the Lord. But the married man cares for worldly things; his aim is to please his wife; and he has a divided mind." The historian of Late Antiquity Peter Brown observes that while pagans and Jews viewed marriage in a positive light, Paul saw marriage as a way of restraining base impulses. "It is good for a man not to touch a woman," Paul noted—but qualified this by adding that not all men have received the gift from God, as Paul had, to be able to keep the promise of celibacy.[22]

Love did not belong in marriage. Sexual passion, in medieval depictions, took place in illicit and adulterous relationships. St. Jerome exclaimed, "Nothing is filthier than to have sex with your wife as you might do with your mistress"—suggesting that sex with a mistress was on another plane altogether. One suggested strategy to maintain purity for wives was to think of God while making love. The Church also sanctioned only the so-called missionary position, suggesting that any variation was sodomy. It also signified the subservience of the wife to her husband.[23] St. Jerome would have been sympathetic with Tolstoy's sentiment, expressed through a character in his 1889 novella *The Kreutzer Sonata* who says that love in practice is simply "a sordid matter that degrades us to the level of pigs, something it's vile and embarrassing to remember and talk about."[24]

In popular and worldly terms, marriage was also portrayed as an economic (rather than a romantic) arrangement, and sex—within marriage—almost a form of prostitution. Chaucer, often cited as the first to use common English rather than Latin or French in literature, has the Wife proclaim in the *Wife of Bath's Tale:*

Praise be to God that
I have wedded five!
Of whom I did pick out and choose the best
Both for their nether purse and for their chest . . .
Why should men otherwise in their books set
That man shall pay unto his wife his debt?
Now wherewith should he ever make payment,
Except he used his blessed instrument . . .

In wifehood I will use my instrument
As freely as my Maker has it sent.
If I be niggardly, God give me sorrow!
My husband he shall have it, eve and morrow,
When he's pleased to come forth and pay his debt . . .

I would no longer in the bed abide
If I but felt his arm across my side,
Till he had paid his ransom unto me;
Then would I let him do his nicety . . .

And I pray Jesus to cut short the lives
Of those who'll not be governed by their wives;
And old and querulous niggards with their pence,
And send them soon a mortal pestilence!

This economic premise, and the prevalence of arranged marriages, illustrates that the shift to a modern romantic sensibility, which would develop from roughly the sixteenth century, was not about making life more rational as such—at least when it came to marriage.[25] At least formally, certain spheres of life in the Middle Ages (and before), such as marriage, were more coolly driven and calculated, from economics to ensuring the continuity of family lines, in contrast to modern concepts of romance.

The key question in the shift to a modern way of life is not "rationality" as such. Rather, the question is who owns the self: the individual herself or fathers and husbands, religious authorities, the community, or a combination thereof? The answer to that question produced, and produces, varied outcomes across different aspects of life, from the family to the marketplace. In the Middle Ages the economic motive in marriage cut across rank.

Of Virgins and Whores

Through the patriarchal prism, virginity is the apex of the good. Prostitution is the nadir, the downfall of men as well as of (especially) women. This is interesting: Whores and virgins represent much more than individuals, fallen or exemplary; they also delineate the contours—metaphorically the genetic code—of a society, decadent or healthy. And that social DNA is fundamentally, unalterably, and inextricably written in gender and sexual terms. The imagery of the woman in the medieval church is divided between virgin and whore, between purity and corruption. Even the mother is portrayed in less glowing light than the virgin.

Virginity reflects a commitment—perhaps a forced commitment—to the community. A woman is—literally, but also, equally importantly, symbolically—the nexus of society, the source of its reproduction. Sex, sexuality, gendered roles, and maternity are the weave of the community in such traditional societies.

The future of the family and the community follows the life cycle of the woman. A woman sacrifices herself for the community. That sacrifice is through chastity or, later in life, through the role of the self-sacrificing mother—in pregnancy the offering of her body is palpable. The continuity of a family's lineage is assured through guarding the chaste lives of its daughters until marriage, where a sanctioned, socially witnessed ceremony affirms the relationship as one of familial and communal worth.

Personal conscience in such circumstances is driven by codes of honor, and honor is a function of performance as a man or a woman. The individual's behavior reflects on the community or family, so the failure or dishonorable actions of others, say of one's sister, is personally felt.

Whores have played a large role in the imagination of societies. This is perhaps less true in their activities than in what they represent: the foil to virgins. On one level, whores have represented the corrupt and wanton in society, in contrast to vestal purity and undefiled morality. Peel away these notions and deeper collective self-understandings are revealed. Whores, significantly, represent commerce, greed, dangerous and unpredictable passion, a wanton expression of the bodily desires, and unbridled selfishness. Virginity represents sacrifice of self and body to the larger good, a spiritual virtue, a commitment to social institutions from family to the community.

The dichotomy between virgin and whore in the communal imagination plays out today among Islamist elements. Christian and Jewish women are portrayed as prostitutes in their very religious affiliations and their association with the West. Thus, as the Imam of a major Viennese mosque recently proclaimed, marriage to "Women of the Book" (Christians and Jews) by a Muslim was forbidden because these women are "prostitutes."[26] Western capitalism and Western sexual mores are of a piece—where everything is for sale and where women are unfettered, they become (in this imagination), for all intents and purposes, prostitutes.

We tend to think of the world in terms of distinct groups such as Muslim, Christian, Indian, Chinese, and American. And we subdivide those groups into even more discrete groups such as Islamist, Sunni, Shi'a, Protestant, Catholic, and the like. We think of the flow of history, or flows, of each of these groups. But equally compelling, if more difficult to grasp, are the threads that weave across societies and across time.

The imperative among so many to sacrifice and give themselves for the greater good, an ethic of self-denial, is a telling example. From the medieval church to twentieth-century Maoism, this same commitment to self-negation, in such vastly different circumstances, leads to striking parallels. Out of this apparent selflessness arose a commitment to an ascetic life, from a contained sexuality to a rejection of materialism. Indeed, when Chinese communist factions wanted to attack Mao himself, they pointed to the debauched and promiscuous habits he took on later in his life.[27]

Curiously, the way Islamists portray the West today has parallels in medieval anti-Jewish and anti-Muslim sentiments expressed by church theologians and in popular discourse. Hostility to the Jews in the Middle Ages was not simply a function of how religious texts were interpreted. The hostility rested in concepts of honor and interest, civic-mindedness and selfishness. Jews were portrayed as driven by avarice and greed, in contrast to the honor-bound and civic-minded members of the Church. Jewish men were "effeminate." Muslim men were "lust-ful." On one side was honor and self-sacrifice for the larger community; on the other, avarice, lust, and a life dominated by base, bodily instincts.[28]

The longing to transcend the body explicitly or implicitly branded bodily desires, and this world more generally, as corrupt. Broadly speaking, two paths promised redemption in this world view. One was the negation of the world altogether, a monk-like withdrawal from towns and cities—in extreme cases, a desire to deny the physical through self-flagellation, vows of silences, celibacy, and wearing clothes full of parasites to remind oneself of the body's corruption.

The other path is revolutionary: to reform the world, even if it has to be destroyed in the process. Catherine of Sienna embodied both forms, but especially the latter, in her worldly activities, namely, involvement in papal politics and in her support for crusades. A revolutionary zeal arising out of aspirations for such transcendence, for the reformation of the world, has marked groups as disparate as the Red Guards and Al Qaeda. Violence thus takes on a celebrated role, cleansing the world of corruption—be it of the bourgeoisie or the infidels. (And as we will note later, the bourgeoisie and the infidels share much.) Indeed, the word *cleansing* is used all over the map—from Frantz Fanon, the Caribbean-born secular ideologist for anti-colonization movements, who wrote of violence as "a cleansing force," to Ayatollah Khomeini, the father of the Islamic Republic of Iran, where violently deposing the Shah was also a "cleansing."[29]

Sex Sells Capitalism

From Catherine of Siena to the Maoists, and in many shades in between, asceticism generates an *entwined* suspicion of sexuality and commerce—both related to the body. Poverty and sexual restraint are prominently celebrated. Conversely, where self-possession is exalted, sexuality and commerce are also intertwined. Today it is a truism that capitalism sells sex, but equally we can say that sex sells capitalism.

Who controls the body is a universal question cutting across history and communities, and the fallout of how that issue is addressed is universal as well. It implicates sexual morality, of course, and institutions from marriage to religion and, ultimately, to politics. When the prerogative of family and community trumps self-possession (as has generally been the case, though to different degrees), the ethic that emerges is wary of the exhibition, enjoyment, or advancement of the self—sexually or commercially. When the body comes to be celebrated—for purposes of calculated commerce (as in physical or intellectual labor, even prostitution), or for unbridled eroticism—gender is still encoded in the social DNA but in vastly different ways.

When valued differently, commerce, romantic passion, and eroticism generate a very different constitution of society. The divergent approaches to the body create mirrored opposites.[30] The principles that order society, such as honor or interest, are respectively viewed as an abomination, a source of chaos, for the opposing party. The parties who make up these paired opposites are, of course, determined by social context. Shades of this contrast are evident between liberals and social conservatives in the United States, for example. But the sharpest contrast is evident in the encounters wrought by globalization.

CHAPTER TWO

A Pirouette in Europe

With Dutch Women in the Lead, History Changes Course

One of the most sumptuous paintings of the Renaissance is Titian's *Venus of Urbino,* painted in 1538 and now hanging in the Uffizi in Florence (plate 4). Venus lies naked, turning toward and holding the eye of the viewer. Little pretense is made of any figurative reference to the goddess Venus. She displays palpable human warmth, an exquisite self-assurance. She also exhibits a remarkable shift in Western art.

The Church celebrated chastity and celibacy. To be naked was to be stripped of dignity, in art as in life. Portrayals of Adam and Eve are an exception, but only in that their nakedness expresses their shame and failure before God. The celebration of the body in art that begins with the Renaissance is a radical break. One has to go back to the ancient Greeks, whose nudes mostly depicted glorified male athletic perfection.

Art is one sign of a changing relationship to the body, one's own and that of others. Across a human canvas of giving and sacrificing oneself for the Church, the Ummah, the community, or the family, the idea that you are your own property is something of a jarring change. But starting from about the sixteenth century in Western Europe, the idea that individuals control their own bodies expanded rapidly, even if in practice such expansion was geographically uneven and gradual, especially for women.

This expansion follows the Protestant Reformation that became manifest in the mid-1500s, with Protestant groups swarming through Catholic churches, destroying the symbols of the church. Protestant churches were much more austere, often entirely bare, save for a simple cross.[1] This reflected a shift from the Catholic Church, in all its grandeur and assurance, to the Protestant emphasis on the individual preoccupied with inner life.

How is this new sense of body and self, and self-possession, expressed? In the first case, it is expressed literally in the grammar and the vocabulary of language. The word *self* as a prefix first appears in the sixteenth century, and its use multiplies rapidly in the seventeenth century.[2] Terms such as "self-control" and "self-determination" reflect a shift in consciousness not only in word but also in grammatical structure. This portends a growing relationship to one's own personal and intimate self—of a sense of belonging to oneself as an independent being and relying on one's own efforts as well as an inclination to be self-centered (not necessarily in the derogatory sense of the term).

There was a veritable flourishing of self-compounds from the mid-seventeenth century—so much so that after about fifty years many of these words dropped away. Many of them are inscrutable to us: self-dilatation, self-diremption, self-disapprobation, self-discoloration, self-maceration, self-panegyric, self-whippings (referring to "Popish Priests"), self-vivacious, and self-fame. It is also clear from the literature of the period that people understood their selves as having multiple dimensions—notwithstanding the unidimensional character that political philosophers would invent to anchor their theories.

Tellingly, Shakespeare, writing in this period, frequently used such self-compounds, for example, referring to "self-will'd harlotry" in *Romeo and Juliet*. Later, for a brief moment in the nineteenth century, there was even a "selfdom," in contrast to a kingdom. The selfdom was the realm of the self. This evolution of language is revealing: As the noted social theorist Norbert Elias commented, "The more or less sudden emergence of words within languages nearly always points to changes in the lives of people."[3]

The sense of "myself" as at the center of "my" world is reflected in the shift in language to the first person singular: The unabashed *I* was now privileged. I could speak on my own authority rather than basing myself on the tradition of speaking through the authority of the Church, of a proverb, or of a saint. Speaking in the third person communicated fatalism, a belief that no action or choice "I" made could change the course of things—that the rhythm of life is predetermined and we are powerless to change it.

Consider this contrast, before and after the shift to self: Maximilian I of Hapsburg, Holy Roman Emperor from 1508 until his death in 1519, speaks of his sadness at the death of his young wife, "for they loved each other a great deal, about which much could be written."[4] In the twentieth century, when Emperor Franz Joseph received the news that his wife, Empress Elisabeth, had been assassinated, he said to his general adjutant, Count Paar, "You have no idea how much I loved this woman."[5]

Historians and social thinkers have generated a still-growing corpus of material about the changes that stirred in the sixteenth century—notably, the beginnings of capitalism, the modern state, and even democracy. How did the pursuit of gain through commercial, mercantile, and other moneymaking pursuits become honorable, after being condemned as the cardinal sin of greed, avarice, and the love of lucre? The most famous explanation is that of the German sociologist Max Weber, who articulated "the Protestant ethic."[6]

But equally striking is the less-asked question of how sexuality and eroticism could come to be celebrated in the shadow of its condemnation as the sin of lust, as sinful as greed for lucre. Why is sexuality so closely linked with an emerging consumer culture? How is this linked to understandings of the body? How did these changes implicate the place of women?

What we find is a transforming sense of self and body, with ramifications for economics, politics, art, language, and psychology, as well as for the stuff of the life—divorce, personal violence, and fashion. In responding to these different threads of change, we begin with the Dutch. As the most prosperous and dynamic society in seventeenth-century Europe, their Golden Age, they proved to be a vanguard in exemplifying the social revolution that would eventually influence all of Europe and large parts of the world.

What had been defined as illicit in medieval Europe, especially around areas of economic pursuit and sexuality, would come to be defined as licit. And yet for significant sectors of the globe today—albeit in very different cultural contexts—the pursuit of gain as its own end and the celebration of the erotic challenge profound beliefs and social architectures of marriage, family, gender, and authority. The literalists of those sectors, notably the Islamists, define themselves through their opposition to the Western world; for them the West represents the contours of the illicit. The same could be said in reverse.

We have at this point a struggle over the body and its control. The transformation that began in Western Europe from about the sixteenth century has come full circle.

Dutch Treats

He struck his pretty flute
Between my breasts.
"Away, away," said I, "you rogue,
What does love mean?
While on your flute, you play.

Play as you should!

It won't bore me:

It's happened often enough!"

—From a seventeenth-century Dutch songbook

In Western Europe in the sixteenth and seventeenth centuries, no nation reflected the changes around the individual, and the interconnected nature of such changes, as much as did the Dutch in their Golden Age. They were a spearhead of the Protestant Reformation, stopping the bloody counter-Reformation forces of Spanish Emperor Philip II as they wheeled through the center of Europe in the mid-1500s. The Dutch established the first republic in early modern history in 1609. The Netherlands was the only republic officially recognized throughout Western Europe in 1648, under the Treaty of Westphalia (the treaty that also establishes the modern states-system). They were known for having the most vigorous economy of the time, essentially capitalist in nature. Travelers from elsewhere in Europe were struck by the participation of women in public and economic life—at least compared to customs in their own countries. And they were positively shocked by the eroticism and sexuality on display—as modern-day tourists in contemporary Amsterdam often are.[7]

Already in the late sixteenth century through the seventeenth century, the Dutch were unusually liberal. Many in this historical moment, including Dutch women, showed little regard for chastity before marriage. They would kiss in the presence of strangers.[8] Mutual caressing in public was not uncommon. Their speech was candid, even ribald, and in cases crudely sexual. Women moved about freely and could be seen feasting in taverns.[9] An open attitude prevailed when it came to eroticism in theatre, popular books, and poetry. Jokes were primarily sexual. How-to manuals on sex were widely available.

Women were also practiced in matters of money. As one Italian visitor, Lodovico Guicciardini, commented in 1567: "The women in this country . . . not only go to and forth in town to manage their affairs, but they travel from town to town through the country, without any company to speak of, and without anybody commenting upon it. . . . [They] occupy themselves also in buying and selling, and are industrious in in affairs that properly belong to men, and that with such an eagerness and skillfulness that in many places, as in Holland and Zeeland, men leave it to women to do everything."[10]

Women were comfortable with, and even flaunted, their looks. The remarkably sexual quality of Dutch art from this period—which generated fascinated interest among the public—shows women at ease with their bodies. Complete nudity was considered offensive, but women were now uncovering their necks and shoulders, and even showing cleavage.

Marriage was now celebrated for its romantic promise. Even marital sex was an expression of a "godly union." Furthermore, sex was celebrated for its expression of love, not only as a means to procreation. "Tender love" was indeed considered essential for a viable marriage. Lack of sex could be grounds for divorce. And, in a reflection of the new authority of the woman over her body, the Dutch legal system became sympathetic to lawsuits regarding wife beating and abuse. Marriage was increasingly viewed as a partnership—a function of two free individuals making a consensual decision—rather than an arrangement reflecting the concerns of family and patriarchy.

The destiny for women was still felt to be, ideally, marriage. But Dutch poetry and literature convey an image of a marriage out of love and free will, often cast in idyllic terms.[11] Yet the courtship is also portrayed as an opportunity for calculation. Jacob Cats, a towering figure of Dutch literature and poetry of the time, wrote:

> I only wish a young maiden,
> When she is proposed to,
> Will not throw herself in a hurry
> And light-heartedly in a loose love affair.
> To hold in consideration
> For no short time,
> A steady proposal, made in true eagerness,
> That is my advice to all girls.
> . . . / . . .
> Before all, pay attention to his virtue,
> Consider the way he has been behaving himself in his young days . . .

When the preeminent authority of family and community declines, women and men are unfettered. The dynamics of relationships change. The partners could in part be calculating, but when it came to courtship and love, the imagery was overwhelmingly romantic. Emblematic are the words of Janus Secundus, a Dutch poet and the most widely read poet in sixteenth-century Europe:

> My Lydia hit me with a ball of snow
> And straight my heart with fire began to glow
> 'Twas strange a conflagration thus should start
> Where frozen water played the leading part;
> But so it was. How can I live at ease,

When I am trapped by perils such as these?
And what is more, no cold this fire can tame;
It must be vanquished by an equal flame.
A mutual warmth will my salvation be;
So come, dear Lydia, come; and burn with me.

Sex in less romantic, more crassly commercial terms was also more wide-spread. The Dutch, famously to this day, were at greater ease with brothels. Though formally illegal, brothels were by and large tolerated and accepted. Commerce and the sex business went hand in hand, and women frequently ran the "whore trade." Brothels were justified with the now-familiar notion that they were a release for men, a kind of safety valve for society.

Many foreign travelers' reports attested to such Dutch mores. Even if they were an exaggeration, clearly the Dutch were a different species than their neighbors elsewhere in Europe, to generate such descriptions from these travelers in the first place.

The root of the word *authority* is author, and indeed Dutch women literally started writing, not just for themselves or for a small coterie around them, but for a public audience. By the second half of the seventeenth century, women in the Netherlands were accepted into the same intellectual and cultural circles as men in an unprecedented way. As a result, at least among the Dutch, women were less the literal and literary subjects of men.

Capital Ideas

Thomas of Chobham, a prominent English theologian in the late twelfth and early thirteenth centuries, spoke of the similarities between prostitutes and usurers (those who lent money at interest). Both traded for money. Usurers were worse in that they sinned against God in every conceivable fashion—everything was up for sale—whereas prostitutes sinned against God only in one respect, in the sale of sex.[12] Thomas was reflecting a broader sentiment. He was also unwittingly pointing to the critical nexus between the body and its control. That is, when an individual was sovereign over herself, there were implications for both economic behavior and for sexuality.

How did the pursuit of gain, of money, become ethically acceptable, even encouraged, from the sixteenth and seventeenth centuries? How did the love of lucre escape its stigma as one of the cardinal sins, along with a hankering for power and sexual lust? Max Weber, in *The Protestant Ethic and the Spirit of*

Capitalism, pointed to a paradox that, he suggested, was resolved among Protestants resurgent in Europe in this period. He identified a seeming contradiction in the very essence of capitalism: the desire for monetary gain, not for consumption, but for capital accumulation in its own right. Certain Protestant denominations, notably the Calvinists, were characterized by an intense desire to reform a corrupt world (which for them included the Catholic Church). In so doing, they brought intensity to their worldly activities, including their work; in fact, they viewed their work as a calling with a divine purpose. Yet they inherited a medieval disdain for monetary gain. So rather than consume the fruits of their work ethic, they lived modestly and saved their wealth or gave it to charity.

It is an interesting argument. After one hundred years of publication, Weber's book is still a mainstay of social thought. It is also an argument that would challenge the thesis proffered here: that the critical turn in this period was the idea of self-possession. Protestant ascetics, whom Weber places at the center of his argument, inherited disgust for the body from medieval Christianity, albeit not quite as extreme. Such aversion would not have allowed a claim of self-ownership, at least in a bodily sense.

But Weber's scenario of self-denial is not how capitalism in fact expressed itself—at least not exclusively, and not in the most dynamic of capitalist economies in this period, that of the mostly Protestant Dutch. When the English traveler William Aglionby made a sojourn through the Netherlands in 1660, he was struck by the opulence of the people and the places in which they lived. The signs of prosperity extended throughout the population, well beyond the aristocracy. He recounted how, for example, country wives showed off gold rings and bonnet pins. The historian Simon Schama, in his book, *The Embarrassment of Riches,* notes how Aglionby's account emphasizes not only the wealth but also the delight of the Dutch in displaying their good fortune. Aglionby wrote: "I know hardly any country where they spend their money more freely. . . . You see everywhere good houses, well furnished, plentiful and elegant tables . . . rich dresses . . . and in the education of their children no expense is spared."[13]

The pleasure of spending—what would come to be called consumerism— quickly took hold of the Dutch. The tales of travelers, Schama wrote, belie the image of an austere and ascetic way of life. Bernard de Mandeville, author of the *Fable of the Bees: or, Private Vices, Publick Benefits* (1714) declared: "The Dutch may ascribe their present grandeur to the virtue and frugality of their ancestors as they please, but what made that contemptible spot of earth so considerable among the powers of Europe has been their political wisdom in postponing everything to merchandise and navigation [and] the unlimited liberty of conscience that is enjoyed among them." The Dutch were consumers living large. Contemporary writers extolled their great *emporium mundi*, the world's emporium.

Protestantism played a critical role, not in the sense of Max Weber's analysis, but in facilitating the individual's self-possession. The Reformation had broken down the hierarchy of the Church, and with it the idea that some believers (priests and other clergy) were closer to God than others. Now, in principle, God was accessible to any believer. If the believer now accounted for his own soul, his body could not be far behind.

To understand the rise of capitalism, we have to look elsewhere than Weber's argument. The Dutch, who became a world economic power within a couple of generations, illustrate a practice of consumption *and* the accumulation of capital. Here we see an interesting development. People have, across time, universally had an interest in consumption (in the broadest sense, from food to material goods). But once the individual has a sense of self-ownership, appetite is married to certain cognitive shifts.

With self-control, the individual understands herself as an actor with *choices* and *opportunities* beyond those scripted by rank and circumstance. That self-control affords the imagination new vistas—in this case regarding material advancement—not merely survival or well-being, but prosperity. Recent work of behavioral economists suggests a further cognitive effect: people rank themselves through comparison, and where a sense of self-determination is present, they believe they can always do better.[14] Consumption in this context is not simply an objective biological drive, but it has a subjective component as well: desires, fashions, envies, and fantasies all play a role.

Honor and Interest

Calculation comes into play in multiple ways: Where do I stand relative to others or to where I could be? How do I advance my fortunes? Here, there is a remarkable fusion not just of objective need and subjective desire but also of the rational and irrational. So I have, if I can put it this way, "passionate interests." The science of economics is built on emotion yet driven (in the marketplace) by calculating individuals. The behavioral economist Dan Ariely captures this phenomenon neatly, in another context, with the term "predictably irrational."[15]

Here we observe another nuance in self-control. In the sense I have used the term, self-control denotes self-ownership, or possession of oneself. But in its everyday sense, it has a connotation of self-restraint. The two meanings are paradoxically intertwined and intricately linked. When we experience ourselves as independent beings, we are in the position to, in Adam Smith's words, "desire the betterment of our condition."[16] Against this background, our self-restraint arises out of that very self-possession.

The historian Albert Hirschman, in *The Passions and the Interests,* observes how the philosophers rehabilitated what was a dangerous vice—the pursuit of gain—by recasting it as an "interest."[17] For example, the eighteenth-century Scottish philosopher David Hume put it thus: "[It is evident] that the passion is better satisfied by its restraint, than by its liberty, and that in preserving society, we make much greater advances in the acquiring of possessions, than in the solitary and forlorn condition." Or, in the words of the seventeenth-century Dutch philosopher Baruch Spinoza, we do not "delight in blessedness because we restrain our lusts; but, on the contrary, because we delight in it, we are able to restrain them." While passions are unpredictable and dangerous, they suggested, interests are transparent, constant and predictable. From this basis arose a science of economics. Self-interest motivates us to do what we do: Farmers have an interest in growing the wheat, and the bakers in baking the bread. The market in principle works without any regulation from above—such was Adam Smith's insight about the "Invisible Hand," the accumulated self-interest that propels the market. And as the term "interest" entered the lexicon, so the stigma of the pursuit of money began to evaporate.

The restraint inherent in "interest" in turn demanded an element, as Hirschman put it, of "calculating efficiency, as well as prudence, into human behavior."[18] Interest, in this regard, is a distinct calculus from, notably, the ethic of honor: one calculating and instrumental; the other passionate and expressive. Interest, when initially broached by the moral philosophers, concerned not just economics but a range—"Interest of conscience, Interest of honor, Interest of health, Interest of wealth," wrote one French thinker of the time.[19] But interest in the narrower, calculating sense came to define economic behavior. Many came to view rational self-interest as the core basis of human personality.

It is in the notion of self-restraint that a *civil* society could arise, where different individuals could mingle in the public arena, protected by an elaborate etiquette. Manners and advice books on etiquette began to flourish in the seventeenth century. Restraint, in this context, is highly textured, an elaborate delineation of behavior and of acceptable conduct. In fact, such civility, restraint, and etiquette were (and are) critical for any society of self-governing individuals to exist at all.[20] Restraint was also essential for social "respectability."

Thus, much of the West, and in time other parts of the world, came to see capitalism, with some constraints, as rational, considered, and essential to human happiness. And yet parts of the world continued to see capitalism as a demeaning expression of selfishness and greed, and the selling of one's labor on the marketplace as the moral equivalent to prostitution. In the most extreme form among many Islamists, when it comes to women's unfettered participation in the market, the merging of capitalism and prostitution is literal, not simply metaphoric. This includes the portrayal of women, the buying of fashionable clothes, conspicuous consumption, and women's independent work.

The Dutch were at the leading edge of a gradual, uneven change across large parts of Europe, distinguished by these signal markers: divorce, violence, and fashion.

Divorce

Anyone who has gone through a divorce (or even broken up with a lover) knows what an excruciating experience it is. As the novelist Pat Conroy famously observed, "Each divorce is the death of a small civilization."[21] But it is also a sign of bodily self-control. Just as marriage becomes a choice, so does its dissolution. ("Divorce is probably of nearly the same date as marriage," the eighteenth century French essayist and wit Voltaire remarked. "I believe, however, that marriage is some weeks more ancient."[22]) The Protestant Reformers rejected the Catholic Church's tenets about marriage. Marriage was no longer a sacrament, an unshakable expression of God's will. With the exception of England's Anglican Church, divorce became an option (with varying levels of difficulty) across Protestant Europe after the Reformation began in the sixteenth century.[23]

Yet it appears that the role of Protestantism in promoting the divorce was more a product of the structural changes Protestantism wrought than of its doctrine. Structurally, the Reformation undermined the centralized, mediating authority of the Church of Rome. In Protestant doctrine, the latitude of the individual regarding divorce was limited. For almost all of the Reformers, marriage was primarily for procreation and chaste (that is, marital) sex. Only secondarily were issues of companionship and affection—or their absence—grounds for parting ways. Divorce was not thought of primarily as a remedy for marital breakdown. Rather, it was granted for offenses against the institution of matrimony—notably adultery.

Still, Protestant law broke significantly from the Catholic Church, even if informed by sometimes similar values. Protestantism led to the consideration of the content of a marriage, rather than its form. The road to no-fault divorce was a long one, but it was in effect being mapped from this early point. Indeed, an important sign of bodily self-control is how easily women today may sue for divorce and how frequently they do it. Women initiate about two-thirds of divorces in the United States.[24] In Saudi Arabia, by law no woman can sue for divorce.

Violence

Levels of violence dropped precipitously in Western Europe, beginning unequivocally in the seventeenth century. That decline began most noticeably in the Netherlands as well as in England, and it gradually spread to the rest of Western Europe. In the late Middle Ages homicide is typically estimated at between 20 and 40 killings per 100,000. By the mid-twentieth century, the European rate was 0.5–1 homicides per 100,000. Moral concern regarding cruelty and violence was growing in the seventeenth century. Infanticide became a severely punishable crime, public executions declined, and torture was gradually discontinued.[25]

Contrast that trend with this description of the popular entertainment of cat burning in sixteenth-century Paris: "The spectators, including kings and queens, shrieked with laughter as the animals, howling with pain, were singed, roasted, and finally carbonized."[26] Violence was a popular spectator sport (though it is not completely absent today in arenas such as boxing and bull-fighting). Men proved their honor through violence.

One explanation for the changing rate of homicide, and with it attitudes toward violence, is what Norbert Elias referred to as the civilizing process, which involved a growing emphasis on self-restraint and on containing one's emotional impulses. But I suggest that in addition to a growing stress on self-interest is a parallel self-referential quality. From the seventeenth century on, we find an increasing interest in personal thoughts, the writing of diaries, and other introspective inclinations—what we would come to call "psychology." This intense interest in interiority, in feelings and emotions, is shadowed by a growing empathy for humans more broadly. Sensitivity to one's own feelings generated, among some, sensitivity to the feelings of others. Such empathy could be limited initially: it might extend, sadly, to fellow English but not to the French, or to Europeans but not Africans.

Fashion

The veil is in a sense analogous to virginity. The covering and effacement of beauty is designed to place the woman beyond reach. On the other hand, fashion—in the sense of wearing attractive or striking clothes, using cosmetics, or even walking in a way that flaunts the erotic—is quite evidently a celebration of the body. Along with bodily self-control, fashion becomes a way of communicating and negotiating with others.

As the designer Christian Lacroix put it, "My fashion is more a way of . . . finding your own true self." It may also involve an inventing of a "true" self.[27] Clothing and fashion are remarkably telling: Who is doing the fashioning—is it, at least in intent, *self*-fashioning? Or is dress answering to community strictures? Clothes express the extent of self-ownership, or tell who is control.

From at least the eighteenth century on in Europe, fashion is understood as a reflection of the self, an "intimate architecture."[28] Fashion captures so much of the paradoxes and ironies of the contemporary age. It expresses individual desire to be special and noteworthy, yet—evident in the very word *fashion*—it is almost always a statement about belonging to one group or another. Dress, in this regard, is about both the "I" *and* the "we." Fashion also captures contemporary angst about status, appropriateness, and about the authenticity of the expressed self. Fashion is the "construction site of the self," a locus of self-expression or self-invention.[29]

For men, modern fashion was determined around 1820 and changed minimally. Women's fashion is quite evidently more fluid, more creative, and more diverse. It has, over time, taken on an increasingly erotic allure (think Victoria's Secret). This is one of the interesting markers of fashion: a shift starting in seventeenth-century Europe from clothes marking class hierarchy—from aristocrat to peasant—to fashion fostering individual self-expression. It is a shift that is also highly gendered. Class is replaced, in terms of dress, by gender and sex.

The self is expressed in how people project themselves—above all in their clothing. "Fashioning" is a process that was initially partial in the extent to which the Europeans who embraced it sought to be, say, risqué. But it would not be too much of an exaggeration to say that through women's fashion the erotic comes to mark mainstream society by the second half of the twentieth century— at roughly the same point that virginity and chastity go *out* of fashion.[30]

Fashion is a social statement. It is also, usually unwittingly, a political statement. In the past, fashion—from jeans to body piercing—reflected generational divides. But today political divides are more severe. A crisis was set off in France from the late 1980s into the 1990s when some Muslim girls refused to remove their veils or "scarves" when attending France's officially secular public schools. A storm followed when a British cabinet minister and former foreign secretary, Jack Straw, stated that the veil was "a visible statement of separation and difference."[31] He was, as a consequence, uncomfortable when women visitors to his office had their faces covered. However, from an Islamist and more broadly traditional perspective, today's eroticized fashions express a "selling" of women as commodities. Women are, in this vision, once more prostituting themselves.

Our Bodies, Ourselves

What do these markers of social change tell us about the *experience* of the self? When are you in control of yourself? How do you experience your body and, through your body, the world? How do such changes become embedded in the individual's "life-world," so that these experiences become presumed—the default, as it were—of individuals and broader society? Language, thinking autobiographically (literally and metaphorically), and selfishness *and* empathy (paradoxically), are foundational to this experience.

One aspect of this social change is to experience physical corporeality, as it were, with self-interested capabilities and wants. The individual is marked as a producer and a consumer, potentially detached from the community. The term *consumer* first appeared in writing in the sixteenth century. This corporeal quality of the individual came to be the basis of much social theory, from Adam Smith to Karl Marx—in essence the bedrock of modern politics and economics.

Another aspect is the beginning of experiencing ourselves in our "subjectivity," where one becomes conscious of viewing the world through one's own mind, making the world (and ourselves) appear to be malleable.[32] This subjectivity is in contrast to viewing the world out there, including our roles, as objectively given, fixed, and taken for granted. (Our physical and subjective selves are often experienced as distinct—yet they clearly intersect. For example, consumption can signify symbolic matters as much as physical desires; purchasing Jimmy Choo shoes is not only about protecting our feet.)[33]

This change presages an extraordinary new act in history, a move away from communally scripted performances upon which honor rested and in which gender had such a critical place. Now one is a human who acts in the world, has interests, and is interested in well-being, materially and subjectively. This is not only a self-interested rationality, which is indeed unleashed in a new economics. It also sets loose a whole new vista of calculations, emotions, sensualities, and sensibilities arising out of a novel ability to fashion ourselves, or self-fashion, and to believe in now being able to fashion the world itself. This parallels a sense of an inner self and an outer self—an intimate, private world and a public, sometimes political world.

The experience of a self distinct from the world (or community) created a remarkable dynamic, as did the duality of physicality and subjectivity now intensely felt—from effecting a rational, calculating, efficient marketplace on the one hand, to the addictive narcotic of romantic and sensual love on the other. A whirlwind was set upon humanity.

Autobiography as a literary genre emerged in the late sixteenth century, most notably in the writing of the French scholar and statesman Michel de Montaigne. He published *Essays* in 1580, popularizing the essay form—the first-person autobiographical style married to a casual familiarity with the reader. His work anticipates a modern sensibility, even a style of journalism. In *Essays*, for example, he writes:

> A French gentleman was always wont to blow his nose with his fingers (a thing very much against our fashion), and he justifying himself for so doing, and he was a man famous for pleasant repartees, he asked me, what privilege this filthy excrement had, that we must carry about us a fine handkerchief to receive it, and, which was more, afterward to lap it carefully up and carry it all day about in our pockets, which, he said, could not but be much more nauseous and offensive, than to see it thrown away, as we did all other evacuations. [34]

Not incidentally, the issue of manners and etiquette arises in this era— though Montaigne takes a contrarian position. People are also learning of the palette of life experiences that they can now at least imagine are available to them:

> In one and the same nation, the virgins discover those parts that modesty should persuade them to hide, and the married women carefully cover and conceal them. To which, this custom, in another place, has some relation, where chastity, but in marriage, is of no esteem, for unmarried women may prostitute themselves to as many as they please, and being got with child, may lawfully take physic, in the sight of every one, to destroy their fruit. . . . There are places where brothels of young men are kept for the pleasure of women; where the wives go to war as well as the husbands, and not only share in the dangers of battle, but, moreover, in the honors of command. [35]

The signs of possessing the self are multifaceted: the new importance placed on washing one's body and on cleanliness (in contrast to medieval neglect of the body); the interest in perpetuating one's image through portraiture; the changes in art and the depiction of the body more broadly; a growing desire for status (and, as the status of born rank erodes, a growing *anxiety* about status); the rise of fashion in the sense we now understand the term. Even an interest in combating spousal abuse developed.

This new subjectivity—viewing the world through the prism of one's own mind, one's own "interests"—can bring about calculated selfishness. Paradoxically, however, such internal sensitivity also leads to empathy and compassion.[36] In a curious way, an era of great selfishness and yet unprecedented humanitarianism begins to unfold. Brutal exploitation would parallel movements to combat inhumanity, from slavery to child labor.

Interest begins to displace honor as the touchstone of daily life from the seventeenth century on, weaving together the disparate trends I have noted here. Interest reflects the sense of the individual as an actor or agent in his or her relations with others rather than assuming a rather predetermined life with little choice or agency. Economic self-interest as we understand the term today is a sub-set of "interest" in this regard, not its *summa*.

Authentic Identities

I have already noted how behavioral economists suggest that one characteristic of individuals' cognition is that they evaluate themselves through comparison. The impact of such a cognitive predisposition will be much magnified when individuals can actually imagine themselves with a palette of possibilities—rich or poor, happy or sad, for example.

In traditional societies—and that covers a broad array from tribal clans to medieval villages—roles are defined at birth. In such contexts the mere imagination of possible paths in life is highly constricted, and the notion of making comparisons is less likely. It would be like watching a bird fly and wondering why I shouldn't beat my arms and fly as well. For the peasant, the concept of becoming a member of the aristocracy was almost literally beyond imagination.

Self-possession breaks some of those restrictions. Over time, ascribed roles based on rank, class, race, gender—and recently even nationality—are less compelling (both in law and custom, and in our own minds). But once cut loose of such social anchors, individuals become fixated by external indications of relative status and respect and, more broadly, by affirmations of a sense of self.

Observers of social life have pointed to the intense anxiety of modern individuals. This anxiety is attributed to a variety of conditions, from being "other-directed" (relying on others for cues to acceptable behavior) to the decline of civil society.[37] But the anxiety is also a function of the subjectivity that comes with self-possession. This augurs an age of a deep preoccupation with the self—an extreme self-awareness and constant self-evaluation. With varying levels of nuance, one becomes the subject, and the object, of one's own actions.[38]

In traditional societies, the principle ethic is one of sacrifice; in contrast, the modern individual, who is sovereign over herself, experiences herself in terms of "needs." Those needs may be as a consumer of commodities. But they are also in the newly felt sense of subjectivity—or what would come to be called psychological needs. The preoccupation with the self, and the accompanying anxiety it brings, leads to a concern about "authenticity" (if not always defined in such terms). Yet paradoxically, individuals will seek to have their authenticity, their "true selves," affirmed by others. Even intimate relationships are sometimes portrayed as a process of mutual self-discovery—a notion alien to traditional societies.

The very term *authenticity* has come into the popular vernacular. The popular talk show psychologist Dr. Phil defines his version:

> When you're asked, "Who are you?" what is your answer? "I'm a mom." "I'm a doctor." "I live in Ohio." Often the answer is not who you are, but what you do, what your social station is, or how you see your function in life. You can't answer who you are, because you don't know.

There is another level of existence that is the true, genuine substance of who you are. It is what Dr. Phil defines as the authentic self:

> The authentic self is the you that can be found at your absolute core. It is the part of you not defined by your job, function, or role. It is the composite of all your skills, talents, and wisdom. It is all of the things that are uniquely yours and need expression, rather than what you believe you are supposed to be and do.[39]

Dr. Phil has come rather late to the game. The elusive authentic self is central to modern literature from Marcel Proust to Sigmund Freud. Literature that ostensibly reveals the inner self—who is the authentic me?—draws an extraordinary interest. Proust's *In Search of Lost Time* is perhaps the definitive example. What Proust does through the narrator is immerse us in his mind, his very subjectivity—his sensory experiences, desires, and obsessions. It is a thoroughly modern novel. Like Freud, Proust suggests an endless search for the self, for part of the self (including aspects of memory) cannot be recovered. The search for authenticity is without end. One aspect of that search is caught in the flow of time: we can evoke past experiences; we can in a sense even repeat them. But there is something irretrievable in the past, which we can at best remember only in fragile ways. When we can evoke the memory of a pleasurable moment, it is an epiphany—a sudden moment of self-recognition. So Proust's now almost universally familiar Madeleine suggests it:

> She sent for one of those squat plump little cakes called "petites madeleines," which look as though they had been molded in the fluted valve of a scallop shell. . . . I raised to my lips a spoonful of the tea in which I had soaked a morsel of the cake. No sooner had the warm liquid mixed with the crumbs touched my palate than a shudder ran through me and I stopped, intent upon the extraordinary thing that was happening to me. An exquisite pleasure invaded my senses . . .
>
> And suddenly the memory revealed itself. The taste was that of the little piece of madeleine which on Sunday mornings at Combray . . . when I went to say good morning to her in her bedroom, my aunt Leonie used to give me, dipping it first in her own cup of tea or tisane . . . and the whole of Combray and its surroundings, taking shape and solidity, sprang into being, town and garden alike, from my cup of tea.[40]

Self-interest and authenticity, two sides of the same coin, are in contrast to the social anchor that is honor, which is maintained through the performance of duty, with interior life secondary (socially at least).

Where the individual ownership of self becomes central and "subjectivity" is increasingly felt, sexuality and gender become a matter of increasing reflection and engagement, individually and socially. This should not be surprising as sexuality and gender—biologically, psychologically, and sociologically—are so integral to being human. The change with self-ownership regards the "reflection" on, and exploration of, sexuality and gender. This is in contrast to the prior notion that, for example, gender roles are fixed and settled—and is the case in honor societies. Indeed, defining ourselves in terms of sexual *identities* (as opposed to practices)—as heterosexual, bisexual, gay, lesbian, transgendered and the like—is a modern phenomenon itself.[41] Thus when the rights of individuals become a point of contention in "culture wars" at varying levels of intensity, sex and sexuality quickly come to mark the contours of the fight.

There is a deep gap between principles that order society on interest and authenticity on the one hand, and on honor on the other. I do not mean, at least solely, between communities or nations; it is a struggle within communities and nations across the world—although, of course, which forces are ascendant varies by place.

The Cult of the Body

Political philosophers of the seventeenth and eighteenth centuries were fearful. As the authorities of the past—above all the Church—began to recede, and even principles of honor and self-sacrifice began to subside, what would hold society together? If each man (never mind each woman) were sovereign, what was to stop the social order from spinning out of control? A variety of solutions were put forth, but a common theme was to re-think the nature of the individual: he was recast as a rational creature, driven by interest.

John Locke, born in 1632, is the English philosopher often thought to be the first in articulating modern conceptions of consciousness and the self. An almost obsessive interest in feelings, autobiography, and diaries, developed in the seventeenth century by anxious Protestants with no "superiors" to turn to. Locke's solution was to suggest that individuality had common characteristics that made people predictable and even uniform in their behavior. Thus, the new subjectivism was not to be feared.

This approach has had a very unfortunate impact on social and political theory. From it scholars have derived a notion of the first principle that all humans can be reduced to the same motives, rooted in rational self-interest. This approach, as the contemporary political scientist Uday Singh Mehta has written, assumes that all differences will become familiar.[42] A belief in such a first principle has misshapen policy, from economic development to plans for democratization. It has led to a situation where we are squinting into the gloom when we try comprehending vastly different societies by simplifying complex realities and by assuming that somehow everyone thinks alike.

In fact, even when we enjoy ownership over ourselves—the more critical pivot than some uniform rationality—we respond in different ways depending on the context. Some situations, notably romantic and sexual, will generate intensely emotional responses that lead to decisions that are far from rational. The behavioral economist Dan Ariely questions whether there is such a thing as a fully integrated human personality. He notes how our motivations are fundamentally different in a world characterized by social exchanges rather than market exchanges.[43] And this is within societies that have a broad consensus on the importance of individual control over their selves.

We have considered in this chapter the genesis of the shift to bodily self-control in Europe. The Dutch in their Golden Age were a vanguard in Europe economically, sexually, and even in terms of women's status. The Dutch case was a precursor, however, to a set of changes that were piecemeal, gradual, conflicted, and stretching over hundreds of years. The concept of the sovereign individual saw a remarkable uptick in scope and geographic reach in the latter part of the twentieth century.

The fault line across the world and within countries cuts across the "cult of the body," or I should say, opposing cults of the body. Not surprisingly, the points of contention shift, from marriage practices, to dress, to whose law is supreme. Ironically, it is in the Netherlands where that struggle has become all the more raw—containing in its borders as it does Dutch citizens who conspicuously (some would say ostentatiously) continue a history of unfettered self-expression, and immigrants, some of whom are fundamentalist.

The contending images of the female body were distilled to their essence in a short Dutch film called *Submission,* released in 2004, and in its aftermath. The film's title was a translation of "Islam," and it was also presented as a critique of conservative Islam. It generated widespread controversy after being shown on Dutch public television. A Dutch Somali woman, the now well-known Ayaan Hirsi Ali, Muslim-born and a refugee, who wrote the script, notes:

> When I sat down to write the script for our film, I decided to use the format of prayer to bring about dialogue with Allah. I pictured a woman standing in the center of a room. In the four corners of the room, four women depict restrictive verses from the Quran. The woman in the middle of the room is veiled, but her veil is transparent at the front, opaque at the back. The transparency is necessary because it challenges Allah to look at what he created: the body of a woman. On her torso is written the opening verse of the Quran.[44]

Her collaborator on the film, Theo van Gogh, was murdered not long after the film's release. The assassin, an Islamist, shot Van Gogh, then cut his throat, almost decapitating him, and stabbed him in the chest. A knife pinned a note to his body, addressing and attacking Hirsi Ali. In both a literal and a figurative sense, statements were made on and through bodies about the freedom to express one's self and about honor, about individual rights and the prerogatives of a community.[45]

CHAPTER THREE

Jerusalem, Rome, Mecca

A Crescent Rises in the Firmament and in Arabia

American soldiers learned of the Middle East's social complexity in the second Iraq war at the dawning of the twenty-first century. A journalist told this story:

Warned by a drone hovering over the "Triangle of Death" in a Sunni area South of Baghdad that men had been spotted burying weapons in a cemetery, the U.S. infantrymen discovered guns and ammunition under gravestones. Those who had hidden the weapons had disappeared. Who were they? Were they the principal target of this particular military patrol, al-Qaeda in Iraq? Or were they Ba'athist loyalists of Saddam Hussein? Or local tribesmen?

In the pre-dawn gloom, with palm trees and shadowed villages nearby, Lt. Thomas Murphy told the journalist, "Here we have so many enemies." Al Qaeda Iraq was just one of myriad groups with overlapping conflicts in this area that drew sustenance from the Euphrates River. Other American officers elaborated:

> "Shiites don't like to shoot. . . . They just EFP [explosively formed penetrator] you," said Maj. Craig Whiteside. . . . "The Sunnis use snipers, RPGs, mortars—they'll attack you in every possible way. . . . Or they'll attack each other." Intra-tribal, intra-Shiite, and intra-Sunni clashes play out against a backdrop of byzantine allegiances and arcane codes of conduct. "We are in the land of the blood feuds," said Maj. Rick Williams, a liaison to tribes in the area. "It's very difficult to tell a tribal fight from a sectarian fight because interests are pretty mixed. You can't just put up a fence."[1]

These American soldiers were experiencing what scores of armies that have traversed the lands of the Middle East over thousands of years have experienced.

When we look at the Middle East, that great global crossroads, we think of the dozens of civilizations, invaders, interlopers, and groups that saw it (and continue to see it) as home, that have placed their footprints on its mostly dusty earth.

Romans, Greeks, Ancient Israelites, the Crusaders, the Ottomans, the French, and the British, among others, left their mark. The region is justifiably seen as having helped shape Western civilization as well as providing the wellspring of Judaism, Christianity, and Islam.

Yet what is astonishing is the extent of social continuity through the travails of multitudes of groups that have marked its landscape. The patriarchal forms we read of in biblical sources—such as in the story of David—are very much with us to this day. Furthermore, the underlying patriarchal kinship, or tribalism, has had a formative impact even on urban life and government in the Middle East—a social system that the Lebanese sociologist Hisham Sharabi has called "neopatriarchy."[2]

This tribalism is the foundation we must look at in discussing the Middle East. Then we can ask how Islam (or Judaism and Christianity) shaped and were shaped by this human landscape. At the heart of tribes, to varying levels, is a severe patriarchy. To refer to the Middle East as "Islamic" sometimes hides as much as it reveals. Or, more accurately, the Middle East has layers—different social forms on different geographic scales—that compete and intersect at times in tortuous ways, generating a sense of utter disorder, and at times in ways that suggest a harmonious sense of purpose. It is akin to bringing your eyes close to a pointillist painting, made dizzy by the myriad and apparently formless multi-hued dots, only to back away to see a sinuous landscape.

Islam is critical to understanding Middle Eastern dynamics, of course, but only if we weave such a pan-religious identification together with the varied social geographies of family, clan, tribe, village, sect, nation, and the like—and ask how and in what ways they interact. Scholars debate the role of Islam, some claiming it is central to understanding Middle Eastern extremism, while others claim that the underlying environment of the Middle East is too varied to make any claims about "Islam." The former approach is too blunt; the latter makes the implausible suggestion that Islam is, in effect, a meaningless category.

Rather, it is the way different social geographies, from tribe to nation to religion, crisscross and shape one another that counts in practice. We need to grapple with a three-dimensional reality. We have to consider all kinds of vertical layers (those social geographies), in unison with the "horizontal" issues that most occupy analysts—struggles between states, militia and terrorist organizations, or, for that matter, religions.

The way Islam intersects with local cultures (including in its historical expansion beyond the Middle East) in part accounts for its varied expressions across the world. In that context Islam has intermingled with a variety of cultural forms, from Javanese in Indonesia to African folk religion. The more recent diffusion by Wahhabi Islamist extremists originating in Saudi Arabia is insidious for such communities in its attempts to create a "pure" global Islam, free of any other cultural influences—from Asia, to Africa and Europe, and beyond. The Wahhabis are what the Indonesian studies scholar Mark Woodward has called a "colonizing" force.[3]

In analyzing the social and political impact of Islam, it is critical to analyze the various parties in play. This includes not just communities, such as tribal or pastoral groups, but different religious sects. These vary from the sometimes welcoming Sufis to the radical Wahhabi Islamists.[4]

In this chapter, I invite the reader to join in exploring how tribalism shaped the birth of Islam in Arabia and Islam's subsequent development. We will discover a nuanced and at times paradoxical relationship in the greater Middle East. In this region, much of Islam is at once in a symbiotic relationship with (especially regarding tribal patriarchy and women), and in opposition to, the "localness" and parochial quality of the tribal societies.

Indeed, as Islam spreads beyond the tribal crescent, it evolves in distinctly different forms—less characterized by tribal patriarchy, and as a consequence not as vulnerable to giving birth to Islamist ideology and to its violent cadres. Indonesia, for example—the largest Muslim country in the world but absent a tribal history—is patriarchal, but it is not of the hard tribal variety. The Islamists, though significant, are a small minority. And militant Islamism did not arise indigenously; the ideology came, primarily, from the Middle East.[5]

Tribal Sojourn

Islam arose and developed in the Arabian Peninsula, and then, after its series of sudden conquests, became a dominant community far beyond its original tribal lands. The Arabian culture that helped shape Islam in its early formation was overwhelmingly Bedouin. Over time, Islam would rule, to a lesser or greater degree, from South Asia to West Africa. Outside Arabia, Islam would evolve in different ways. But in the beginning the social context was that of the Arab tribes.[6]

The Bedouin exemplify, then and now, the Arab tribal structure. Camel nomads, they could maintain themselves on camels' milk and occasionally on their flesh. This was supplemented with the wheat and dates they obtained from the agriculturalists—the farmers—who were limited to oases. The farmers, in turn, could acquire other herd animals from the nomads and other products brought in from far afield.

The Bedouin life assured a good degree of independence, which afforded lucrative trading and, under the right circumstances, the extraction of tribute from farmers and villagers. Villages, caravans, and herds were and are targets of predatory raiding. "Protection services" were offered for caravans and oases, which may have been honest help or simple extortion. But even those in the commercial towns or agricultural oases thought of themselves as "settled Bedouin."[7]

If women in these tribal societies are the promise of reproduction of family and culture, men are the bedrock of security.[8] The honor of virginity and fidelity is matched by the honor of the martial courage of men. This is not to suggest there was or is some kind of egalitarian complementarity (or equity) between men and women, as some have argued. The senior man has authority over everyone else in the family, and the women are subject to distinct forms of subjugation. Indeed, as we observed in the story of David, the women are a form of property of the men. Even young boys can have authority over their mothers in their fathers' absence.[9]

Family and community security in Arab culture, from the pre-Islamic period until today, has rested on "balanced opposition."[10] Regardless of sex, almost everybody belongs to numerous nested sets of kin groups, from families to clans, tribes, and confederations of tribes. Each group, at all levels, is responsible for protection of its members and for the harm its members may do to others. It is a mix of collective responsibility and "self-help." If there is a confrontation, groups face off: family vs. family, lineage vs. lineage, clan vs. clan, tribe vs. tribe, and so on. The anthropologist Philip Carl Salzman suggests this can go all the way up to the Islamic Ummah vs. the infidels.[11]

Balanced opposition is a way to organize security. But it also means that violence, or the threat of violence, is an organizing principle of society—at a basic personal and communal level. Any potential attacker knows he may trigger a formidable collective response. It is the very antithesis of the civil republican form, where the state monopolizes violence (in principle) and social relations are conducted on the basis of restraint, etiquette, and norms of civility. The role of violence explains why, in good part, the prowess of males is so valued. Group loyalty rather than the rule of law prevails in the tribal milieu. The tribal form is decentralized in that there is no central authority. It is democratic for men in that every male has a say and decision making is collective.[12]

Blood feuds are often kicked off—and some last for generations—due to loss of property, injury, or death. Because many group members are implicated in such feuds, the group can often pressure its members to act prudently and cautiously and to avoid entering into conflict if it can be avoided.

That social pressure is clearly not always effective. In present-day Albania, for example, thousands of men are under the threat of revenge killings. For any act of murder, victims' families feel compelled to find a male relative of the murderer to ensure vengeance. This spirals into family and clan blood feuds. Even young boys are at risk. Often those under threat remain at home indoors—permanently—so as not to expose themselves to retribution. The women may have to do the farm work as the men hide.[13]

Individuals have two reasons to enter into collective arrangements. One is practical: you act on the basis of reciprocity; fellow group members will defend you if the need arises. More important is honor: your reputation rests on martial prowess (akin to the sexual honor of women). Tribal societies do not afford the relatively easy "exit" from family ties that modern functioning states do from kin dependencies, so to dishonor oneself is to live a life of humiliation and shame. Furthermore, it will be difficult for the dishonored to find partners for any social or economic endeavors.[14]

The tribal arrangement can encompass hundreds of thousands of individuals without the need for centralized institutions or hierarchy. Individuals are interchangeable, in essence, because individuals can undertake a variety of tasks—riding, fighting, bartering, and the like—and are not necessarily divided into specialized roles.[15]

The great Muslim historian Ibn Khaldun was the first to recount, writing in the fourteenth century, what he saw as the fundamental instability of the greater Middle East. Warriors of a tribe conquer a weak state with its traders, merchants, and settled urbanites and village supporters. But such tribes themselves are "urbanized" over time and lose their tribal warrior ethic. Kin ties lessen as they divide themselves geographically and politically over dispersed sinecures. They become a weak state, vulnerable to other tribal warriors.[16]

Many village peasants have a tribal origin—some even shift between living in villages and in tents—and it is fairly common for peasants to have group loyalties based on tribal, patrilineal descent. Indeed, tribal forms reach into towns and cities. More than demography, tribal life has, in the Middle East, a mythic status, felt to be the primordial essence of the pure, desert life.[17] It is in this environment that we see the rise of Muhammad in the seventh century.

Muhammad: Kinship and Ethics

Muhammad was born in 570 in Mecca. He married at the age of 25 and worked at different times as a merchant and as a shepherd. Later in his life, retreating to a cave outside Mecca for meditation, he experienced his first revelation from God. He was 40 years old. Three years later he started preaching. He proclaimed that there is a single God and that his listeners had to completely "submit" (the root of the term Islam) to Him. Muhammad himself, he said, was the prophet and messenger of God.

The faithful have held that the Qur'an was revealed from God to Muhammad from 610 to 632 c.e., the year Muhammad died. Muhammad (who could not write) had recited the Qur'an to his followers and dictated it to his scribes. The third caliph after Muhammad's death, Caliph Uthman ibn Affan, brought about a standard version of the Qur'an among the variety of versions that were in circulation. "Non-standard" texts were burned. Muslims hold the present Arabic form of the Qur'an as exactly the same as that revealed to Muhammad.

Muhammad was one of those remarkable historical figures who defined a new vision, based on an ethical system and helped to institutionalize that vision. The Qur'an declares to Muslims, "You have become the best community ever raised up for mankind, enjoining the right and forbidding the wrong, and having faith in Allah" (III, 110). This prophecy makes clear that Islam is based on universal ethics.

As such, Islam was in tension with the seventh-century tribal society of Arabia, where kinship, not impersonal ethical injunctions, defined allegiances. Islam demanded a trans-tribal communal belonging, the existence of a society that was distinct from those that had preceded it, and demanded that Muslims must collectively endeavor to realize the faith. This realization of the faith was not simply about internal *beliefs* but was a set of daily *practices*. Muslims were part of a common social body, a shared community. And yet even pious Muslims differ on what the "best community" should be like.[18]

The tensions and interactions that emerged between a new ethical framework that is universal in its import (and as it turns out, its export) and the localized, kinship-based society, shape Islam and its internal struggles to this day—especially for Arab Islam. The way this tension plays out is not necessarily a simple zero-sum game, but is more nuanced. The Islamists, for example, project a tribal-like patriarchy globally, while rejecting local or national cultures. (Muhammad himself was an orphan, and it is interesting to consider if this shaped his turn to universal ethics over traditional tribal kinship.) These contrasting expressions of Islam are reflected in different practices and in doctrinal disputes around the world, from the Middle East to Indonesia. What is of special note, however, is the way the "social location" of women is defined is critical to the different expressions of the faith.

The early parts of the Qur'an speak of many moral injunctions and demands for generosity, purity, and chaste conduct. The morals, the historian Marshall G. S. Hodgson observed, were not unprecedented and seldom diverged from older Bedouin norms. What was new was the way these norms demanded that lives be lived—with an ethical orientation as humans, rather than as a function of a specific family, clan, and tribe. So it is revealed in the Qur'an's portentous imagery of the Last Day:

> When the sun is darkened, when the stars fall and disperse, when the mountains are made to move away, when the camels, ten months pregnant, are left untended, when the wild beasts are brought together, when the seas are set alight, when men's souls are paired (like with like), when the infant girl, buried alive, is asked for what crime she was slain, when the records are laid open, when the sky is stripped bare, when Hell is made to burn fiercely, when Paradise is brought near, every soul shall know what it has put forward. (LXXXI, 1–14)

Humans cannot *choose* to be good of heart. They cannot control their own ways—the evidence of failure of will was too great. They can achieve rectitude only by submitting themselves to the will of God. The human choice was between submitting to God or turning to the personal desires of the moment.[19] Condemnation of the infanticide of girls (as a result of tribes favoring boys) in the imagery of the Last Day was not new as such, but its presentation as an undeniable ethical imperative was a new turn. In a very real way, humans had to give up control of their bodily selves if they were to be moral beings. Once more we find a set of internal tensions and interplays, from the sense of tribal notions of self-sacrifice to the idea of universal humanity.

Women became a central gauge of that strain within the faith and culture, and here the Qur'an shows elements both of tribal practices and of a relatively more moderate approach. At the center of the Qur'an's exposition of the family was the standardization of one type of Arab family, with some amendments. The man maintained authority over his wife (or wives), superseding that of her family or his. He was responsible for his wife and children's welfare. The children were defined through his line, including their religious identity. The children belonged to him. Inheritance was to be primarily through the immediate family and not to be spread more thinly through the clan.[20]

Yet wives and daughters were bestowed with more status than in the traditional Arab family on which the Qur'anic family was based. Bride-price (or *mahr*) was given by the groom to the bride's family in Bedouin families. Under Muslim law the *mahr* was given to the bride herself. (This had often been the practice in pre-Islamic Mecca as well.) If substantial enough, this bride-price gave the bride a certain amount of insurance and dignity. A man had the prerogative of divorce from a wife, but if he brought about the divorce he could not reclaim the *mahr*. He also had to support his wife and children from his own wealth, such as it may be, and not draw on his wife's property.

Wives and daughters had rights of inheritance, though sons were given twice as much as daughters. Infanticide of girls, as graphically described in the Last Day, was strenuously prohibited. Muslims could not enslave other Muslims, though Muslim men could take female slaves as concubines.[21]

Sharia legal discourse, as it evolved, made for further norms in the arena of the family. (Sharia is made up of a complex set of derivations, but it stems from the Qur'an and the *sunnah*, or practice of Muhammad, which in turn is based on God's word and on scholarly consensus and analogy.) Men could have up to four wives—whereas in pre-Islamic Arabia having more than four wives was not uncommon. In Islam, all the wives had to be treated equally. Over time, rules could be interpreted more strictly. Thus Qur'anic injunctions about women's modesty were stretched, through *hadith* (reports on the sunnah), to physical seclusion in the household and to burqas and the face-covering niqab.[22]

Thus Muslim communities could evolve in ways more conservative or more moderate. The status of women has been a primary in gauging the trajectory. John Esposito, the scholar of Islam, has argued that Islamic law, as it was established in the early period of the faith, reflected the dominance of conservative jurists over those who sought an Islamic jurisprudence that was more flexible and retained room for interpretation.[23] Over the long term, sociological factors were critical. The underlying culture—be it tribal patriarchy or, say, a community of merchants built on trade—played an essential role in determining what form the local Islamic practice took.[24]

Other tribal practices, such as the importance of honor and male martial prowess, remained central. Concepts of "balanced opposition" now extended to the level of Islam as a whole. Honor could now be invoked for ethical—or, in modern-day terms, ideological—causes that transcended the skeins of family, clan, and tribal ties.

But equally, in this emerging religion, a very different ethic could show itself. From the start, some individuals sought a personal piety that stressed inwardness and a more mystical contemplation. This form of Islam, which came to be called Sufism, was frequently disconnected from the historically oriented and politically minded Islam. It was even detached from the idea of an Ummah. For the most ardent Sufis, Sharia law was just an outer matter, a shell. Such written law could at best be incidentally related to the character of the soul. Sufis honored the Qur'an, not through the letters of its words, but in repeating the felt *experience* that Muhammad had receiving God's word. The Sufis wished to relive the spiritual experience of Muhammad—which in turn reflects the "palpable" meaning and transcendent states for which mere words can only approximate true inner feeling.[25]

Sufis have traced their origin to Muhammad himself, rejoicing in the Prophet's very illiteracy. For Allah to reveal himself to humanity through the Qur'an, he needed a vessel, a person "unpolluted" by intellectual knowledge represented in text and script. Muhammad's illiteracy as such was a sign of his purity.[26]

One of the most important of the Sufi figures was al-Hallāj from Persia, who died in the year 922. For him, the mystical life was to revisit our encounter with the divine essence, taking us back to the primordial moment that is each person's creation. In contrast, for the Sharia conservatives the word of God was explicit and unequivocal. No spiritual states should cloud a man's head. Nothing should obfuscate prescribed daily duties. But, like Christian and Jewish mystics, al-Hallāj rejected ritualistic practices that he felt hid the true experience of divine love. He favored the "drunkenness" of divine responsiveness to "sober" responsibility. Al-Hallāj was tried and condemned for his heresy. He was crucified, his hands and feet cut off, and quartered and burned. In an eerie parallel to Catherine of Siena, he bore his agony with delight, so it was said, since he was suffering for the sake of God.[27]

The individual soul and its relationship with the All-in-All is a common motif across mystical groups, Jewish, Christian, and Muslim alike. That stress on the individual soul has often (if not always) been an opening for women to take on a more equal role. Thus in Sufism women could be guiding torches of the faith. Rābi'a al-Basrī, born in 717 in Basra, in what is today Iraq, was one. Her words captured the spiritual sense of Sufism and the deeply contrarian view vis-à-vis the orthodoxy:

> In love, nothing exists between breast and Breast.
> Speech is born out of longing,
> True description [comes] from the real taste.
> *The one who tastes, knows;*
> *The one who explains, lies.*[28]

It was claimed that even men who looked down upon women accepted Rābi'a as a model of selfless love: in the unity of God, lovers do not have a separate existence; and as such, a distinction between a man and a woman cannot be made.[29]

Still, Sufism has had its political offshoots as well. Across sects, there are points when they seek to institutionalize themselves to ensure their continuity. Or they organize politically to protect themselves. This has been true across mystical and other-worldly groups of all faiths and has the effect of changing the character of the sect in the process. The Safavid dynasty, which was one of the most historically important dynasties in Iran (ruling from 1501 to 1722), had Sufi roots. Sufis established many Islamic states in West Africa, including the Sokoto Caliphate in Northern Nigeria (founded in 1809, and continued through British colonial rule, albeit much weakened).

Islam Transcendent

Islam expanded much beyond its tribal roots in theology, custom, and geography. It is this transcendent or overarching Islam that is the framework for arguments within the faith. Moreover, it is primarily this broader religion that generates engagement and opposition from without. Internally, all Muslims, no matter how diverse, orient themselves vis-à-vis a shared Sharia. Such shared lodestars—even if engendering vastly different interpretations—undergird a certain commonality.

Globalizing forces, however, have had the effect of fostering Islamist movements that see "pure" historical Islam as transnational and free of local cultures—thus generating internal Muslim conflict. Paradoxically, movements for a global Islam—such as Salafi Islamists—find authenticity in the ancient patriarchy of Arabia, albeit in a "revealed," adapted, and universalized form.[30] The Arabian tribal cultures themselves are, as such, rejected.

The outer contours of Islam can be productively elicited through contrasts with its older siblings, Judaism and Christianity. These contrasts also help reveal the dynamics, civil and uncivil, between and within these creeds. Islam, Christianity and Judaism, the three great monotheistic faiths, have always been acutely aware and suspicious of each other—due not only to political and military challenges but also their intertwining histories and theologies. They have recognized their commonalities less frequently (or at least did not often recognize them in a spirit of fraternity). Judaism and Islam have shared legal traditions, with regulations and customs determining the rhythm of daily life as well as governance. Christian distinctions of "rendering unto Caesar the things which are Caesar's and unto God the things that are God's" (Matthew 22:21), and separation of church and state, or religious and political authorities, were foreign to classical Islam and historical Judaism.[31]

On the other hand, Islam and Christianity had commonalities distinct from the Jews. Judaism claimed universal truths, but all peoples and religions could reach the world to come, or heaven. Indeed, as the "chosen people" Jews had (and have) more extensive obligations than Gentiles in order to reach that Eden. For much of Christian history (and still today for many Christian denominations), and for all of Muslim history, one's place in paradise could only be assured for their own believers. Christians and Jews in turn shared the Hebrew Bible (with Christians adding the New Testament). Muslims let go of the Hebrew and Christian scriptures, while recognizing the prophetic and historical importance of many biblical figures.

Yet what unites the three faiths theologically has had the most dramatic impact on human history: the concept of a singular, universal and transcendent God. Here we find built-in oppositions and tensions between self and other, or believers and non-believers; and between the imperfect if not outright corrupt world in which we live and the idyllic heavenly world that we can imagine. The many ways in which those tensions are (in theory) resolved tells us much about these three faiths and the myriad sects that make them up.

Thus we find similarities among sects cutting across Judaism, Christianity, and Islam—mystics, for example, who seek to escape the corruption of this world in order to achieve union with the All-in-All: "[to] be uplifted to the clarity of ecstasy, to wander the solitary heights of contemplation stripped of forms or images, tasting union with the only and absolute principle." Such mystics will be, at the same time, in theological opposition (or worse) with groups *within* their respective religions.[32]

In the Hebrew Bible God's, or Yahweh's, singularity is invoked on a number of occasions and is the essence of the most central prayer, *Shema Yisrael* ("Hear, O Israel"), said in morning and evening Jewish prayer services: "Hear, O Israel: the Lord our God, the Lord is one" (Deuteronomy 6:4). In Christianity, the story has been more complicated because of the trinity of the Father, Son, and Holy Ghost. But since the three are viewed as being of the "same substance," they make up a unity—in effect, a monotheistic God.[33]

The doctrine of the "oneness of God" is foundational in Islam. The doctrine is termed *Tawhid,* and it stipulates that God, or Allah, is unique and indivisible and that Allah is transcendent and independent of creation. Allah's universality also points to the moral and just coherence of the universe. Both good and evil arise from the act of creation, but evil forces do not have any power independent of Allah. Allah is a universal God rather than local, place-based, or tribal—an issue that is of core importance for the struggle within Islam. Tawhid is the first part of the *Shahada,* the Muslim declaration of belief, which in English is "There is no god but Allah, and Muhammad is the Messenger of Allah." Recitation of the Shahada is the most important of the Five Pillars of Islam for Muslims.[34] Converts to Islam are required to publically recite the Shahada.

The life of Muhammad, a model for all pious Muslims, falls into two parts. In the first, during his years in his birthplace of Mecca (570–622), he was in opposition to the ruling pagan oligarchy. In the second period of his life, after his move to Medina (622–632), he was a head of state. These two periods—one of resistance and one of rule—inspired, the scholar of Islam Bernard Lewis writes, two traditions in Islam: one radical and activist, and the other authoritarian and quietist. Both traditions are reflected in contemporary as well as historical Muslim writings and practices. The inspiration of the Prophet for Muslims is reinforced in that he triumphed in his lifetime and died a ruler and a conqueror. In contrast, Christ was crucified, and Moses died before he reached the Promised Land. These narratives profoundly influenced their respective religions.[35]

The succession of the three faiths also proved critical. Just as Christianity saw itself superseding Judaism, Islam taught that it superseded both Judaism and Christianity. In this teaching, the Jews and Christians had failed their custodianship, allowing the revelations entrusted to them to be corrupted. However, as religions that had preceded Islam, they did have certain rights in Muslim lands that made possible the practice of their faiths and maintenance of their places of worship—with certain discriminatory practices that ensured recognition of Islam as the privileged religion of the three.

The Politics of Religion

After the terrorist attacks of September 11, 2001, it became common in Western countries to lament that Islam had not had its own reformation similar to the Protestant Reformation in the sixteenth century. By this, commentators were referring to the process of democratization and pluralism that, in time, came out of the Reformation. Aside from the problematic tendency to project one's own historical evolution on other religions and societies, this revealed a certain misreading of Islam. Islam does indeed have more in common with Protestantism than with Catholicism—but with critical differences.

For Islam, as for Protestantism, there is no papacy or religious hierarchy. There is no definitive body to determine authoritative interpretations of the holy texts. The holy texts (such as the Bible or the Qur'an) themselves take on a "fundamental" importance in revealing God's word. Absent an authoritative hierarchy, a certain kind of democracy of the sacred takes over within the faiths. In both Protestantism and Islam we have a history of theological disputes, schisms, break-offs, new sects, and contending schools of thought, each claiming a better understanding of the holy writ—sometimes expressed violently, at other times more peacefully.

In Islam, the most notable division is that between the Sunnis and the Shias.[36] This schism began with a dispute over who should succeed the Prophet Muhammad as the caliph. The Sunnis have believed that the *Shura*—the community of Muslims or their representatives—should choose the caliph. The Shias have believed that the caliph should remain within the family and descendants of the Prophet. With the Iranian revolution of 1979, the Shias moved from a more quietist group to one with a more centralized authority based around the mullahs, but an authority that is in question, to say the least. It may have moved in a more papal direction, but it is without the authority over Shias that Rome has for Catholics.[37]

Thus Islam, "horizontal" in its organization, is egalitarian in this regard. Protestants share this sentiment that the believer experiences God directly, unmediated by any priestly body organized in a more "vertical" way. Protestant ministers and the Muslim *ulema* (religious scholars) are, in principle, no closer to God than any other believers. Both religious groups had some sects that were (and are) more or less exclusivist: Protestant Calvinists, for example, felt you had to be a Calvinist to be saved. In Islam, the militant Islamists view even other Muslims as *kafirs*, as unbelievers. Muslim groups rarely go to the extent of the more inclusive Protestant sects that see all—including non-believers—as having the potential to reach the gates of heaven.

(Little known outside South Africa is that many white South Africans used the word "kaffir" as a nasty epithet for black Africans, especially in the Apartheid era but even today. Such whites were overwhelmingly Christian, and completely unaware of its origins in Islam—a religion they did not think about much, and when they did it was generally with disdain.[38] The white South African use of the term likely has its roots in the African slave trade and Muslim slave traders. The term *kafir*, in both the religious and racial milieus, does not simply describe a category of people. It conjures up a contemptuous disgust, on a deeply visceral and aesthetic level.)

Especially noteworthy is the extraordinary pluralism that characterizes both Protestantism and Islam. Given this diversity, it is a mistake to typecast Islam, as frequently happens in Western countries. Muslims range from other-worldly mystics to violent, politically minded Jihadists, with a broad mainstream of Muslims in the middle. That is not to suggest that we cannot point to certain parameters that characterize Islam, parameters of great consequence—for example, the role of monotheism or the absence of a priestly hierarchy. But in analyzing the ebbs and flows of Muslim politics, it is essential to keep this diversity in mind.

Notwithstanding their similarities, the differences between classical Islam and Protestantism are equally telling and help us understand some of the dynamics of global politics. The differences can be thought of in terms of two broad but interconnected ways of acting in the world—namely, in terms of *time and space* and the *sacred and secular*.

The Navel of the World
Time and Space

Islam and Protestantism arose in distinct settings, in ways that affect us to this day. Islam took root in the seventh century in a tribal, honor-based society, and the initial expansion involved the conversion of different tribes to the faith. It was in this reality that Muhammad prophesied. Islam was shaped as well by the local human landscape. In the longer term, pluralism within Islam created space for a variety of theological and social leanings—but that came later.

Protestantism gave impetus to an embryonic system of European states, from the Netherlands to England, from Germany to Sweden, and then in Western Europe as a whole through the Peace of Westphalia in 1648 (which recognized Western Europe as being made up of independent states). Protestantism propelled more centralized governments and, specifically, the birth of republics (as opposed to the then-prevalent monarchies). The first was the Dutch Republic in 1609. In other words, Protestantism foreshadowed and drove forward the emergence of a new kind of state and civic politics (limited at first to propertied men). It also sowed the ground for a new international politics, founded on principles we now call sovereignty and national self-determination. Furthermore, multiple sects and churches, active across Western Europe, represented Protestantism from the beginning; whereas Islam was initially more unified through the figure of Muhammad.

These respective origins created an indelible mark for both religions and provided, for Islam, a cardinal point of reference. Unlike Protestantism, Islam calls on adherents to look to history, to the beginnings, for their Golden Age. In Protestantism, time propels us forward, progressively, to the moment of truth, the *Eschaton*, the end of time, when the kingdom of heaven becomes one with earth. This is the early modern seed of secular ideas of "progress." It is this dynamic that gives energy to economic development and scientific creativity. Western Europe, long trailing the science and thought of the Muslim world (and that of China and India), begins from about the seventeenth century on to surpass the rest of the world in science and technology.[39]

Islamic history, especially the period of the Prophet and his companions, is of significance for Muslims as it reveals the working out of God's purpose for the Ummah. But Islam's boundaries (or *Dar al-Islam*, the House of Islam) are more fluid and are matters of debate among the believers. The very fluidity of Islam generates tension within Islam and wherever Islam is present (such as in Europe), since political claims can follow assertions of a country—say, Spain—lying in the jurisdiction of the House of Islam.

Because the time of Muhammad and his companions is felt to be the Golden Age, many wish to emulate that period. The Muslim past is palpable for the believer, especially those who read the Qur'an and the commentaries in a literalist fashion, such as is the case of the Salafis. The word *Salafi* is from the Arabic root for "the companions," the first three generations of the followers of Muhammad. The Salafis include the Wahhabis and other Islamists. Not all Salafis are violent—the other-worldly and non-violent Salafis will, as it were, "mentally" travel to that time in history, while withdrawing from the corruption they see in the societies around them.[40] But for the militant Salafis, the images that beckon to them are those of the warrior, Jihad (in its martial and expansionary sense), a "pure" transnational faith, and the tribal patriarchy of medieval Arabia. It is an ideology of the patriarchal, honor-based tribe writ global.

Notions of time impact space: The desire to transform the world to reflect the image of a Golden Age—either of the past or the promised future—has driven expansionary impulses.

Interestingly, while both classical Islam and the West use spatial metaphors to describe authority, they employ them in distinct ways. In the West, the imagery is up-down and front-back (and it is better to be up and in front, so to speak). Classical Arabic rarely uses such imagery. Instead, the spatial metaphors refer to near and far, in and out. In Islam, power is horizontal—what matters is how "close" you are to the ruler. Hierarchy and privilege are rejected in principle, and justice demands equidistance from authority. Power is horizontal, not vertical; power and status are a function of nearness to the ruler and depend on his (always his) favor, not on rank and birth. Though violent Jihadists do not represent mainstream Islam, they do reproduce this horizontal imagery of the organization of power. This is evident even in the so-called franchise model of terror groups, notably with Al Qaeda (tellingly, the Arabic word for the foundation, or the base).[41]

The Caliph al-Mansur built his new capital in Baghdad in the middle of the eighth century. He designed a round city because a circular city meant that the sections of the city would be equidistant from him, in the center. This was necessary for justice (and, of course, control). The caliph was at the center of the city, Baghdad was the center of Iraq, and Iraq was the center of the world. To emphasize al-Mansur's caliphate's centrality, his chroniclers described it with the metaphor "the navel of the world." A navel of a body, that is of the social body.

In the radical Islamist imagination, that sense of being part of a singular communal body is turned to a more revolutionary purpose. The faithful are now part of a great epic, the instruments of a singular and transcendent authority. Believers bask in that reflected glory, moving history to the Golden Age.

The Sacred and the Secular

The reader will recall that we discussed the changes in the English language that took place in the seventeenth century, notably the emergence of "self" as a prefix, as in self-determination or self-realization. Classical Arabic is equally revealing in the way its world is articulated. In classical Arabic as well as in other languages that draw their political vocabulary from classical Arabic, there was no pair of words that matched religious and secular, or lay and ecclesiastical, or church and state. ("Mosque" refers only to the physical structure, the building, rather than an institution or an abstraction.) Only in the nineteenth century, under Western influence, were words found to articulate the "secular," first in Turkish, then in Arabic.[42]

The idea of a laity is equally absent. Sharia, after all, is not a narrowly legal document governing merely the scaffolding of society in the sense of, say, the U.S. Constitution. Sharia regulates the whole of the human experience, including the cadences and rituals of daily life; in this context, "laity" does not make sense.[43] As a consequence, the political and the spiritual are intertwined. In Muhammad's lifetime, the Prophet was the head of state, and he led a victorious, expansive community—at once a political and a religious community.

In the Protestant Reformation, the rebels rejected the Church of Rome and its claim that the papacy and the priesthood mediate the believer and God. Instead, every believer could experience the spirit of God, expressed in the Latin phrase *unio mystica*. Within certain parameters—more tightly drawn among

Calvinists and more liberally defined among Baptists—Protestantism derived from *unio mystica* an egalitarian ethic. Just as the hierarchy of the Church was rejected, so political hierarchy was rejected as well. In some congregations, decision making, from the very beginnings of the Reformation, became increasingly democratic. Quakers went so far as to hold meetings in which congregants sat in circles in order to avoid any sense of a leader.

The broader consequences of these Protestant movements were clear in the language of freedom and liberty increasingly in the air. Thus the era of revolutions was set in motion: the Dutch Revolt from the mid-1500s, the English Glorious Revolution of 1688, the American Revolution of 1776, the French Revolution of 1789 and onward. Revolutions were driven by the unprecedented and exhilarating human sentiment that we can create societies from scratch, based on *our own* visions for more equitable futures. Not coincidently, this change is associated with the rise of science and the growing belief that humanity could control nature for its own purposes.

Humans self-consciously wrote these stories of revolutionary emancipation without necessarily making claims of divine writ. Of course, in a good number of cases there was much buyer's remorse: the awful bloodletting of the French, Russian, and Chinese revolutions are instances that come to mind.[44]

But in classical Islam, God is the legislator. His sovereign word has been revealed through the Qur'an. The first-known account by a Muslim of the British House of Commons at the end of the eighteenth century expressed his consternation and pity that a people lacking a divinely revealed law were forced to enact their own laws.[45] In an environment that was through divine revelation ethically and legally made whole, and where Sharia was all encompassing, the issue becomes not so much the creation of law but the application and execution of law. So in classical Islam the focus of concern is not liberty or freedom, in the conventional sense, but *justice*. The law, given through revelation, is in principle not subject to change. In practice *fiqh*, or Islamic jurisprudence, allows for a more fluid approach to law (and with it social change) through the rulings and interpretations of Islamic jurists. Even *fiqh*, however, has a distinctly judicial tilt.

Indeed, in the languages of the Middle East, there is no word for "citizen" or for "citizenship." It is only in the nineteenth century, under the influence of the West, that terms for citizenship are derived from cognate words, for example, using the words for "compatriot" in Persian, Turkish, and Arabic. Even today, the concept of "civil society," drawn from the West, has different nuances in the Middle East.[46]

The idea of "Muslim citizenship" is still ambiguous where it is proffered, especially in Europe. One conundrum: European countries often wish to promote citizenship as a means of integration to create a common "French" or "British" society. But it is frequently the politically minded Islamists who promote a purported Muslim citizenship. And the Islamists' objectives may in fact be counter to the "host" society's objectives of integration.

In classical Islam, the near-seamless ties of religion and politics, and of the public and the private, inspired a sense of loyalty and community in Islam that transcended the idea of a faith and concerns of religious doctrine.[47] Islam was the revelation that could create a shared community and identity for much of the Middle East and beyond. No wonder the Ummah could (and can) be so compelling, socially as well as religiously, for the believer. You are at one with history and on a providential path. In the shadow of today's tragic conflict in the Holy Land, it is an irony that Islam and Judaism parallel one another in merging religious inspiration and peoplehood. Curiously, it may be that the Arabic *Ummah* and the Hebrew *am*, both meaning people, as in the People of Israel, are linguistically related.[48]

Reconciling the Faith

Like any major religion, Islam faces internal theological and social tensions, oppositions, and even contradictions. In Islam tensions that are especially resonant in the present moment are those between tribal patriarchy and transnational global values, more exclusionary and more inclusionary definitions of the Ummah, communal and individualistic expressions of faith, and revolutionary (Jihadist) and quietist (traditional) approaches to the world.

Women and their status is an "anchor point" for addressing these internal tensions. This is especially notable in the relationship between Islam and tribal patriarchy. The way women's place in society is articulated becomes crucial to addressing (in different ways) theological and ideological oppositions and intersections—by taking seeming contradictions and resolving them on another plane. Notably, Islamists take insular tribal patriarchy, which is generally indifferent to anything except for the most local of concerns, and project this patriarchy onto a global ideology.

Women's place in classical Islam was—and largely remains in the Middle East to this day—distinctly inferior. Islamists can refer to the time of the Prophet, which they wish to emulate, and see a still highly patriarchal society. Islamic feminists, seeking to transform the place of women in Islam, counter this patriarchal reading by pointing to the progressive intent of the Prophet.[49]

The key question, then, is: How do the different sects and streams of Islam absorb tribal patriarchy as a seamless part of the faith, or to what extent do different sects disengage from tribal patriarchy? This is the key that also opens or closes the door to others. Those "others" can include different Muslims, such as Sufis, as well as Christians, Jews, Hindus, and the like. Radical Islamists, violently or non-violently, have slammed that door shut (or at best left it slightly ajar)—and other Muslims, whom they deem to be *takfir* (apostates), have been the primary victims. Prominent among these victims are those Muslim women who take advantage of globalizing trends to try to better their individual positions in society.

HOW GLOBALIZATION
ADVANTAGES WOMEN

Having considered the historical settings that shaped the lives of women, in Part II we turn to the present-day forces of globalization. One remarkable shift is how globalization is changing women's access to education and to the job market. Indeed, women in many areas of the world are outpacing men educationally, and often they are adjusting better to a global economy. Such changes are not simply economic. Women, once subject to traditional lives, are increasingly in control of their own lives. This novel "adventure of the self" is starkly evident in the world of fashion. The greater Middle East has, however, lagged behind the rest of the world in the overall scope of change.

CHAPTER FOUR

Global Markets

Putting *Homo economicus* on the Defensive

Much of the academic literature on women and globalization paints a dark picture—of cross-national prostitution, sweatshop conditions, uninviting export zones like the *maquiladoras* in Mexico, or the prison-like circumstances of domestic maids in the Persian Gulf. Part of this grim portrayal is accurate.

But in fact, on the whole, globalization has appreciably improved women's conditions in terms of education, the expansion of rights (and, in a patchwork fashion, their application), health conditions, and, most importantly, participation in the labor market and income. Significant problems in attaining gender equality remain. But curiously, there are also deepening signs of men falling behind women in certain areas in the world, especially in education.

This positive outlook for women is tempered by exceptions like the sex trade. However the extent of this problem may be exaggerated in the public eye because the large amount of public and private money raised to combat it drives more publicity. A case in point is the migration of Eastern European women to the West, often thought of as a major source of prostitution. In fact, it is estimated that only a small fraction of that migration is related to the sex trade. This does not mitigate the ugly exploitation that is involved in much of this business. But overestimating the extent of the problem prevents a sound analysis of globalization's impact on women.[1]

Let us consider two related issues in order to make sense of globalizing dynamics and women. First, we need to figure out how women's status and sexuality are entwined with globalization. Second, we need to ask why globalization, from the late twentieth century onward, has generally advantaged women's status—in economic terms and also in terms of education, human rights, and cultural expression.

In addressing these concerns, we find that at the crux of cultural change, if it is to be meaningful, is change in bodily conduct. Globalization has reshaped the status of women in much of the world by effecting greater sovereignty over their own bodies. This has a remarkable impact in many areas of women's lives, from work and fashion to marriage patterns. Even prostitution can sometimes reflect a shifting use of sexuality by independent women (and men). In a brief voyage to Cuba, we will find out how.

The changes in women's conduct are a function of economic restructuring and associated changes in human rights, media, and other global developments—and the agency (the autonomy to act for oneself) that globalization makes possible. Women, as a whole, have increasing control over themselves. This autonomy is leading women to re-fashion themselves in sometimes dramatic ways, including their sense of their roles in society, their self-presentation, and their sexuality. In short, women's very identity is increasingly rooted in their bodily autonomy.

The fact that one region in particular—the Middle East and North Africa—lags well behind all other regions in terms of women's participation in the labor market as well as in political empowerment is indicative of continuing patriarchy in the region. Note that Muslim countries outside this geographic ambit—countries that do not have the tribal-patriarchal legacy to the same extent—do not lag behind the rest of the developing world. The positive dynamics of globalization in Indonesia, the largest Muslim country in the world, is especially worthy of attention.

Globalizing Bodies

Changes in women's status and sexuality are central in the progression of globalization of recent decades. Perhaps because the impact of global economics, politics, and culture is now such an all-present part of our lives, we don't notice this core quality of our globalizing world. We do not fully comprehend the scope of cultural changes relating to gender.

We have an intuitive sense of what *politics* is about: power, its distribution, and the struggle to have it. *Economics?* It is about the production of commodities for our consumption, in one sense or another. *Finance,* in principle, oils the whole process—money, loans, and interest make all these transactions possible.

But *culture?* In this concept we a have a breakdown of any consistent, intuitive sense of meaning. Is it "high" culture—Sanskrit documents, the arts, symphony orchestras, and fine wine? Or is it popular culture—Hollywood, Bollywood, the late Michael Jackson, sports, gossip, and the overly exposed Britney Spears? Or is culture, more abstractly, the symbols and patterns of behavior in a society? Sociologists and anthropologists have their own internally disputed definitions. But unlike the disciplines of economists and political scientists, a foundational concept of the sociological and anthropological craft—culture—is lacking, at least in terms of popular understanding.[2]

Think of culture this way: Everything we do involves our bodies: eat, pray, or love. We can't do anything without, so to speak, our bodies. Less obvious, but equally true, everything we do involves culture: eat, pray, or love. Culture is *embodied*. Acts, gestures, the way we carry ourselves, self-representation (for example, through forms of dress), consumption (such as food customs), how we shelter ourselves (through architecture), work and play—all involve the intersection of body and culture.[3]

Take a basic cultural artifact like language. Language allows us to interact with others and is, furthermore, intrinsically expressive of specific values, beliefs, and understandings. It is a core basis, the "expressing," of culture. In invoking the vocabulary and syntax of language, we draw on an enormous repository of understandings and rules that don't belong to us personally; in this sense, language transcends us and is rooted in the society around us. But we express our culture through the manipulation of our bodies.

Language itself—its vocabulary and rules—is not inherent, but the ability to learn it is inherent. Culture and body, body and culture are seamlessly intertwined.

Similarly, language is in large part built on metaphors of space, place, and movement—which in turn are rooted in the experience of the body itself: he feels like the world "weighs" on him; it "turned my stomach"; she felt "moved" by his gesture. We extrapolate from ourselves—that is, from our bodies. Bodies are our "lived experience." When we empathize with others, we "embody" their experience. This much we sense: Language as word or text is the language we *feel*. We cannot, as intellectuals and academics are wont to do, categorically separate "knowledge" and "feeling." This much we need to know: Language as a bodily act and language as culture simply cannot be separated.[4]

Thinking about language as culture and as bodily act raises a question: What does that mean when we meet, as individuals and as intersecting cultures? It means there is no "neutral" or transcendent set of cultural norms. There is no disembodied culture. Nor is there a body absent culture, except for the extremely young or the ill. So when cultures intersect, someone has to make concessions, convert—or resist. There is no transcendent "third way."[5]

Let me illustrate this point with a true story. When the British colonized what is today Kenya, they wanted to build a railway line in East Africa, joining what is now Kenya and Uganda.[6] To do so they needed local Kikuyu tribesmen for labor. The British administrators came up with an incentive: money. But like any other human artifact, money is culturally embedded. We impute value to money and exchange it for goods.

The Kikuyu, however, had a subsistence economy based on barter. Money was meaningless to them. The colonial overlords could only change behavior through coercion: they imposed a poll tax, and money was necessary for paying that tax. So the Kikuyu were forced to work on the railroad to earn money to pay the tax. But even then the structure of work as defined by the British—say, the tyranny of the clock, as opposed to the cycles of nature—proved problematic. For example, the concept of "profit," or generating surplus goods for profit making, was absent.[7] So why work more than was necessary for one's basic needs? [8] The resolution of such culture clashes, and an alignment of values, has been gradual and sometimes faltering across the globe—that is, when it did not involve extreme coercion.

Sex and gender take on a particular importance as bits and pieces of cultures traverse the world.[9] Sexuality epitomizes this unity of body and culture. It is about our biological identity *and* about how our sexual identity is socially expressed (or "gendered")—from Yemeni tribes to South Beach in Miami. Sexuality is also about the erotic and how it is displayed or hidden. This complex of sexuality is such an intrinsic part of us that, together with food and security, it is felt as elemental and primordial.

So what happens when *cultures* meet is what happens when different *bodily practices* meet, from economics to the ways men and women pair up (or the various permutations thereof—from polygamy to same-sex couples). The body acts as a bridge—a crossing point between cultures, or a point from which to fight back. Values and conduct are expressed through the body, such as in the economic values of the British and the Kikuyu.[10]

Women's bodies, as we have learned, have been fraught with meaning. Honor and dishonor are expressed from the way a woman dresses, to a woman alone in a souk. Bodies are a nexus, a point of mediation, for the interaction of groups and societies, metaphorically as well as literally.

Women's bodies have been notable points of engagement. This can be quite direct, as in the case of reports of Tahitian women showing "their beauties" to British sailors of HMS *Dolphin* in 1767. More somberly, women's bodies become a point of civil conflict, of struggle, and of systematic dishonor—of the victims and of their communities—through rape. So we learned of the systematic use of rape by different combatant parties in the civil war in (the former) Yugoslavia.[11]

Globalization in roughly the last three decades has involved the body and sexuality in particularly vivid ways. Why? Global media and the Internet may have opened the world to the endless streaming of digital sex. They may have also revealed new vistas for some oppressed women—a new knowledge of women's rights or of alternative economic opportunities. But such media, though important, are not the primary driving force linking globalization, the body, and sexuality.

Let us start thinking about that question with another story, one taking place in Cuba.

Havana Nights

Cuba is the setting for a graphic, if unrefined example of the body as the conduit of globalization and of the ways that global changes are inscribed in bodily conduct.[12] When the Soviet Union ended its contributions to Cuba in 1991—which had represented 40 percent of Cuba's gross national product—Cuba began a tentative foray into the global economy.[13] Tourism was a central part of the strategy to attract foreign investment and currency. And sex tourism became a mainstay of the tourism trade, alternatively suppressed or met with a blind eye by the communist government in the style of Captain Renault in *Casablanca*.

This ambiguity is reflected in a statement by Fidel Castro. "We had to accept tourism as an economic need, but we said that it will be tourism free of drugs, free of brothels, free of prostitution, free of gambling," Castro told the Cuban National Assembly of the People's Government in 1992. He continued: "There are hookers, but prostitution is not allowed in our country. There are no women forced to sell themselves to a man, to a foreigner, to a tourist. Those who do so do it on their own, voluntarily, and without any need for it. We can say that they are highly educated hookers and quite healthy, because we are the country with the lowest number of AIDS cases. . . . Therefore, there is truly no tourism healthier than Cuba's."[14] Be that as it may, the tourism industry, of which the sex business is a substantial part, is good business for the political and business elites in Cuba and has been an important part of Cuba's integration into the global milieu.[15]

But prostitution in Cuba is different from that in other parts of the world. Prostitutes are called *jinteras,* literally translated as "jockeys." (Some make a distinction between jinteras and prostitutes as such, the former less stigmatized and associated with what has been termed the "girlfriend experience"; that is, the transaction is not just about sex.) These jinteras "ride" the tourists in all manner of speaking. Women (and men) of all strata engage in sex work because the money is so much better than the miserable wages of a Cuban worker at any level. A jintera's single night's activity can earn forty dollars, double the monthly salary of a Cuban university professor at the turn of the twenty-first century.[16] Even professionals will—and some do—become sex workers in such conditions.

Because of the money, the jinteras are able to wear brand-name clothes and, through their clients, enjoy fine restaurants. These simple luxuries are essentially unavailable to the average Cuban citizen working only for Cuban pesos, so jinteras are not viewed as shameful in the way prostitutes are in most other places—and they are even envied in Cuba. Furthermore, the jinteras work mostly directly with their clients, independently, and third parties or pimps are relatively rare. Because the level of AIDS in Cuba is low, the country becomes an attractive site for clients, especially from Europe.[17]

Bodies are at the intersection of cultures and, for Cuba, sex tourism became a principle nexus of global and local linkages. For the tourist client, he (and it is mostly he) is looking for the supposed exoticism and unrestrained sexuality of the Cuban women. This evocative image has unfortunate roots going back to European slave owners, who saw their mulatto women slaves, freely available to them, as "hot constitution'd and sensuous in an animal-like way."[18]

The rather interesting aspect of the Cuban jinteras is that in general they view this whole process favorably, not just for the money but also as an opportunity to find a husband with whom they will immigrate to countries like Spain. This is not the unattainable dream—many do, in fact, do exactly that.

The sex trade's global linkages are not an abstraction, nor are they limited to face-to-face business transactions. Internet sites promote jinteras, indicating where they can be met, how much to pay, and how to deal with the police. YouTube videos display the adventures of visitors and the expectations of different jinteras. One jintera, interviewed by an Italian tourist on video, declared her desire to fall in love with a foreigner and just to "be happy." Clearly, there is a desire, perhaps more so than in prostitution elsewhere, for deeper emotional connections on the part of jinteras and even the clients.[19]

Globalization involves in part the unprecedented flow of media, information, finance, and bodies across borders. Sex tourism to Cuba is characteristic in this regard, including the use of tourism as a mechanism for integration of the country into the global economy. As many writers note (in the academic argot), we see the "commodification of male desire and women's bodies" in global capitalism, in this case here in Cuba. More importantly, sex tourism has brought a *culture* of capitalism to Cuba—the jinteras' earnings support many more than themselves, and through conspicuous consumption they display a new ethic that others want to emulate.

Despite the Cuban government's attempt to create what has been called "tourist apartheid"—trying to keep Cubans away from the corrupting influences of the tourists—a new culture, with a new set of bodily practices, is increasingly seeping into Cuban society.[20] The approach to the body, of women and men alike, is steadily breaking away from the ascetic, self-sacrificing ethic of Cuban communism.

Cuba is a particularly colorful case. But the impact of globalization on women, gender relations, and sexuality is much more pervasive than only in Cuba. Growing autonomy and sovereignty over the self have broad implications in the "gendering" of individuals and their identities everywhere. That is to say, with increasing self-control, issues of gender and sexuality come to the fore.

The ways in which a globalizing economy enables such personal sovereignty of women are the start of a process. The social, cultural, and political implications—from fashion to political movements—quickly follow.

Women in a Globalizing Economy

Marking the beginnings of globalization in economic terms, let alone in cultural terms, is as much an art as it is a science. Some historians point to 1492 (when Columbus reaches the Americas in search of spices) or 1498 (when the Portuguese explorer Vasco da Gama rounds the Cape Coast of Africa up to India, driven to develop a lucrative trade route to India). Others go back deeper into history, to expanding civilizations such as the Romans.

Economists Kevin O'Rourke and Jeffrey Williamson point out that the world economy was fragmented and not truly global before the nineteenth century. But O'Rourke and Williamson also note that none of these approaches to economic globalization indicate the difference between trade expansion driven by supply and demand *within* the trading economies (such as population growth), and trade expansion that is a function of the actual integration of markets *between* trading economies (which would show itself in the equalization of the prices of like commodities across trading regions, or "commodity price convergence"). By that measure, they calculate from empirical data that there is no evidence that the world economy was integrated in the context of 1492 or 1498. On the other hand, they cite abundant evidence that the nineteenth century contained a "very big globalization bang."[21]

Some argue that, depending on the data and methods used, important commodities such as tea, textiles, tobacco, and sugar (and also slaves), do trend toward price convergence prior to the nineteenth century. The deregulation of protectionist, mercantilist policies during the seventeenth and eighteenth centuries had a "highly significant effect" upon the prices of traded commodities.[22]

Be that as it may, these studies, including that of O'Rourke and Williamson, focus on just one dimension of economic globalization—the international trade of commodities. They do not consider, for example, the shifting flows of capital and finance or the migration of labor (or what economists call international factor mobility). I argue that for a profound impact on women's status, international factor mobility—including foreign direct investment, the growing role of global corporations, and migration—is more critical, as it is most propitious (as we will see) for shaking up existing cultural patterns as they relate to women. International investors and global corporations are not invested (figuratively speaking) in local institutions and customs that restrict women's economic role, and migration often (but not always) frees women from the restraints of patriarchal villages and families. Indeed, such patriarchal structures can be—and often are—obstacles to economic expansion.

In this light, a much more recent marker of economic globalization is a good deal more significant. *Financial* globalization, from the 1980s on, makes for a remarkable contrast to the past. The turnover of foreign exchange trading globally went from $590 billion in 1989 to $1.19 trillion in 1995.[23] This is a change in excess of 100 percent in six years. The proportion of the international banking sector as a share of world output has grown astronomically, from 0.7 percent in 1964 to 8.0 percent in 1980, to 16.3 percent in 1991. This amounts to a change, between 1964 and 1991, of over 2,200 percent. Cross-border bank credit to non-banks went from 54 billion dollars in the early 1970s to 1.8 trillion dollars in 1990—an increase of about 3,200 percent.[24] As some have argued, the story of economic globalization at the turn of the twenty-first century is finance, not trade.[25]

Trade—in and of itself—does not necessarily upend existing economic structures; it just may re-direct them. That is to say, the same economic entities—from individuals to business concerns—can simply expand or reorient their base of suppliers and customers. The global flow of finance and capital, in contrast, is seeking the most profitable outlets. This in turn has fundamental social implications, notably for women. That is why finance is the more interesting story regarding globalization in comparison to trade.

Furthermore, the emergence of truly global corporations, which are not dependent on any one country for the bulk of their revenues and profits, is a function of this financial revolution. They can operate financially, and in terms of their organizational operations, on a transnational basis. Once you have such corporations, you have states competing for their investment and largesse. Finance, more broadly, in an environment of now-instant communications (the transmission belt making this general economic shift possible), can move much more easily around the world. The growth of shipping made global trade possible; the Internet and communications technology made the financial revolution possible.

The dramatic expansion in cross-border economic transactions and the increasingly global production process in the decades leading to the turn of the twenty-first century generated furious global competition. Governments in this environment sought a number of structural changes—including reducing the role of the state through the privatization of industries, deregulation of domestic markets, encouragement of more flexible labor markets—and gave tax incentives to attract foreign direct investment and foreign corporations.

Protectionists of varying shades questioned this approach, and these voices, such as that of the well-known economist Paul Krugman, are even more vociferous in their criticism following the Great Recession.[26] These voices may be correct that deregulation was centrally responsible for that economic crisis. But in fact, women's entry into the labor market in the aggregate benefited from these economic policies. Indeed, women also weathered the recessionary storm better, on the whole, than did men in a number of national economies.

Competition for the resources of international finance and corporations by many governments (not just at the national level but also at the provincial, state, and various regional or sub-national levels) led to some fairly evident conclusions regarding women. From a strictly economic perspective, it clearly does not make sense to keep half of the population out of the labor pool contributing to the GNP. The share of women in the labor force and in education is also statistically correlated with economic growth. This is a direct effect of greater use of a country's workforce, but women's share is also attributed to indirect effects such as the impact of women's education on lowering fertility rates, the subsequent child survival rates, and greater investment in children's education. Women also save more of their earnings than do men.[27]

So a clear conclusion—and certainly a part of a global ideology promoted by United Nations agencies, international non-government organizations, and Western governments—is that if half of a country's population is cloistered, restricted, or severely discriminated against, a proportional part of economic growth is being held back. Thus it is increasingly important to include women in a highly competitive global environment.

During the last decades of the twentieth century, millions of new factory jobs were generated in the developing world. Historically, men had far outnumbered women in the formal manufacturing sector. Women reached parity or beyond in many countries in just one to two decades and are now a significant part of the working class, especially in countries that went through rapid industrialization.[28]

However, the readiness to employ women was uneven.[29] Where there were strong unions, women made less progress. More importantly, in terms of global politics, the Middle East and North Africa lagged badly in the integration of women.

World Economic Forum (WEF, the group behind the Davos meetings) studies also show that the gender gap has narrowed in many parts of the world. By 2011 the educational attainment gap narrowed to 93 percent (100 percent meaning that women would have reached equality). The gender gaps in political empowerment and economic participation have also narrowed, although they remain wide. In 2006, the economic participation gap had been closed by 56 percent, while in 2011 the gap had been closed by 59 percent. The political empowerment gap is wider, although it continues to narrow as well. The gap had been closed by 14 percent in 2006, and the number increased to 19 percent in 2011.[30]

However, the Middle East and North Africa region significantly lags in gender measures. In the overall performance on the Global Gender Gap Index 2011, this region holds the lowest position (other regions include Sub-Saharan Africa, Asia and the Pacific, Latin America and the Caribbean, Europe and Central Asia, and North America). The Middle East and North Africa fall behind other regions, especially in two categories: (1) economic participation and opportunity, where the region had by 2011 closed the gap a little over 40 percent; and (2) political empowerment, where the region by the same year has closed the gender gap in the low single digits in percentage terms. The region holds the second-to-last rank in educational attainment, surpassing only Sub-Saharan Africa.[31]

Within the Middle East and North Africa itself, Israel—which ranks fifty-second globally—holds the top position. Excluding Israel, all the other countries in the region rank below the top 100 globally. Yemen remains in last place, both within the region and among the overall 134 countries. Yemen, whose performance declined even further after 2008, is the only country in the report that has not closed the gender gap up to the 50 percent mark.

It is worth noting that there have been improvements in the Middle East and North Africa mainly in educational attainment. Literacy rates for women are higher than for men in United Arab Emirates. Kuwait, Tunisia, Bahrain, and Mauritania are above average in their performance on educational attainment. Qatar and Jordan also perform well in educational attainment. Some of the richest countries in the region have invested more resources to increase the level of women's education. Nonetheless, some countries still lag behind in educational attainment. Egypt, Morocco, and Yemen are among the countries from this region that occupy the lowest rank of educational attainment globally, together with several countries from Africa and Asia.

The World Economic Forum has noted that substantial investments in the Middle East have "dramatically reduced the gender gap in education, but the gender gap in economic opportunity remains the widest in the world."[32] Because opposition to women's participation in the job market is at the family and societal level—as opposed to state-supported education—the impact is more marked in the Middle East than in other developing regions. The Arab Spring rebellions that were initiated in late 2010 aimed at authoritarian governments and thus do not as such displace the cultural challenges to women's advancement.

In the categories of economic participation and opportunity, and political empowerment, the situation is less promising in the Middle East and North Africa. Only a few countries within the region made a notable gain in closing the economic participation gap. Saudi Arabia and United Arab Emirates each made a notable 2 percent increase in the women's labor participation rate from 2009 to 2010. However, both countries—together with Qatar, Egypt, Jordan, Morocco, and Yemen—occupy the lowest ranks on the global level. Yemen holds the lowest rank in economic participation among the 134 countries included in the WEF report.

The Telling Case of Indonesian Women

Indonesia is an especially interesting example of a nation that undertook a vigorous strategy of encouraging foreign investment and of developing export-oriented industry from the 1980s. In Java and other parts of Indonesia, women have for centuries been working in the markets and interacting with men. For this and other reasons noted earlier—such as the smaller (albeit significant) presence of Islamist movements compared to the Middle East—Indonesia is a test case, as it were.[33]

In her detailed study on Indonesia, the political economist Terri Caraway traced the way labor-intensive, export-oriented industrialization generated an enormous demand for labor, including that of women. This growth also allowed employers to hire women without firing men. Caraway argues, however, that as industries matured and became more capital-intensive, "masculinization" ensued: the sexual division of labor did not disappear but was re-drawn. As a result, though women's wages were equal to men's in lower-paying sectors of the manufacturing workforce after a decade of "feminization," men's wages were on average higher. Nonetheless, women were drawn into the formal labor market—and this is the critical element in the social shifts that followed.[34]

Let's consider these processes a little more closely to demonstrate the role of economic globalization for women. This is evident in the role of export industries explicitly aimed at the global market. First, it is worth noting that the percentage of change in women's employment in manufacturing between 1971 and 1996 is highest in industrial sectors that are export-intensive. With the exception of the rubber sector, every sector categorized within industries with medium-low, medium-high, and high labor intensity experienced an increase in women's employment. The highest increase occurred in export-intensive sectors such as footwear, garments, textiles, and wood processing. Women workers also became the majority in six sectors that are all export-intensive, although men still held their majority status in 16 out of 24 sectors of the manufacturing industries.[35]

Second, the role of foreign direct investment (FDI) is of particular interest, since by definition it too represents the role of a globalizing economy. Furthermore, international capital is less likely to be weighted by local customs, including gender biases. Some argue that international capital is drawn to the "docility" of women workers, though this is contested. Another factor may be that women coming from outside the labor force are not unionized. At first, the number of job openings for women in Indonesia's manufacturing industries increased along with the increase in foreign investments. The data from Indonesia's Department of Manpower indicate that the job openings for women increased from 29 percent in 1983 to 53 percent in 1996. This correlates with the increase in FDI from $292 million in 1983 to around $6 billion in 1996.[36]

Equally significant is the impact of "mediating" institutions, from government policy to trade unions and religious groups, according to Caraway. Strong unions *negatively* affect women's participation in manufacturing (negatively influencing the share of formal employment of women in Brazil, for example). Islamist groups equally resist (if for different reasons) the integration of women into the labor market. Likewise, if traditional patriarchy is broadly characteristic of families, resistance will ensue. Thus, Indonesia is a relatively positive story in terms of women's labor integration because, in short, unions were weak, an authoritarian government suppressed the Islamist movement, and the tribal kind of patriarchy present in the Middle East and North Africa is largely absent.

Significantly, foreign manufacturers relied more heavily on labor than did local manufacturers, and export industries led foreign investment—and the burst of labor employment that sowed the ground for female labor integration. Improvements in the education of women and reductions in the number of average children (fertility rates) also made women more attractive as workers. Moreover, Caraway suggests that women are not so much more "docile," but that the unions in these cases are "docile."

Further examples of the link between economic growth and the integration of women in the job market—in good part based on export and integration into the global market—are the so-called Asian Tigers: Hong Kong, Korea, Singapore, and Taiwan. All exemplified rapid and prolonged industrialization between the early 1960s and the 1990s. Over the period 1970–2008, the participation of women in the job market increased by 26 percent in Singapore. In the other three countries, the increases grew at approximately 10 percent each.[37]

Global Autonomy

As people in these developing regions are integrated into the global environment through the media, they are also engaged by a global ideology regarding women's rights, education, and economic autonomy. States generally support these influences—at a minimum through lip service and if only due to global competition. Equally important, with growing independent income, women attain a certain degree of autonomy over their bodily selves—though of course less so where patriarchy is most entrenched. The expression of that autonomy, to its varying degrees, comes to be much more than economic.

CHAPTER FIVE

Fashioning Herself
Women Unbound by Tradition

A television correspondent for the Lebanese Broadcasting Corporation reported on Saudi women and webcams:

> Behind closed doors and far from any supervising eyes, they remove their shame and turn their backs on all customs and traditions. Girls display their bodies in chat rooms on the Internet, in most cases free of charge. As soon as one of these girls places the camera in front of her, she begins to strip, displaying her seductive charms to more than three hundred young men of different ages. Some believe that the phenomenon of stripping over the Internet may be understood within the framework of social hypocrisy, especially since they believe that our religious and educational discourse does not attribute importance to the strengthening of self-restraint, and prefers the appearance over the essence. This drives some people to play several roles and wear several masks.[1]

When we own ourselves, we make ourselves—in contrast to community fiat in effect making us. We define careers. We shape and define ourselves through consumerism, career building, and, perhaps most importantly, through relationships. There is a preoccupation with the subjective sense of self to varying degrees. In desired sexuality, we find the most direct sense of self, body, and expression.

The report of the Saudi woman and the webcam is telling. Through the Internet, the woman obtains a certain freedom to explore and to display her erotic sway. It is a palpable presentation of the linkages between globalization, individual autonomy, and self-discovery. As we have observed, globalization is not only economic; it involves culture, human rights, media, and politics. The capital that globalization affords is not only monetary but can take various forms—including, as for the Saudi woman, "erotic capital." The sexual and erotic can now be displayed, in varying degrees of subtlety, rather than hidden. At first, as in the report, it may be furtive; usually it is more subtle, as expressed in fashion.[2]

As globalization changes the circumstances of many women, providing greater income, access to global media, more mobility, and, in general, more autonomy of body and self, how do these changes matter? How do such women, from hitherto traditional environments, conduct themselves and think of themselves? How do such women experience "their bodies, their selves"? These questions are critical in a number of ways. If globalization is significant, it is through the ways it shapes our behaviors and thoughts. In those actions we can gauge the directions it takes for both women and men, and in the ways it may be "Western"—or something else altogether.

As we ventured into seventeenth-century Western Europe, especially the Netherlands, we learned of social transformations that dazzled and titillated travelers of the time: an interest in autobiographical depictions of life and in the psychological inner life; curiosity about the larger world and the palette of experiences it provides; a hedonistic delight in satisfying one's senses, including the epicurean (and not just for the aristocracy); a calculating economic logic, driven by enrichment and not just survival; a concern with, and anxiety about, self-presentation; a growing interest in finding the ever-receding "true" self. Results of these social transformations include choosing one's marriage partners; women owning property and speaking in candidly sexual, even crude terms and displaying their beauty and eroticism in public; couples openly kissing; a broad, if mostly tacit, acceptance of prostitutes; and erotic art and literature for the wider (yet still respectable) public's edification.

Not all the Dutch at the time—much less Europeans in general—celebrated this social revolution. In retrospect, however, a turn had been taken in Europe. And now that same path (albeit with twists and detours) is crisscrossing the world.

As women today now take on increasing levels of autonomy—of self-control—in otherwise traditional contexts, we see different kinds of transformations than those in historical Europe. But there are parallels: the sense of discovering one's body through the lens of *self*-interest, of an economic, social, or political character. That discovery is equally introspective—of exploring the sensory, subjective, and the psychological self. It is an exploration with tribulations and doubts for many, with the challenge of finding the median between liberation and respectability, or of having to live divided lives across often sharply divergent social worlds.

But one constant that we see from the descriptions of women unfettered by custom, from the seventeenth-century Dutch to women globally today, is that the control of their own bodies includes the control over their own capital. This includes control over their labor power and the freedom to sell it in the market-place as well as control over the disposable income that is the fruit of their labor. But the shift is more profound than that. It includes a growing emphasis on erotic capital as well. Fashion and the growing accent on beauty and aesthetics reflect this fundamental societal change. It affects the very sense of self, from duty defined through honor and custom, to self-discovery and development. This has its clearly negative side: the immense pressure to appear attractive in socially defined ways will cause some to suffer emotional problems associated with body image.

We can take measure of these changes through fashion, consumer behavior, the use of the Internet (as in the case of the Saudi women in the television report), approaches to work, and attitudes toward sexuality. I focus in this chapter primarily on fashion and beauty, and the role of erotic capital.

Issues such as fashion tend to be viewed as part of the entertainment sector of media, essentially trivial information useful only for gossip and for disparaging celebrities. Even scholars of fashion can dismiss its significance. As fashion historian Valerie Cumming wrote, "In all honesty, both the construction of fashion across the ages and its consumption are innately frivolous."[3] It is true that changes in fashion as well as in aesthetics and beauty more broadly are felt in the realm of social life; such issues are not usually an impetus for political mobilization. But this approach misses how conduct in this arena has deep political implications and often profound religious and sociological significance as well.

This is especially the case when it comes to the experience of aesthetics—how beauty is conveyed and understood, from art, architecture, poetry, and theatre to relations between women and men. It is curious that we do not think of aesthetics or beauty as political issues, since questions of beauty and presentation have taken a major role in contemporary conflict. Aesthetics are expressed in arguments over topics ranging from women's dress to how drawings of the Prophet Muhammad are presented in Western media.

The fights over aesthetics are often tied to the place of women in society. An important part of a community's control over women is through their clothing and adornments—showing, for example, whether they are married. Dress also reflects whether community norms are being followed or the individual is shaping her own self-presentation.

We humans have gone from wearing dress that marks our rank or caste—in which case our conduct from family to work to marriage is largely scripted—to carefully fashioning ourselves as part of a planned autobiography in career, romance and other pursuits. As globalization draws a class of women as well as men outside the hold of traditional patriarchy and into the public arena, so tensions come to the fore.

Erotic Capital

At the point where we become autonomous, self-determining individuals, we are also at the point of "selling" ourselves—of advertising our merits as corporeal and intellectual beings. As a consequence, we are also in a position of constantly negotiating our place and status in society. This is most obvious on the job market. Rather than continuing in a vocation defined by tradition—say, as a peasant—or by a particular caste or by our sex, we sell our labor power. This, of course, is a very basic premise of classical economics and, in different ways, of Marxist thought as well.

But we also have to sell ourselves on the dating and marriage markets. Of central importance in this regard is what the British sociologist Catherine Hakim has called "erotic capital."[4] It is important not only in romantic contexts but also in work, media, advertising, the arts, and everyday life. Erotic capital grows in importance as cultural life becomes increasingly sexualized—and that, in turn, is a result of globalization's erosion of patriarchal institutions or of any institutions that subordinate the individual to larger collective concerns.

Eroticism, Hakim suggests, is not just beauty, the standards of which vary across cultures. Sexual appeal, social grace, physical fitness, presentation skills, and sexual playfulness and competence (generally only known to lovers) are also important. Great beauty and sexual appeal are especially in short supply and therefore highly valued. Consequently, they can be used as erotic capital.

Women have more erotic capital than men (women, suggests Hakim, work harder at it). It generates competition among women as well as men. It also contributes to real anguish—and actual diseases, such as bulimia and anorexia—and distress about body image among some women (and men) in response to the extraordinary expectations generated by the media. Age diminishes erotic capital beyond a certain point. This can be tempered through cosmetic surgery, but that is an expensive alternative with often questionable results. It could be argued that extraordinarily attractive women engender such a level of envy and unwelcome attention that erotic advantages are not linear with rising beauty, but are more like an arching parabola.[5]

Numerous studies show that in prosperous modern societies people have more sex than in the past, and its importance has grown. Men generally want sex more than women—and this is the case across cultures. Standards of beauty and sexuality have evolved and grown. The effect of all this is to give women with high erotic capital great leverage in certain labor market, dating, and marriage opportunities. This leverage can be used to overcome other disadvantages such as relative financial deprivation.[6]

What is telling is the backlash against erotic capital—its suppression, at least in public, by men with patriarchal interests or by women and men who resent the competition. As Hakim notes, women who display their beauty and sexuality are frequently disparaged, labeled as "stupid" or as "bimbos." Beauty contests are often belittled. But most of the backlash is more insidious, more everyday, and is expressed in a variety of contexts, especially in the workplace.

One can point to two sources of opposition: one counterintuitive, the other much more dangerous. In the first case, a good part of academic feminism has rejected the importance of erotic capital. Academic feminists, especially in the English-speaking world, ignore or even attack beauty and sexual allure among women for a number of reasons. Feminist literature tends to focus almost exclusively on educational and economic attributes for measuring women's mobility. Furthermore, as with almost all academics, academic feminism privileges intellectual qualities above all others.

More importantly, there is an overwhelming tendency among those scholars to reject what may be viewed as *any* biological determinants. In this view, sexuality and gender should be viewed as wholly determined by extraneous social factors. The body is, in effect, putty to be shaped accordingly.[7] Among some feminist writers, even heterosexual sex is suspect, and for a woman to sleep with a man is to partake in her own oppression.[8] Famously, Naomi Wolf, in her book *The Beauty Myth*, attacked the rising importance of beauty and female sexual attraction as dangerous to women and feminism.[9]

Ironically, what is implicitly "popular feminism" is very different from much of academic feminism.[10] In other words, many women who revel in their autonomy also embrace their varying forms of capital, whether it be cultural, social, intellectual, or erotic. This is evident, for example, in fashion trends.

Women's autonomy and the wherewithal to deploy her own self in areas from work to love to politics faces a much greater threat, however—and not just in terms of eroticism. More than a threat, such women's autonomy has been frequently prevented or undermined. The tribal-patriarchal blowback to the public display of feminine beauty—and at the same time equality—is vehement. This engagement goes beyond women themselves and seeks to reshape societies and institutions to conform to their extreme patriarchy. The aspiration for this reformation goes hand in hand with a belligerent resistance to the moral embrace of the West.

Beauty Eternal

Why is beauty so captivating, both on a personal and a political level? Beauty compels us and draws us in, whether in architecture, in religious symbols, or in women. The philosopher Elaine Scarry has suggested that beauty mesmerizes us because it invokes the sacred, as if it contains a transcendent and holy truth. Beauty "quickens . . . adrenalizes. It makes the heart beat faster. It makes life more vivid, animated, living, worth living." Beauty evokes the eternal, "the perpetual duplicating of the moment that never stops."[11] No wonder there is a desperate struggle over how we "picture" the world, from the depiction of women to cartoons.

To paraphrase Emerson, beauty is its own reason for being (or acting, or reacting), and therein lies its power—as opposed to the more instrumental considerations of money or politics.[12] Beauty—whether in art, in political symbols such as flags, or (perhaps above all) in a woman or a man—is its own motivation to act. To the captivated observer, beauty is its own end rather than a means to an end. Beauty is power, a command in itself. It is no surprise, then, that for some, beauty is to be hidden, covered up, and protected.

If beauty evokes the eternal, it is only the eternal that can be beautiful. Thus one thread that winds its way through Judaism, Christianity, and Islam dictates that the very portrayal of human beauty is sacrilege: it is idolatry, the worship of an image that is not God. Portrayal of human beauty violates God's admonition in the Hebrew Bible: "You shall have no other gods before me. You shall not make for yourself a graven image, or any likeness of anything that is in heaven above, or that is in the earth beneath, or that is in the water under the earth; you shall not bow down to them or serve them; for I the Lord your God am a jealous God . . ." (Exodus 20:4).

The beauty of women is consciously underplayed in patriarchal communities to the point—as in the case of the burqa—of women covering themselves entirely. In fact, in Islam the human form is wholly absent in sacred art. Rather, the most noble of the arts in Islam, its very aesthetic, is literally inscribed into its holy writings, in the calligraphy of the Qur'an. The concern with beautiful writing extends to all the arts, from nonreligious texts to inscriptions on buildings and cloth.

Calligraphy is thus held as the most revered and gracious of the arts. Islamic art and architecture are also characterized by a mesmerizing depiction of geometric designs and organic patterns (like the arabesque). One is drawn into the impression of unending repetition as if to experience the infinite presence of God. Ibn Khaldun, the medieval Muslim historian, observed, "[Writing] is the outlining and shaping of letters to indicate audible words which, in turn, indicate what is in the soul. It comes second after oral expression. It is a noble craft, since it is one of the special qualities of man by which he distinguishes himself from animals."[13] The Qur'an reports that "Allah said to the Prophet: 'And thy Lord is the Most Generous, who taught by the Pen, taught Man what he knew not.'" Calligraphy is the way of revelation from Allah to the Prophet Muhammad, and thus its exalted status in Islam.

The splendor of the Christian Middle Ages also compelled something other than the human and feminine form. Think of the beauty of a medieval cathedral, its architecture sweeping up to the spire and beyond, as if beckoning God. The church itself was a virtual cornucopia of tapestries, stained glass, and statues. The believer could not but be entranced by this sensory feast. And such was the art of the Middle Ages, with its recurrent depictions of the Virgin Mary, baby Jesus, and broader religious symbolism. Women as depicted in the art of the period are flat (literally and metaphorically) and uninspiring.

The Reformation becomes manifest from the mid-1500s, with Protestant groups swarming through Catholic churches, destroying the symbols and the art of the church. Protestant churches would be much more austere, often entirely bare save a simple cross. But the individual now became central. The depiction of humans in art became more embodied, more rounded. The images of women's beauty and sexuality in art multiplied rapidly. A new era was beginning, if in uncertain and in fragmentary ways, in Europe.

In different but also uneven ways, that experience of depicting human beauty has in recent decades been playing out globally—becoming ever more visible with the integration of more women into the global economy, media, culture, and even politics.

The Erotics of Culture

To truly comprehend the world in front of us, we have to understand the ideas behind the various cultures. But understanding the ideas, the theory, behind, say, honor cultures is not sufficient. We need to empathize (which is not the same as sympathize) with the experience of honor. That is, we must be cognizant of the emotions it generates, its texture, its *feel*.

This is not just an analytical problem, but it is also an aesthetic challenge— that is, to try to comprehend something that is experienced bodily and is palpable through sight, hearing, smell, touch, and taste. Think of the power of beauty, of the stylized text of a prayer book, of architecture, or of art. To experience the sight and "feel" of an iconic presence can generate strong emotions that are beyond dispassionate and reasoned evaluations. Some of those reactions will be uplifting; others may cause anger. For example, those in the West found incomprehensible the rage that overcame many Muslims at the Danish cartoonists' portrayal of Muhammad.[14]

So we need to access the "feel" that comes when the construction of gendered relations in a tribal-patriarchal society is upended, when honor is questioned. The response is not only one of "interest"—that the labor market is now more challenging for men, or that it will be difficult to find a traditional bride, for example. A violation of honor is a deeply emotional, physical experience. If someone breaks a contract, this is felt not only on the level of profit and loss but also as a physical violation—an aesthetic sensation less pleasant than that of beauty.

The late critic Susan Sontag long ago attacked the tendency in literary studies (and one could add in the humanities and social sciences more broadly) to reduce literature to ideas, or to the author's ideology, or the viewer's "gaze." In an essay titled "Against Interpretation," she called for replacing this kind of interpretation with an "erotics of art" in order to appreciate the "sensuous surface" of art, including literature. Reading, Sontag argued as a case in point, is (or should be) a physical, embodied experience, not just an intellectual one.[15]

As the literary editor Lindsay Waters writes in regard to most literary criticism in our universities today, nothing is left up to the senses, and everything is a proposition to be affirmed or denied. Once "you've reduced art to politics and virtue, you either toe the party line or face the consequences."[16] (Oh, yes.)

This is not to say that analysis, rational self-interest, and logic are not critical in understanding social and political issues. After all, if society had no pattern, we would not be able to go about our daily lives with a reasonable expectation that the "rules of the game" of daily life are in the main being followed. But such patterns are powerful because they reflect what people feel as well as calculate. And this is especially the case when we are dealing with how the body is experienced and what it means to be a woman (or a man) in a changing society.

The experience of the self is going to be very different if the organizing principle of a community is honor rather than one's own interests and a search for self-realization and "authenticity." Or it will be different if that experience reflects the bewildering feelings of being caught between disparate life-worlds, as it surely is for the Saudi women exploring their very selves through the Internet.[17]

So in thinking about how women in extremely patriarchal societies respond to changing circumstances in which they have a newfound autonomy—financial, political, legal, even geographical and spatial or in access to global media—what are the implications? How is such autonomy felt and acted upon? How do they understand themselves when they attain increasing control over their own bodies, their own selves?

Muslim Fashionability

The traditional veil is related to chastity. The concealment and the effacement of displayed beauty are designed to place the woman beyond reach. Conversely, fashion—wearing attractive or striking clothes, using cosmetics, walking in a certain manner, and the flaunting of the beautiful and the erotic—is a celebration of the body. Women's fashion, in its finery and splendor, is a fête of femininity. Fashion calls attention to the wearer. With bodily self-control, fashion becomes a way of communicating and a form of negotiating with others.

So the varying sartorial trends among women in Muslim communities—from the Middle East to Indonesia to Europe—are telling. But is not a simple shift from traditional dress to Westernized dress under the influence of globalized media and additional income (although that shift is not absent). One can see the developments in different ways from Yemen (a country that has been very orthodox, but without the strict policing of dress as in Saudi Arabia); Iran (with its private, underground explorations of fashion); Indonesia (where Javanese culture has shaped Islam in distinct ways), and in Europe (where Muslim immigrants have migrated to, or been born into, a decidedly Western ambience).

One writer, Anne Meneley, describes returning after a decade to Sana'a, the capital of Yemen, in the 1990s, to find a society that had undergone profound changes. The gap between the rich and poor had widened, with suburban villas, fancy Western cars, and satellite dishes multiplying. Globalization was palpable and evident, but so were the beggars and the visible stagnation of the economic status of many. All kinds of new consumer products were now available in the *souks*, the lively Middle Eastern markets made up of small stalls, including what could be taken as Barbie dolls.

This was not Mattel's Barbie, however, but an imitation. This Barbie was wearing a *chador* and was concealed in ways that California Barbie would find, well, foreign. Yet the Yemeni Barbie displayed in the souk had her own coy sexuality. This Barbie beckoned the eye through the use of henna, her exposed lips had lipstick, and the open-front chador revealed a form-fitting dress. This Barbie was clearly Middle Eastern, yet comfortable in a more cosmopolitan world—and in being sexy.[18]

We observed earlier how the Iranian government responded to such dolls—including the real Barbie—with their doll "Sara." Sara donned a conservative floor-length chador. Her "brother," Dara, had a long coat and the turban of a mullah (see plate 6). Sara and Dara's designer, Majid Ghaderi, complained about how Barbie was never interested in having children and held onto illusions of eternal youth. Barbie was a Trojan Horse, he said, which would unleash pernicious Western influences.[19]

But Sara is not the only doll with "Muslim values." In the Arab world, as opposed to Persian Iran, a doll named "Fulla," introduced by a Syrian company in 2003, has been much more popular (plate 7). Fulla shares Barbie's proportions, but she steps out of her pink box wearing an *abaya* or similarly modest outfit and a matching headscarf. She has outside-of-the-home clothes that are traditional, with her legs, arms, and hair covered. Her clothes for inside the house can be more form-fitting and akin to Western public dress. She comes with her own little prayer rug. Like Sara, she does not have a boyfriend like Ken. Indeed, boys rarely appear in Fulla's television advertising.[20]

Fulla, however, does not escape Western aesthetics or images of beauty. She has a button nose, bow mouth, and a lithe figure. (She is olive skinned instead of Barbie's peach-like color.) Furthermore, Fulla's merchandising does reflect a certain self-consciousness about her place vis-à-vis the West. The "Singing Fulla," one advertisement states, "shows that although she may not be dressed like the rock stars and pop princesses on MTV she is every bit as talented as they are. Fulla shows that talent has nothing to do with how provocatively one dresses but everything to do with the purity of a girl's heart and intentions." The "Dancing Fulla" dispenses with the "lewd costumes." Though Fulla does not have the repertoire of careers that Barbie has, she is available in traditionally respectable professions, namely, Doctor Fulla and Teacher Fulla.[21]

The Arab League introduced Laila, a nonreligious name, to appeal to both Christians and Muslims. Laila's costumes include Western-style outfits, while also including traditional folkloric dress from Egypt, Syria, Palestine, North Africa, and the Persian Gulf region. Laila, the sponsors state, is a "representative Arab girl," and like Sara, has a brother.[22]

The story of Barbie, Sara, Fulla, and Laila actually reflects a more profound phenomenon. Beyond the small minority that fully assimilates into Western modes ("Barbie"), three broad trends can be discerned: fashion that is adopted to assert a conservative Muslim or even Islamist aesthetic ("Sara" or "Fulla"), effacing any expression of feminine sexuality; modernist shifts that lead to a mutual accentuation of religiosity, nationality, and cosmopolitanism ("Laila"); and a continuation of customary dress that is patriarchal but not necessarily Islamic in its impetus (which has yet to find its representative doll).

Especially conservative Muslims—some simply traditional and others Islamist—would reject even the existence of a doll like Fulla. Such a doll is construed in this light as an "image" of a Godly creation and thus is Islamically wrong. Thus some Islamic toymakers in Europe are now making stuffed dolls without faces. These small children's dolls are gender-neutral and not sexualized in any way.[23]

Throughout the central countries of the Middle East, wearing Western styles of dress, together with discarding the veil and headscarf, spread in the early twentieth century. This form of dress went in tandem with the rise of secular nationalist and socialist movements in the region. But as the nationalist and socialist movements waned, and as the authoritarian governments that took on the mantle of nationalism and socialism lost credibility, a new turn took place.

From the 1970s onward, a growing number of women began to veil themselves.[24] This was a conscious grass roots movement expressing a pious response to the secular governments and secularization of everyday life. For many women, this was a form of piety that differentiated them both from the West and from their own authoritarian governments.[25] This was an *anti-fashion* movement: the style of dress involved covering up, a sober anti-consumerism that erased the sartorial markers of class, social status, and liberalism in countries such as Egypt and Malaysia.[26]

However, by the late 1980s and the 1990s, an *Islamic consumerism* emerged. With affluence and easily accessible Western luxury goods, style and fashion that were more individual in their expression came to the fore, and identities were increasingly expressed through consumption (such as expensive fabrics, brand names, and conspicuous display).

Aesthetic considerations, taste, status and, importantly, the availability of more income and products had by the 1990s taken Islamic dress and "fashionized" it. Emerging from the oil-rich Gulf States, even Islamic dress did not escape consumerism. This is not a simple matter of the clothes women happen to wear; it changed the public life of such women, who were self-consciously expressing their own personality and taste or worldliness even in public—by, for example, draping their bodies with Swarovski-encrusted *abayas* and concealing their hair with Hermes scarves. Sometimes this was done in a selective manner, in private (as in Iran, where clothes were policed in public) or in universities.[27] This fashionizing distinguished such women from traditional or Islamist women whose

Islamic wear is uniform. In the latter case, their absence of fashionability makes them largely indistinguishable from other traditionalists or Islamist women in their community.

Muslim fashion is at the very nexus of globalization. Not only are images of fashion rapidly globalized through media and advertising throughout most of the Muslim world, but the changes in Islam itself make more of its religious movements, schools, and groups susceptible to fashion statements. The response is to try to express a self that is both individualized and, say, Islamic, Arab, Pakistani, or Indonesian.

Many Muslim women are engaged in creating a fashion that is both "authentic" and international at the same time. Importantly, the Islamic restrictions of keeping beauty private (the covered body, concealed face, and the use of henna) are pushed. Yet all the while, beauty is playfully and teasingly revealed, for example, with heavy kohl and made-up eyes, and with fitted and decorated *abayas*.[28]

The surprising thing is that globalization influences not only modernists but also fundamentalists who seek to efface the West's influence (and gaze) through highly concealing dress. In being anti-fashion, the Islamists respond to globalization through their very resistance. Curiously, in Indonesia, where radical Islamism is in a distinct minority, such beliefs are marked frequently by wearing Arab dress or what is *thought* to be Arab. (Even Afghani Pashtun dress is worn by Indonesian Islamists under the misconception that it is Arab.)[29] Only those who wear customary dress—and they may do so because it is culturally accepted and not for reasons of piety—stand relatively apart from this globalizing milieu.

Fashion Markers

Yemen is an interesting example of fashion developments in the Arab world. Most Yemeni women in the capital, Sana'a, still wear black loose outer garments that hide any underlying contours of their figures. Most cover their hair, and many veil their faces. Yet underlying this cover are important trends. For example, by the turn of the twenty-first century, young educated women and university students were more drawn to the *abaya*. While modest by Western standards, the *abaya* is made of thinner fabric and has a more dress-like appearance than do the traditional garments and the *balto*.

The *balto*, which came into fashion in the 1970s, is a long overcoat, sometimes with a belt. (The 1970s was also a period with migration of Yemeni men to the oil-rich Gulf States, which in turn brought money flowing into the Yemeni economy and a consequent rise in consumer goods.) While the *balto* could appear fashionable, its modesty also met the approval of the Islamists. But Islamist women were stricter about fully covering their hair—so already at this point, social delineations became apparent. But the 1990s pushed more in the direction of fashionability, mostly for the more educated women (the ones more likely to have disposable income and to be more attuned to global trends). This development earned the ire of the Salafis. In booklets, they issued warnings:

> A dangerous phenomenon is spreading amongst Muslim women and that is that some women wear the *abaya* on the shoulders and cover their heads with a headcloth that in itself is an embellishment. Such an *abaya* follows the body and shows the chest and the shape of the body. This dress is worn as fashion.

Wrote another:

> O daughter of mine. Beware of the revealing *hijab* that is spreading amongst the women these days and that is characterized by:
>
> 1. The tightly cut *abaya* following the body, that shows the attractiveness of the woman. Such an *abaya* needs another *abaya* to cover it.
>
> 2. Wearing the *abaya* on the shoulders, as the original way of wearing it is on the head in order that it covers the body completely. Showing the head of the woman and her shoulders attracts the gaze towards her.[30]

What is critical for the Islamists (and all Salafis) is that beauty and sexual allure be hidden. When women claimed, with the support of moderate clerics, that it is religiously acceptable for women to show their face and hands, the Islamists and Salafis rejected this. (The Qur'an itself actually stipulates the covering of hair and the bosom, not the face.) As one commentary put it, "[I]t is known that desire and attraction are located in the face. . . . This means that the face is the first thing that needs to be covered." Nor is it acceptable to use clothing strategically, for example by "wearing a *niqab* that covers what is ugly and shows what is beautiful."[31]

This is a struggle over aesthetics. Think again of the story of David and Bathsheba: David spies Bathsheba on a rooftop of a house in Jerusalem, lustrous with sexual promise. What follows is a moral collapse both for David himself and for the House of David. In other words, the issue of aesthetics is not superficial; it is a *palpable* experience of ethical struggles and decisions, in this case of turning away from God to what is personally desirable.

Islamists radiate this strict patriarchal-tribal aesthetic: women must be covered up almost completely. Aesthetics capture the reality that ethics are not something worked out solely on an intellectual level. Aesthetics, furthermore, have deep social and political significance. The Islamist reaction is all the more viru-lent as the erotic becomes so much of the visual texture of contemporary life in a world sutured together by global media, advertising, consumerism, and the Internet.

But the more progressive—that is, fashionable—Muslims in Sana'a and else-where have embraced the modern and the global. They believe in at least a modi-cum of autonomy for women. They have taken possession of themselves and wish to shape their self-presentation. They "make" their selves through consum-erism, through buying certain fashions, displaying certain brands—and even literally reshaping themselves through cosmetic surgery. Cosmetic surgery is especially popular in Iran—indeed a status symbol is to display the bandages on your nose after a rhinoplasty. Cosmetic surgery is also growing in popularity elsewhere in the Muslim world, such as in Pakistan. Indeed, globalization ap-pears to be creating a globalized sense of the perfect body and face, not least the shape of the nose.

Fashion empowers the individual. Fashion makes it possible for the wearer to disclose how she wishes to be seen, what she wishes to disclose about herself, and how she will comport herself, publically and privately. It is a part of her "adventure of the self."[32] The very act of "being fashionable" is a statement of cosmopolitanism. It is about standing out and embracing beauty and, to some extent at least, about the erotic as an ethical value. Implicit in fashion is a rejec-tion of seeking status in (only) chastity, honor, and communally defined norms. It implies a desire for achievement and personal success in social life and in work. It is a celebration of the self—albeit with a high degree of trepidation for many.

But fashion also involves differentiation, of distinguishing oneself. The play of the global gaze—that is, the sense of defining oneself in relation to others in an environment rich in images, ideas, ideologies, beliefs, claims and counter-claims—paradoxically causes an inward turn. This itself causes, especially for those outside the West, a heightened awareness of ethnic, religious, and cultural roots.[33]

Fashion also lends itself to bridging these worlds. Fashion can involve the act of differentiating oneself, simultaneously, from the West, the Islamists, and the customary traditionalists; while selectively (an expression of individualism in itself) choosing from across these palettes of fabrics, adornments, styles, disclo-sures, and enclosures. This is the story behind the Yemeni "Barbie": an open chador, face unveiled, some cosmetics, yet distinctively Middle Eastern. Further-more, it is a form of dress that is rooted in the argument that this dress is perfectly acceptable under Islamic strictures. The Laila doll is similar but draws equally on cultural and national as well as religious traditions.

We see a similar yet distinct echo of this story in Indonesia, where there was an upswing in the use of scarves and markers of Islamic dress from the 1990s. Islamists of, notably, the Wahhabi mold introduced their form of clothing strictures into Indonesia, and it continues to play a role. But the changes in the way women dressed responded mostly to other forces.[34]

Under the Suharto dictatorship, which lasted from 1967 to 1998, a "modern" and secular sense of Indonesia and its women was promoted. As Suharto's rule waned, many Indonesian women, especially students, donned a very Indonesian style and pattern of dress, with a loose-fitting headscarf. It was an act of independence that expressed both Indonesian and cosmopolitan identity. It was distinct from Suharto's "modernism," but it was also in opposition to the Islamists, who demanded an austere, transnational Islam, free of local cultural identification. Relatively small numbers now wore the Saudi-style *chador*, the black body cover.[35] As *fashion*, this Islamic-Indonesian dress empowered individuality in shaping one's own self.[36] It drew (and draws) from Javanese tradition but in innovative, individual ways. A diversity of styles and a multitude of colors marked the multitudes in Jakarta and beyond in Indonesia.

Individual fashions that draw on both national and Islamic motifs are evident elsewhere as well—for example, in the breathtaking haute couture designs coming out of Pakistan. These are as pleasing to the eye, as appealing in terms of ready-to-wear, as offerings on the Parisian catwalk.

Other women, for example in Yemen, still wear the veil not only because of religion but also because of custom. The tribal-patriarchal customs weave in and out of Islam, but they are not considered necessarily a part of Islam. Islamists, in contrast, completely fuse these customs into their religious doctrine (often interpreting it even more strictly, as in dress) and then making their ideological stance into one of global import. But as in the case of those who follow certain sartorial practices out of custom not religion, such tribal-patriarchal styles can have an autonomous status—that is, they can be independent of Islam.[37]

Negotiating Public Space

Uncovering the face in places like Yemen or wearing a *chador* in Indonesia is more than a religious statement. It implicates the individual's experience of public space. And conversely, the character of the public arena, from France to Iran, shapes the kinds of statements that are being made. In most Muslim societies, complete cover may afford certain anonymity. But in Western countries like France or even the United States, an all-enveloping burqa will draw unwelcome attention—while deflecting attention from the individual wearer and depersonalizing her.

The Turkish Cypriot designer Hussein Chalayan metaphorically and literally unveiled these fault lines in an exhibit titled *Veils* in 1998. He first displayed a model fully veiled and covered from head to toe. One model followed another, progressively removing a layer of clothing. Finally, a naked woman appeared, her sole covering a small mask, suggesting the image of a dominatrix. "The paradox of Islam is that it has women wearing veils to eliminate their beauty and appeal," Chalayan suggested. "But the desire to remain anonymous and unseen has a boomerang effect. When you dress in a veil, you become enormously conspicuous . . . in Western culture. And who controls the gaze? The Muslim woman peeping out from behind her veil, or the person who sees her?"[38]

Still, the exposure of the face and the wearing of distinct fashions in public have a particular psychological effect on the individual. Absent face cover, the individual has a new accountability. She becomes a "personality." Once out in the open, so to speak, there is a growing onus to present oneself in the most flattering light and show oneself to be fashionable. Fashion is so pervasive that even its rejection—dressing sloppily—becomes a statement. In being in the open, publically, as the fashion historian Gilles Lipovetsky notes, we then observe each other endlessly.[39] We critique each other's looks, appreciate fetching outfits, and envy the wearer of those Louboutins.

The individual and her self-presentation are at the center of it all, so this changes the character of public space. Rather than the classic sense of public space as the area of shared identity, it is an arena of "mutual display." But shared background can also be quickly evaluated.[40] As Muhammad Velji, a philosopher who studies fashion, writes: "[H]air worn as a side pony tail is the signification of the 80s. If one were to wear this side pony tail with bellbottoms signifying an intimacy with the 60s it suggests a new disclosure of the spirit of both decades. Fashion is a communicable language that can only be intelligible because others take it up and it becomes a shared background."[41]

This participation of the individual in public is not only of psychological import. The individual openly displaying herself fashionably is shaping the civic arena. She helps shape the social "body" of society and, as such, the nature of its political life (the body politic). We are observing this phenomenon in a very explicit way in the debate in France about veiling in schools or the wearing of burqas in public. The supposedly prosaic issue of dress in public is a politically crucial issue for all societies.

Fashion is thus a social statement. It is also, usually unwittingly, a political statement. In the past, fashion—from jeans to body piercing—reflected generational divides. But the political divides are, today, more severe.

From an Islamist and more broadly fundamentalist perspective, however, the eroticized fashion of today expresses a "selling" of women, and that turns them into commodities. Women, in this vision, are prostituting themselves. For the majority of people, across religions, once a person is in possession of her bodily self, she is in a position of self-presentation and thus negotiation. Individuals "sell" their labor and intellect at work. They flirt and seduce when seeking a romantic partner. They use their élan and education at cocktail parties in order to impress for all manner of purposes. They have been unfettered, and unleashed.

Fade to Black

Black as a fashion color has always had a special place, especially in French couture. The little black dress is exemplary. Black conjures up the night and the promise of sin. Black exposes. "To set off to advantage the freshness of a blonde or the fairness of a red-haired woman, it is a soft and deep black that is wanted," wrote Charles Blanc in an influential book from 1877, *Art in Ornament and Dress.* Black is anterior to light; it suggests the moment before revelation, the frisson of the (yet) unseen intimate.

Yet black, when it hides, can summon repulsion. And such it is for many in Europe, and especially in France, at the sight of the all-black, all-concealing burqa. "It is as if," said the French writer Guy de Maupassant, "death went out for a walk."[42]

In the play of dress (and undress), we see the essence of a global divide—a divide over the place of the body and the nature of the self.

PART III

EXPLAINING THE ISLAMIST BACKLASH

As the economic and social positions of women progress with globalization, so has a patriarchal backlash became evident. This is especially noticeable in the greater Middle East, where the backlash has also taken on a political, anti-Western form among Islamists. The Tribal Patriarchy Index, introduced in this part, allows us to explore the linkages between tribal patriarchy, Islamists, and religiously motivated violence. In addition, we consider the ways patriarchal hostility is expressed in Islamist thought.

CHAPTER SIX

Loathing the Feminine Mystique

The Islamist Resistance

The Algerian general heading the fight against the Armed Islamic Group (GIA) described one way he evaluated the successes and failures of the fight against the insurgents.[1] He drove to different parts of Algiers and elsewhere in the country, he said, and observed how the women were dressed. If they dressed in an Islamist or traditional fashion, the fight was not going so well for the government in that area. If the dress was secular, then the war was proceeding more hopefully.[2]

This battle for Algiers is fought on the streets, not just with guns and bombs but also through ostentatious display of the body and its sartorial embellishment. After General Zeroual won the presidential elections in 1995, the radicals were pushed out of the Belcourt neighborhood once controlled by Islamists. Now young people publically drink and smoke, and young men brazenly wrap their arms around their girlfriends. Young women dress in miniskirts, expose cleavage, and wear heavy makeup. Hedonism and consumerism confront the asceticism of the radicals. The cabarets and nightclubs are in turn targeted by the GIA, who have at times summarily executed their patrons. One woman, aged 19, wearing make-up and tight pants, is defiant in the face of such dangers: "If they kill me, I die beautiful. At least I lived."[3]

Understanding the symbolism behind such a declaration reveals the underlying dynamics of the Islamist backlash in, notably, the Middle East and North Africa. What drives this determined resistance, in word and deed, to the equalization of women in a world that is integrating economically and culturally—even when such resistance is against the economic self-interest of men and women alike? In what social and cultural circumstances does such a stance regarding women take root? And when does opposition go beyond familial and communal hostility, to political and even violent rejection—as in the case of militant Islamists?

Surprisingly, given the wide media coverage, we have until now lacked a systematic explanation of the drivers behind the Islamists' vociferous opposition to sexual and gender equality. We know that the data show a lag in the integration of women into the job market in the greater Middle East relative to other developing countries.[4] A wealth of books and journalistic reportage depict the challenges for women in the area. We also know from United Nations data that a number of Middle Eastern and North African countries have made some progress in recent years.[5] Yet in other respects the information is very sparse. For example, data on violence against women in the region is sketchy and limited. The data that we do have suggest a severe problem but do not allow us to compare information over periods of years or between countries.[6]

So how can we go about examining this patriarchal backlash and, specifically, the dynamics underlying militant Islamist groups? Two sets of issues confront us. One is the patriarchal backlash against women that plays out at myriad *cultural* levels—in couples, families, and broader communities—and across religions. The other is the *ideological* and sometimes violent attack, not just on women but also on the institutions and societies viewed as advancing an agenda that corrupts women. A significant segment of Islamists support violence as a legitimate expression of such opposition. This chapter will focus on this sharp edge of the resistance.

Understanding the backlash demands an illustration of the linkages between severe patriarchy and the ideological foundations of Islamist militancy. (It must be noted that the great majority in even the most patriarchal communities, Muslim as well as non-Muslim, do not resort to such ideologically inspired hostility.)

To respond to these issues, I draw on a statistical tool developed for this book, the Tribal Patriarchy Index, or more succinctly, the Tribalism Index. The findings will help us parse the distinct role of patriarchal tribalism (including, centrally, women's status), the circumstances under which Islamist groups prosper most, and how tribal-based notions of honor and grievance assume ideological and global import.

Tribal conflicts, in the narrow sense, tend to be kinship-based. Disputes and even tribal war also tend to be circumscribed geographically. However, the Tribal Patriarchy Index demonstrates that the mix of tribal patriarchy and Islam does provide the grounding for globally oriented and anti-Western militant Islamist movements. The Index also shows, however, why a focus on Islam in isolation is of limited use in explaining the dynamics of the conflict.

I will also illustrate how tribalism serves as the organizational model of important militant networks.

The Tribal Patriarchy Index

One commentator, alluding to the wars involving Western powers in Afghanistan and Iraq—and less overtly in Yemen, Somalia, North Africa, and elsewhere—suggested that the "Global War on Terror" was actually a global war on tribes.[7] In fact, the role of tribal regions in this conflict is not incidental—and it is tightly interwoven with the severe patriarchy of these regions.

Tribalism has played an extraordinary role vis-à-vis the struggle against militant Islamists from Afghanistan and Pakistan to Yemen, the Horn of Africa, and across North Africa. Even societies that are urbanized, and certain diasporas, maintain qualities of tribalism. Those with a national origin in the more tribal-patriarchal societies play a disproportionate role in religiously motivated violence. Men of Pakistani and Somali descent, for example, tend to play an outsized role in incidents of extremist violence in both the United Kingdom and the United States—even if those individuals make up a tiny fraction of their respective communities.

Yet, oddly, little attention has been paid to the role of tribal patriarchy in initiating and perpetuating religiously motivated violence. In truth, understanding the links between tribalism and Islamist movements is fundamental to revealing the sociological dynamics of the broader conflict. This is the case not only in the wars in Afghanistan, Pakistan, Yemen, and Somalia, but in the ideological struggles from the Middle East to Western Europe and among diasporic communities.

But there needs to be a nuanced understanding. This is not simply a linear relationship of tribal patriarchy to religiously motivated violence. Even among tribes themselves, their relationship to violent ideological groups is extraordinarily varied. The Pashtuns in Afghanistan have in many cases a close relationship with the Taliban and even Al Qaeda. Yet the Tuareg tribe in the Sahel region in Africa—a region that includes Mali, Mauritania, Niger, and southern Algeria—has had limited ties to Al Qaeda in the Maghreb (AQIM). Some Tuareg are involved or cooperate with the AQIM, but others have engaged in firefights against AQIM cells. The Tuareg do not show the same patriarchy of the Pashtuns (and are organized on matriarchal lines). Tuareg Islam is, furthermore, restrained and even quietist. So the threads linking patriarchal tribalism to Islamist violence demand a subtle analysis.

It also needs to be recognized that tribal societies can display, cumulatively, an unusual degree of personal and social violence. This is also true of other decentralized societies where kinship is the organizing principle of social and political life. Medieval life, with its decentralized state structure and lack of coherent monopoly on the legitimate use of violence, was much more violent than contemporary Europe on a personal level.[8]

Why would tribes, as a whole, exhibit such violence? We observed earlier that balanced opposition is a way to organize security and served to organize many societies for millennia. This also means that the threat of violence is an organizing principle of society—at both a personal and social level. Such a threat is the very antithesis of the civil, republican form of the modern state, where the state monopolizes violence and social relations are to be conducted on the basis of self-restraint and civility.

The need for security is the reason why, in good part, the prowess of males is so valued in tribal contexts. Group loyalty, rather than the rule of law, prevails in the tribal milieu. The tribal form is decentralized; that is, there is no recognized central authority. The blood feud is the ultimate tool of accountability. Honor becomes essential in ensuring lineage, continuity, and martial values.

Yet tribal conflicts tend to be fairly insular and rarely take on a global importance in terms of international security. If the fight is based on kinship issues, the quarrels will be on the level of families and clans. In more extreme cases—witness the genocide among tribes in Rwanda—the bloodletting will take on a broader reach. But even then, the violence rarely spills beyond one or two countries. In other words, the violence does not become global or transnational. So it is not sufficient to simply look at tribes and tribal patriarchy in isolation.

Rather, I suggest the following: militant Islamists (as well as Islamists more broadly) are most likely to develop in tribal-patriarchal environments. Those Islamists will nationalize and, increasingly, internationalize what have been mostly local conflicts. Furthermore, Islamist groups turn tribal-patriarchal concepts—such as honor, gender, and grievance—into ideological rather than kinship-based concerns. Clearly, this analysis presumes that it is at an intersection of tribal patriarchy and Islam where these militant groups are best nurtured. Keep in mind, this does not mean that militant Islamists will be the majority in such communities. They may still constitute a relatively small number. But such militant Islamists are more likely to prosper in such a social environment.[9]

Think about the patterns in terms of social geographies. We have Muslim societies, such as Indonesia, whose roots as we noted are not tribal. Indonesia has generated little in the way of homegrown extremism. Clearly, extremism is a problem in Indonesia, notably in the terrorist organization Jemaah Islamiyah (JI). But such extremist ideology has been imported primarily from the Middle East. Furthermore, the Islamists receive rather limited support in Indonesia. This is evident in the low support of Islamist parties in elections in Indonesia, in contrast to the extraordinary support of Islamist parties in the greater Middle East.[10]

Conversely, tribes outside the Islamic ambit can display great violence—such as in the cases of Rwanda and the Congo—but, as we noted, the violence is relatively localized. In such cases we are seeing humanitarian catastrophes to which the world has turned a largely blind eye. The reason is that these conflicts remain contained within the domain of one or two states.

From the national security perspective of Western states, the most severe problem arises when tribalism intersects with Islamism. Tribal patriarchy of this sort cuts across North Africa and the Middle East, and arcs up to Pakistan and Afghanistan.

How can we go about examining the arguments proffered here, and illustrating its import? We have to be able to tease out the impact of tribalism as such and then its interplay with Islamism. This involves two steps. The first is illustrating the linkage of tribal patriarchy with religiously motivated violence. The second involves demonstrating the connections between tribal patriarchy, Islamism, and the export of violence.

To date, no systematic, quantitative measure of tribal patriarchy has existed. To develop such a measure requires a determination of the social dimensions that characterize tribal patriarchy. We then find statistical measures for those social dimensions. From there, we can develop an "index" of tribal patriarchy. Although I simplify a complex and involved process, this is the essence of quantitative index creation.[11]

In developing the Tribal Patriarchy Index, it is not sufficient to examine only gender inequalities, though gender is the primary consideration. Gender is the hinge, but tribal patriarchies are a bundle of interconnected factors: hostility to centralized states (unless the tribe in question controls the state), which leads to corruption; nested grievances and feuds, from the family to the clan and on up; and pervasive fractionalization between kinship, ethnic, and sectarian groups.[12]

Tribes resent the impingement of the state on their autonomy and resist it—unless, of course, a tribe can seize the powers of the state for its own benefit. Thus tribal societies can be to one degree or another anarchic, associated with weak or failed states—or, indeed, a tribe may manage to enforce its rule on others.

Modern examples of tribal societies with weak centers include Afghanistan, Somalia, and Yemen. In the case of certain tribes enforcing their rule on others, one can point to the success of the Saud's, a tribal family, instituting control in the eponymous Saudi Arabia. The control of Saddam Hussein and his Takriti clan in Iraq, and the rule of the father-and-son Assad regime in Syria, who represented a relatively small clan, the Alawites, are other examples.

Yet even in a number of cases of tribal societies with strong governments, we see the festering of extremism from within (notably the radical Wahhabis from Saudi Arabia, including a number of the 9/11 attackers). Or these centralized tribal governments sponsor extremist groups themselves. This is true, for instance, in the case of the Assad regime in Syria.

In order to construct the Tribal Patriarchy Index, I bring together critical factors that characterize tribes and tribal qualities that often extend into urban and even diasporic environments. These factors or dimensions include gender inequalities, corruption, grievances, and fractionalization. The measures of such qualities come from a consolidated database of some two dozen databases, allowing us to systematically measure this phenomenon of tribalism. The database sources include, among others, the United Nations, the World Bank, the World Economic Forum, Transparency International, Freedom House, and the Fund for Peace. From this study, degrees of tribalism can be measured in each nation-state.[13]

The role of gender in tribes and tribalism is foundational. In keeping with the importance of gender and women's status, that dimension is the most heavily emphasized (or "weighted") dimension of the Tribalism Index. This gender component statistically summarizes national gender disparities in education, health, political participation, and labor force opportunities.[14]

Perceptions of corruption are the next most heavily weighted component of the Tribal Patriarchy Index. Corruption is endemic in tribalistic environments since, by definition, civic government or society is weak. In a functioning civil society, universal rules apply irrespective of clan, religious, sex, or other parochial considerations. In highly tribalized situations such universal rules are weak or nonexistent. The legitimacy of the state is often highly questionable in such environments, as is evident in the recent graphic cases of Libya and Syria.[15]

The next component, "group grievance," speaks to the effects of persecution, perceptions of injustice, scapegoating, and atrocities committed between groups and by the state.[16] Following the Arab Spring we have seen these dynamics visibly at work—again, Libya and Syria are telling cases. As levels of tribalism in a country increase, so group grievance ratchets higher.

Additional dimensions of the Tribalism Index include fractionalization and the presence of indigenous groups. Fractionalization speaks to the level of linguistic, religious, clan, and ethnic variety within a state. Again, tribal societies are

by definition highly fractionalized. We measure fractionalization broadly, drawing on ethnic and other lines of division, not just clan and tribal breakdowns.[17]

A "score" of tribal patriarchy, by country, is statistically derived from the ag-
gregation of the different dimensions of the Tribal Patriarchy Index. The index
goes from 0 (lowest level of tribal patriarchy) to 1 (highest level), with values av-
eraging around 0.5. Afghanistan, for example, measures 0.988. Somalia also
measures 0.988, and Iceland, at the other end, garners a lowly 0.060 (notwithstanding its Viking roots).

It is important to note that *all* countries will accrue some measure of a tribal
patriarchy score—whether deriving from even minimal gender inequalities,
ethnic fractionalization, or perceptions of corruption. Even if a society has no
tribes as such, elements of tribalism will be apparent to varying degrees. We
capture certain social qualities here, not just tribes in the narrow sense—but the
extent of such qualities varies.

It is not surprising that Latin American countries will be middling—such as
Brazil at 0.438 or Argentina at 0.300—or that Central European countries, with
mean scores of 0.500, will be higher than Scandinavian countries, with means of
0.080. Table 6.1 gives Index scores for countries with populations over 5,000,000.
The scores are based on data from years 2000 to 2010, depending on the availability of source data.

The Tribalism Index is able, on its own, to explain a remarkable 68 percent of
rates of religiously motivated violence (based on data drawn from tabulations of
the National Counterterrorism Center [NCTC] for 2005 to 2010.) This influence
is dramatic—the likelihood of a national from a country with a tribalism score
of 1.0 causing a terrorist incident is 6.5 million times higher than a national
from a hypothetical state scoring 0. If we add additional variables of social globalization, Muslim percent of population, and per capita GDP, we can account
for 93 percent of the religiously motivated violence.

But what is especially interesting is that if we factor out the presence of tribalism, a larger Muslim population actually has a modestly *negative* relationship
with violent religious terrorism.[18] Simply, as tribalism increases, so does violence; but as the population becomes proportionally more Muslim, religiously
motivated violence modestly decreases.

What does this mean? In essence, we are able to isolate tribal patriarchy as a
major factor in driving religiously motivated violence when we seek to predict
the patterns shown in NCTC data. We are able to state, with assurance, that a
state's movement from one end of the tribal patriarchy spectrum to the other

TABLE 6.1
Tribal Patriarchy Index Scores by Country (countries with populations over five million)

Country	Score	Country	Score	Country	Score
Afghanistan	0.988	Greece	0.413	Peru	0.500
Algeria	0.850	Guatemala	0.525	Philippines	0.475
Angola	0.675	Guinea	0.688	Poland	0.325
Argentina	0.300	Haiti	0.388	Portugal	0.263
Australia	0.088	Honduras	0.338	Romania	0.463
Austria	0.238	Hungary	0.338	Russia	0.500
Azerbaijan	0.788	India	0.475	Rwanda	0.563
Bangladesh	0.550	Indonesia	0.625	Saudi Arabia	0.800
Belarus	0.488	Iran	0.938	Senegal	0.613
Belgium	0.400	Iraq	0.863	Sierra Leone	0.650
Benin	0.663	Israel	0.400	Slovakia	0.388
Bolivia	0.600	Italy	0.375	Somalia	0.988
Brazil	0.438	Japan	0.288	South Africa	0.463
Bulgaria	0.425	Jordan	0.825	Spain	0.400
Burkina Faso	0.650	Kazakhstan	0.763	Sri Lanka	0.450
Burundi	0.563	Kenya	0.738	Sudan	0.900
Cambodia	0.538	Korea,	0.500	Sweden	0.063
Cameroon	0.725	Republic of		Switzerland	0.263
Canada	0.238	Kyrgyzstan	0.838	Syria	0.913
Chad	0.863	Libya	0.875	Tajikistan	0.825
Chile	0.200	Madagascar	0.488	Tanzania	0.625
China	0.488	Malawi	0.625	Thailand	0.600
Colombia	0.450	Malaysia	0.463	Togo	0.600
Cuba	0.375	Mali	0.675	Tunisia	0.438
Czech Republic	0.400	Mexico	0.463	Turkey	0.825
Denmark	0.150	Morocco	0.863	Turkmenistan	0.550
Dominican	0.338	Mozambique	0.550	Uganda	0.700
Republic		Nepal	0.700	Ukraine	0.550
Ecuador	0.488	Netherlands	0.200	United Kingdom	0.363
Egypt	0.825	Nicaragua	0.438	United States	0.250
El Salvador	0.338	Niger	0.725	Uzbekistan	0.800
Ethiopia	0.725	Nigeria	0.725	Venezuela	0.475
Finland	0.088	Pakistan	0.999	Viet Nam	0.463
France	0.288	Papua New	0.550	Yemen	0.900
Germany	0.263	Guinea		Zambia	0.638
Ghana	0.563	Paraguay	0.375	Zimbabwe	0.575

predicts an extraordinary increase in the production of religious violence on the part of nationals.

Although increasing tribal patriarchy is associated with increasing violence, tribal patriarchy had a *negative* relationship with the *export* of violence across borders.[19] This makes sense, since tribal violence tends to be more geographically insular. But the percentage of Muslim population had a *positive* relationship with the *export* of violence. Simply put, Muslim societies are somewhat less violent than their non-Muslim counterparts if we factor out the presence of tribalism.

However, when increasing Muslim population is *combined with* high levels of tribal patriarchy, religiously motivated violence is more likely to be exported across national borders.

This intriguing finding describes a reality in which high levels of tribalism can be associated with bellicosity. However, Islam (in its Islamist form) projects tribal patriarchal qualities onto a global stage—in terms of women's status, honor, grievances, and feuds, among other considerations. Higher scores on the Tribal Patriarchy Index mean more violence (independent of Islam)—but greater proportions of Muslims in a country mean a higher likelihood of violence exported abroad.

The finding that Islam appears to lend, through its Islamist forms, a global framework to the otherwise insular violence endemic to tribal patriarchies is striking. These findings present a more subtle view of the intersection of tribal patriarchy and Islam than previously understood. Certainly, given that higher percentages of Muslims are associated with lower levels of violence, the view that Islam is *ipso facto* a cause of violence is untenable. Overall, this gives us a subtler picture of the dynamics involved than the view of a civilizational clash or, conversely, the claim that religion is irrelevant to the conflicts that confront us.

The greater Middle East graphically stands out on the high end of tribal patriarchy scores (see fig. 7.1). It is no coincidence that this region is also, in the summation of the senior diplomat Richard Haass, "by most measures the least successful region of the world, one characterized by frequent wars, seemingly insoluble conflicts, the spread of nuclear materials, terrorism, weak regional institutions and poor integration, and a near total absence of political legitimacy within many of its countries."[20] How those challenges are addressed is, of course, another issue altogether and will be a continuing conundrum.

However, the level of tribal patriarchy is not uniform across the region, and different histories and sociologies have filtered tribal patriarchy in different ways. The scholar Mounira Charrad, for example, studied Tunisia, Morocco, and Algeria in this context. All three countries were colonized by France and had similar cultures, with tribes prominent. However, Algeria had no central government to speak of when conquered by the French. The tribes by and large were completely independent of central government. Morocco, prior to French colonization, had no central government capable of extracting taxes, and the tribes were in constant conflict with the political center. Tunisia, on the other hand, had the most cohesive government that was capable of levying taxes. By the time the French arrived, there was already a college for the training of civil servants.

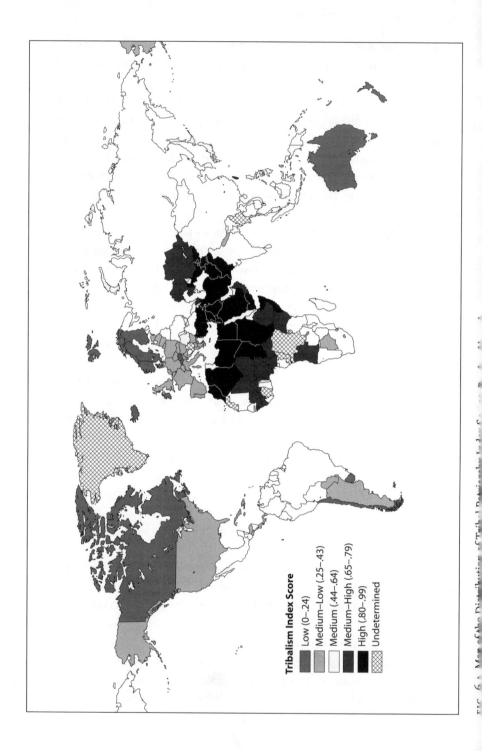

Tribalism Index Score

- Low (0–24)
- Medium–Low (.25–43)
- Medium (.44–64)
- Medium–High (.65–79)
- High (.80–99)
- Undetermined

FIG. 6.1 Map of the Distribution of Tribal Patriarchy Index Scores Around the World

The government had the ability to enforce its decisions in most of its territory, which had recognizable borders (unusual when tribes dominated). The French reinforced this national and central government, something they were not able to do to the same extent in Algeria and Morocco.

After Tunisia became independent, a reforming national elite emerged that was largely independent of the tribes. As a consequence, Tunisia enacted progressive family laws that recognized women's rights (seen as a marker of a "modern" state). In Morocco and to some extent in Algeria, family law after independence was less progressive. Stricter interpretations of Islamic law were retained in order to appease the tribes.[21]

A Global War on Tribes

What is also compelling, and points further to their tribal-patriarchy roots, is the extent to which tribal structure informs the organization of Islamist groups. This is true for Al Qaeda and in certain respects other Islamist networks like the Muslim Brotherhood.

The scholar of Islam Peter Mandaville compares the Al Qaeda network to the Internet, a recurrent analogy. Like the Internet, Al Qaeda is a "network of networks." The Internet was in its early forms designed by the American military to be an impervious communications network in the event of a nuclear strike. Redundancy was built into the network, so messages could be sent even if entire sections of the network were destroyed. The Internet is also decentralized in its structure, so there is no "central choke point" on which all other operations depend. Thus the Al Qaeda analogy: it too has the redundancy capacity in that its network of operations can continue to operate even if a part of the Al Qaeda network is destroyed. The killing of Osama bin Laden was a clear blow, but in itself not a fatal one.[22]

But while the Internet is an essential *mechanism* for the operations of networks like Al Qaeda, there is a more direct way for deciphering them: these networks mirror tribal patriarchy—and do so consciously. The tribe is not simply an analogous social form; rather, the networks are in critical ways tribes writ large. It is the form of society that the leaders of the different networks know, so it informs their organizations. It illustrates the extent to which the tribal patriarchy is not simply an "ideology" but is rather a lived experience. The Internet is a tool rather than a model of organizing.[23]

In what ways is this tribal experience integral to the networks? There are numerous threads making up the fabric: relations and trust based on kinship and organic systems; the trust-based conduct of financial relations; the way segments of the network mirror each other in form—and as such can be sacrificed and reproduced, if need be; the stress on male martial honor to the point of suicide; the culture of honor and vengeance; the horizontal organization with only a loose hierarchy (among males); the network that unites factions or clans (in the name of the Ummah) against the common, infidel enemy; the principle of self-help; and, of course, the stratified relationship of men and women (often elided in discussions about the horizontal nature of the network). Even the nomadic quality of such networks mirrors—albeit for distinct reasons—the tribes. Cells of the network are akin to, and often called, "families," or can allude to clans—or what we call fraternal networks or sub-networks. These fraternal organizations have been called in the West "franchise" organizations.

This attachment to a patriarchal-tribal kinship mold became publicly evident in the trial of Osama bin Laden's driver, Salim Hamdan in 2008. This was the first war crimes trial held by the United States since the 1940s. "Mr. bin Laden seemed to take an almost paternal interest in his hireling, who hailed from Hadramout, Yemen, the ancestral home of the bin Ladens," reported the *Wall Street Journal*. The former FBI investigator Ali Soufan described how bin Laden told Hamdan and a fellow Al Qaeda member of staff to return to Yemen and marry sisters. This was explicitly designed to create blood ties within the AQ network. Bin Laden played host to their wedding feast back in Afghanistan.[24]

This arrangement is not unique to Al Qaeda. Jemaah Islamiya (JI) is the Indonesian group responsible for, among other attacks, the Bali bombings of 2002, which killed more than two hundred people, mostly Australians and other foreigners. After those attacks, Indonesia made a concerted and extensive attempt to eradicate that group. It has survived in significant part as a result of its built-in, widespread kinship ties. Members of JI, once inside the group, augment the ideological ties through marrying sisters and daughters of their comrades-in-arms. Brothers are sometimes recruited together.

Whole families or a variety of family linkages—brothers, sons, daughters, sisters, and in-laws—are implicated in JI activities. Two sets of brothers were involved in the first Bali events. Arranged marriages are used to forge alliances, with JI spiritual leaders playing matchmakers, much like Osama Bin-Laden. Converts' loyalties are cemented through marriage: Jack Thomas, an Australian convert, married an Indonesian woman, Maryati, in South Africa on the recommendation of his JI friends. Thomas, who adopted the name "Jihad," married her the day he met her.[25]

Though observers have noted operational advantages to such arrangements—it limits options for betrayal by members of JI; they have additional motives to protect fellow members' identities under interrogation; and it increases the trust essential for clandestine operations—clearly something more fundamental is at work here.[26] Other terrorist groups, like the Irish Republican Army or the neo-Nazi groups, have not demonstrated the same degree of kinship ties. Indeed, with the militant Islamist groups, is it kinship augmenting ideology, or ideology augmenting kinship? In fact, both forces are at play, making such networks a hybrid of "traditional" kinship organizations and modern voluntary organizations.

This hybrid quality is notable in the Muslim Brotherhood. The Brothers are organized systematically, with a defined administration and professional support. Yet the notion of kinship was infused in the very name of the organization and in the way the building blocks of the Brothers was conceived from the 1940s. They were defined as "families," composed of up to ten active members. These families, observers have argued, were the real source of power in the Muslim Brotherhood.

Another advantage of tribal- and kinship-based organizations is the extent to which operations and logistics can depend on social trust. Bin Laden, for example, used the *hawala* method to conduct financial transactions. In this arrangement, sums of money can be transferred between towns or countries, based on the honor and performance of large networks of brokers. No record of the transaction exists—so there is none to track. The transaction costs—such as commissions—are generally lower than in formalized banking. This practice can be traced back to eighth-century Islamic jurisprudence and was in different ways practiced over the centuries by kin networks of different religions and cultures. After the September 11, 2001, attacks, the U.S. government cracked down on such practices as a source of terrorist financing.[27]

This tribal quality of the networks is palpable in a description by Gen. Stanley A. McChrystal, who led the Joint Special Operations Command from 2003 to 2008 and served as commander of U.S. and NATO forces in Afghanistan in 2009 and 2010:[28]

Like all too many military forces in history, we initially saw our enemy as we viewed ourselves. . . . By habit, we started mapping the organization in a traditional military structure, with tiers and rows . . .

But the closer we looked, the more the model didn't hold. Al Qaeda in Iraq's lieutenants did not wait for memos from their superiors, much less orders from bin Laden. Decisions were not centralized, but were made quickly and communicated laterally across the organization. . . . Money, propaganda, and information flowed at alarming rates, allowing for powerful, nimble coordination. We would watch their tactics change (from rocket attacks to suicide bombings, for example) nearly simultaneously in disparate cities. It was a deadly choreography achieved with a constantly changing, often unrecognizable structure.

Over time, it became increasingly clear—often from intercepted communications or the accounts of insurgents we had captured—that our enemy was a constellation of fighters organized not by rank but on the basis of relationships and acquaintances, reputation and fame. Who became radicalized in the prisons of Egypt? Who trained together in the pre-9/11 camps in Afghanistan? Who is married to whose sister? Who is making a name for himself, and in doing so burnishing the Al Qaeda brand?

All this allowed for flexibility and an impressive ability to grow and to sustain losses. The enemy does not convene promotion boards; the network is self-forming. We would watch a young Iraqi set up in a neighborhood and rise swiftly in importance: After achieving some tactical success, he would market himself, make connections, gain followers, and suddenly a new node of the network would be created and absorbed. The network's energy grew.[29]

Honor is foundational to the operation of these networks—in financial transactions and even more so in terms of combat and "self-help." The concept of self-interest in itself does little to explain the commitment of foot soldiers in these organizations or their motive to join. The Islamist networks and the organization's statements, communiqués, and publications are infused with the language of honor and of grievances, retribution, and humiliations to overcome.

It is important to remember that while Islamist militants incorporate much that is tribal into their networks, they also seek to transcend the tribes. Islamist ideology focuses on a universal Islam, stripped of local or national culture. Such Islamists aspire to a singular, global Islam that cannot be in any form identified in terms of local or national groups, including tribes. "A Muslim has no nationality except his belief," wrote Sayyid Qutb, the most prominent of the Islamist thinkers.[30] We will delve more deeply into this issue through the work of Islamist ideologists in the following chapter.

As a consequence of this emphasis on honor, in part, actual relations between groups like Al Qaeda and tribes can either be symbiotic or conflictual. In Iraq, for example, Al Qaeda in Mesopotamia (also known as Al Qaeda in Iraq, or AQI) failed to pay due respect to the elders of the Sunni tribes. It was a terrible mistake on their part, since this presaged the "Awakening Councils" that cooperated with U.S. forces in routing the Al Qaeda elements. Arguments can erupt over such issues as the legitimate number of wives. In Afghanistan, the Al Qaeda quarreled with otherwise sympathetic Pashtun tribesmen, since the tribesmen did not feel bound by the Islamic sanction of four wives only.[31]

Al Qaeda does learn. As the insurgents moved into Yemen following the Iraq setback, they were more careful to work *with* tribal elders. One top Al Qaeda leader married into a local tribe. Financial assistance was provided to tribesmen in the poorest areas. Messages of global jihad were tailored to fit local grievances. Longer-term Al Qaeda ties with tribes—including the fact that Bin Laden's family was from the area—helped. In exchange, some tribal leaders welcomed Al Qaeda members, protecting them from government troops, and permitted their sons to sign up. "As long as al-Qaeda respects the tribes, some tribes will welcome them," said Sheikh Abdulqawi Sherif, the head of the pro-government Bani Dhabian tribe.[32]

Articulating the Cause

Too much explanation of militant Islam has relied purely upon the words of major thinkers of the genre. Islamist ideologists can only win support if the underlying social and cultural dynamics are promising, if they "make sense" in a given set of circumstances.

Islamist thinkers are critical in that they provide a structure, organization, and purpose in times of social change; they also legitimize the expression of certain emotions, thoughts, and ideas. They can ideologically explain and reconcile social worlds in times of transition—for rural people facing urbanization, for example. In essence, intellectuals with mass appeal are those who are able to provide a meaningful story for individuals caught in the maelstrom of history. They link their personal stories of such individuals to the larger sagas of religions, tribes, and nations. To do so, these thinkers often draw on metaphors, imagery, and aesthetics of the faith, interpreted in ways that serve the militant cause.

At the bloody spearhead of this global conflict, one can clearly discern the ink of these Islamist scholars.

CHAPTER SEVEN

Thoughts and Consequences

The Ink of Scholars and the Blood of Martyrs

Part of what gives militant Islamist movements their lethality is the way they escalate highly personalized tribal concepts—for example, a feud with a particular individual, which may be extended to his family and clan—to an ideological level. The feud, the vengeance, the promise of restored honor, is now projected ideologically and morally. The enemy is now the West, the United States, Christians, and Jews. Such targets represent capitalism, pornography, and fornication (all of which is epitomized, in this view, in Western or Westernized women). Western ideas of interest are judged against Islamist honor. Perhaps beyond anything that classical Islam could have envisaged, the infidel becomes a pollutant to be cleansed.

In this chapter we turn to the articulation of ideology by the foundational thinkers of militant Islam. The imagery and use of the body in this articulation is primary. The use of the body includes women—especially Western women. Like most ideological tracts, the foundational and subsequent Islamist writings are also theatre. At the extreme point, this theatre is acted out through the ultimate sacrifice of suicide bombing, which I will also consider here. The theatre has its scriptwriters and its actors, a linkage that was merged by, among others, Osama bin Laden. In the words of one such scholar, Shaykh Abdullah Azzam:

> The life of the Muslim *Ummah* is solely dependent on the ink of its scholars and the blood of its martyrs. What is more beautiful than the writing of the *Ummah*'s history with both the ink of a scholar and his blood, such that the map of Islamic history becomes colored with two lines: one of them black, and that is what the scholar wrote with the ink of his pen; and the other one red, and that is what the martyr wrote with his blood.[1]

Although discussions of the intellectual history of Islamism and the status of women in Islam more broadly have been extensive, they have not sufficiently elicited the role of women and the image of woman as fountainheads of the Islamist movement.

Intellectual Roots of Islamism

The Islamist resistance to secularizing or Westernizing trends, especially regarding women, goes back at least to the early twentieth century. The focus of the Islamist movement's resistance changed to reflect the shifting focus from the national level to the global level as the world itself came to be seen as a singular space through globalization.

As Arab countries attained independence after World War II, the first challenge for the Islamists was that of the largely secular or royalist Middle Eastern and North African governments such as in Egypt and Morocco. Their center of attention was initially national or regional. Islamist movements gained momentum from the late 1960s in the Middle East as the Arab socialist and the monarchist governments were seen as failing—economically, politically (as authoritarian and corrupt regimes), and as a result of the Arab's defeat by Israel in the 1967 War.

The core Islamist intellectuals most mentioned are al-Wahhab, al-Banna, Mawdudi, and Qutb. Many other commentators complement these figures, making for skeins of intricate distinctions on issues of permitted violence, strategy, *takfiri* Muslims, and suicide bombing. With the rise of the Internet, numerous, often quite influential "Internet Jihadi Scholars" have caused even more dense deliberations.[2] (Muslim activists in England often joked about the rising influence of "Sheikh Google.") Still, the foundations of Islamist thought and the framing of much of the internal debates were established by these founding thinkers. I focus here primarily on Qutb, since he has a special importance for the globalizing of the Islamist movement.[3]

Muhammad Ibn Abd al-Wahhab was an eighteenth-century reformer in what is today Saudi Arabia. He sought the "purification" of Islam from any innovation that had been introduced after the time of the Prophet—an idea known as *bid'a*. The Prophet's companions and near-contemporaries are known as *salaf* or *Salafis*. Salafis today are those who seek to bring Islam back to what they view as its true, original state of the companions of the Prophet. The Wahhabis are one group among the varied Salafis—some violent, others not.

Al-Wahhab interpreted the "oneness of Allah" (*tawhid*) as prohibiting the worship, or even the semblance of worship, of any man or man-made object. The Sufis, who venerate saints and visit their graves, have suffered in particular from this approach. The Wahhabis even destroyed the Prophet's house in Mecca so as to preempt any idol-like worship.[4]

Al-Wahhab made an alliance with the tribal family of the Sauds in 1740.[5] In this regard, Wahhabism came to epitomize the Islamist form through a marriage of tribal patriarchy and Islam. Wahhabism was a political arrangement that prospered through violent conquest and through winning the allegiance both of other tribes in Arabia and other Muslims, whom they deemed *takfiri*, or apostates. These apostates, though allies of convenience, were considered little better than *kafirs*, or non-Muslims. They also held, and continue to hold, a special disdain— to put it mildly—for the Shia in general and the Iranian Islamic Republic in particular.[6]

Hassan al-Banna (1906–1949) founded the Muslim Brotherhood. He had been distressed by the decreasing role of religion in Egypt in the wake of Western colonization and modernization. Al-Banna developed a message of anti-colonialism, rejecting Western influence and calling for a return to a supposedly purer Islam. His popularity as a speaker grew, and in 1928 he founded the Muslim Brotherhood to carry his mission forward and to advocate for a full role for Islam in public life. In the 1930s and 1940s the movement expanded dramatically.[7]

Al-Banna's emphasis was foremost on social reform, rather than on the creation of an Islamic state as such. Later leaders of the Brotherhood, however, would stress the need for an Islamic state. Still, one should not leave with the impression that this movement was simply a civic reform movement under al-Banna. Violence was very much part of the movement.

Sayyid Abu al-Ala Mawdudi (1903–1979) was a contemporary of al-Banna, but was from South Asia. He developed a more elaborate theoretical foundation for Islamism than did al-Banna and was the founder and ideologist for the Jama'at-I Islami party. That party, in turn, is closely associated with Pakistan, though it was founded in British India in 1941, prior to the founding of Pakistan in 1947. The party has offshoots in Bangladesh (formerly East Pakistan, broken off as an independent state in 1971) and Sri Lanka. It seeks an "unsullied" Islamic state based on Sharia.

For Mawdudi, the Muslim's role is to realize Allah's will on earth through a "democratic caliphate" or a "theo-democracy." Society in this context would be an organic whole, a shared political body. Although Mawdudi believed that the state's role was to bring about an Islamic way of life, he believed, like Al-Wahhab, that social reforms were the most urgent undertaking. Women would have a very limited role in society; he was, like the others, severely patriarchal. He also supported violent jihad to reach Islamist goals.[8]

The Egyptian Sayyid Qutb's (1906–1966) interests initially were mostly literary; as far as the Qur'an was concerned, he first stressed its aesthetics. But following a trip to the United States at the end of the 1940s, he joined the Muslim Brotherhood in 1952. He took an increasingly confrontational role against the government. He supported the coup by the (secular) Free Officers in Egypt against King Farouk in 1952, the same year in which he joined the Muslim Brotherhood. But he was deeply disappointed by the secularism and Arab socialism (including, notably, an evolution toward women's rights) that followed, especially under the leadership of Gamel Abdel Nasser. In 1954 he was arrested in a roundup of dissidents after an attempt on Nasser's life and was sentenced to fifteen years in prison.

In jail he wrote the seminal text *Milestones on the Road,* his strongest and most influential statement on removing the taint of the infidels. The government banned it. After he was released in 1964, the Muslim Brotherhood asked him to become their spiritual adviser, and he apparently agreed. He was subsequently charged with seeking to overthrow the Egyptian government and to assassinate the president. He was hanged in 1966. But his ideas, especially those described in *Milestones,* became core principles for the Islamist movement—especially for the radicals, and especially for a more globalized movement.[9]

Wahhabis are viewed by scholars as distinct from Islamists. Islamism, like Wahhabism, is a doctrine that seeks an Islamic political order, from legal practice to the daily structure and rhythm of life. It may be advocated violently or nonviolently. But Islamist ideology seeks to resolve the difficult paradoxes that have arisen in the modern age. Islamists, more than Wahhabis, have theologically accepted modern science while continuing to reject modern culture. Islamists are more closely associated with the Muslim Brotherhood and, in its early origins, with al-Banna.

But in practice, Islamism and Wahhabism today can be ideologically distinct but often involve a merging of beliefs in addition to their shared sociological roots in tribal patriarchy. In that light, the Wahhabis belong to the spectrum of Islamists, albeit with all kinds of political and ideological conflicts among these groups. After the assassination of Egyptian President Anwar Sadat in 1981, many of the Egyptian Muslim Brotherhood—implicated in Sadat's assassination—took refuge in Saudi Arabia with the Saudi government's welcome. The Wahhabis and "Brothers" combined to create a lethal, puritanical zealotry. Thus we witness both strains in figures such as the late Osama bin Laden.

Fighting Usury and Fornication

Not long after 9/11, a communication in the name of Osama bin Laden titled "Letter to the American People" was circulated on the Internet and among Islamists. The letter purportedly answered the question, "What are we calling you to, and what do we want from you?" After noting that the first "want" or demand was for the American people to convert to Islam, the second regarded morals:

> We call you to be a people of manners, principles, honor, and purity; to reject the immoral acts of fornication, homosexuality, intoxicants, gambling, and trading with interest . . .
>
> It is saddening to tell you that you are the worst civilization witnessed by the history of mankind: You are the nation who, rather than ruling by the Shariah of Allah in its Constitution and Laws, choose to invent your own laws as you will and desire . . .
>
> You are the nation that permits Usury, which has been forbidden by all the religions. Yet you build your economy and investments on Usury. As a result of this, in all its different forms and guises, the Jews have taken control of your economy, through which they have then taken control of your media, and now control all aspects of your life making you their servants . . .
>
> You are a nation that permits acts of immorality, and you consider them to be pillars of personal freedom.
>
> You are a nation that exploits women like consumer products or advertising tools calling upon customers to purchase them. You use women to serve passengers, visitors, and strangers to increase your profit margins. You then rant that you support the liberation of women.
>
> You are a nation that practices the trade of sex in all its forms, directly and indirectly. Giant corporations and establishments are established on this, under the name of art, entertainment, tourism and freedom, and other deceptive names you attribute to it.[10]

These words capture the moral heart of the Islamist project—though it is important to emphasize that not all Islamists favor the path of violence, at least tactically, to reach the goals that Osama bin Laden so fervently preached. Usury (strictly, interest, but more broadly, capitalism) and fornication (in the main, any sexual activity outside heterosexual marriage) characterize the West, and the heart of darkness. This outlook is extraordinarily resonant of medieval Church doctrine in terms of sexuality. As the letter notes—if in a tone we do not share—those in the United States consider sexual and economic liberties, to one degree or another, as "pillars of personal freedom." Rather than following a sacred, heavenly scripture as such, we in the West also collectively write our own laws. We individually "author" scripts and desires for life and use our bodies accordingly.

In essence, what is contested is what it means to be human, what is righteous and what is evil conduct. The letter conveys an alternative sense of the body and of the battle for control of the body. The letter expresses the very antithesis of sovereign individuals free to trade (in Bin Laden's sense) their bodies for all manner of interests—economic, sexual, or otherwise.

The letter itself builds on radical Islamist themes that go back to Al-Wahhab but were developed most effectively for the global stage by Qutb.

Qutbism

In Qutb's *Milestones*, two parts are of particular significance for the political and social struggles occurring around the world. First, Qutb seeks to demolish foundational Western and liberal beliefs about individual sovereignty. In essence, our daily life should be completely under the guidance of Allah, and we must surrender ourselves to Allah and Allah's laws. Second, having rejected the provincial groupings of tribe, ethnicity, and nation, Qutb re-introduces patriarchy as a critical foundation for a globalizing Islam.

Qutb takes the term *Jahiliyyah*, referring to the time of moral and social chaos preceding the time of the Prophet, and extends it to all modern and Western civilization:

> If we look at the sources and foundations of modern ways of living, it becomes clear that the whole world is steeped in *Jahiliyyah*, and all the marvelous material comforts and high-level inventions do not diminish this ignorance. This *Jahiliyyah* is based on rebellion against Allah's sovereignty on earth. It transfers to man one of the greatest attributes of Allah, namely sovereignty, and makes some men lords over others. It is now not in that simple and primitive form of the ancient *Jahiliyyah*, but takes the form of claiming that the right to create values, to legislate rules of collective behavior, and to choose any way of life rests with men, without regard to what Allah has prescribed.[11]

For Qutb, slavery rests in the very understanding of freedom that the West (and now much of the world) holds dear, namely, that we control our own selves.

For Qutb, such individual sovereignty has the effect of making us tools of each other, economically and in a debauched sexuality. Furthermore, in having author-ship of ourselves, we invariably give license to base bodily impulses. By extension, that individual corruption applies to collective self-determination—democracy—which violates Allah's prerogative as the sovereign of the universe.

We become slaves to each other and to the moral chaos that ensues: "The result of this rebellion against the authority of Allah is the oppression of His creatures . . . and the exploitation of individuals and nations due to greed for wealth and imperialism under the capitalist systems are but a corollary of rebel-lion against Allah's authority and the denial of the dignity of man given to him by Allah."[12] Western freedom of choice and consumerism is an extension of this exploitative fabric, and it leads us astray, cognitively and in our conduct. Either Allah is sovereign, or we are sovereign; we cannot have both.

The world is at the brink of a precipice, Qutb declared at the beginning of *Milestones,* as "Western civilization is unable to provide healthy values."[13] Though issues of economic exploitation are referenced, Qutb's core argument regards the moral implications of the entwined Western and capitalist values. He refers to the times of *Jahiliyyah,* and describes how fornication was "rampant in vari-ous forms and was considered something to be proud of, as is the case among all *jahili* societies, old and new."[14]

Islam, Qutb expounds, is not a theory or a belief, but a life in which Islamic *practice* determines the whole cadence of life, day and night, cradle to grave. It is an "active, organic and vital movement."[15] It is a way of life. There is nothing reflective or subjective in Qutb's rendering of life as it should be practiced. We are not agents of our own destiny, but rather we *enact* the scripture. Islam, he says, abhors being reduced to pure thought or belief. The believers acquire integrity—in the sense of wholeness, as well as displaying ethical conduct—by following the strict and literal word of Islamic law. This bestows freedom rather than the corrupting and dehumanizing practices of the West and other *jahili* communities.

Qutb's Islam is both a religion and a movement to wipe out tyranny and cor-ruption and to introduce freedom for mankind through *Jihad bis saif* (striving through fighting). He states explicitly that Islam is not a "defensive movement." But this fight against tyranny has definite stages, "each of which [will utilize] new methods"—alluding to the tactical considerations of political violence. By definition, all Jewish, Hindu, and Christian societies are *jahili* societies.

Even if in modern society we seek to author our lives and we seek control over our bodies, Qutb says, we are in fact products of Allah's law, and Sharia is also part of that universal law that "governs the entire universe, including the physical and biological aspects of man." Man, he writes, "breathes Allah's air in the quantity and fashion prescribed by Allah; he has feelings and understanding, he experiences pain, becomes hungry and thirsty, eats and drinks—in short, he has to live according to the laws of Allah and he has no choice in the matter." As such, Qutb claims that there is no difference between man and other objects, animate or inanimate, in the universe. All parts of the universe "unconditionally submit to the Will of Allah and to the laws of His creation."[16]

Invariably, an essential part of this natural order that Qutb describes is the traditional role of the woman. Indeed, the family and the "relationship between the sexes" *determines*, in Qutb's thinking, the character of society:

> [I]f . . . the division of work is not based on family responsibility and natural gifts; if woman's role is merely to be attractive, sexy and flirtatious, and if a woman is freed from her basic responsibility of bringing up children; and if . . . she prefers to become a hostess or a stewardess in a hotel or ship or air company, thus spending her ability for material productivity rather than in the training of human beings, because material production is considered to be more important, more valuable and more honorable than the development of human character, then such a civilization is 'backward' . . . or 'jahili' in the Islamic terminology.[17]

Many have suggested that Qutb must have been driven by his experiences as a visiting student, sponsored by the government of King Farouk's Egypt, to the United States in 1949 to 1950. In a now-celebrated recounting, Qutb described with a mix of fascination and revulsion a church dance in Greeley, Colorado, using graphic imagery: The pastor, doubling as disk jockey, dimmed the lights to impart "a romantic, dreamy atmosphere," and put on a record of "Baby, It's Cold Outside." Qutb wrote of how the "dance floor was replete with tapping feet, enticing legs, arms wrapped around waists, lips pressed to lips, and chests pressed to chests. The atmosphere was full of desire."[18]

Humans, left to their own authority, are driven by their crass bodily desires, as Qutb describes Americans:

> There is no doubt that this fascination with physical strength is indicative of the vitality of this nation and its sensuality. If this fascination were tamed and sublimated, it could lead to the creation of a great art that would remove the gloominess of life and infuse the human spirit with fragrance, and bind the sexes with ties higher and more beautiful than the ties of thirsty bodies, burning passions, and eye-popping sex that beckons through the limbs, and is embodied in motions and gestures.[19]

As the writer Jonathan Raban put it, "We're in the psychodrama of temptation here—the language tumescent with arousal, even as it affects a tone of detachment and disdain."[20]

In his Qur'anic commentary, *In the Shade of the Qur'an,* Qutb described how the believer's task would be "purifying the filthy marsh of this world." He was telling a story that many in the most patriarchal corners of the world, especially the Middle East, could identify with, in the face of the sensory assault of the West. He not only legitimized those feelings but also gave some of them an Islamist program for action—expressed with or without political violence.[21]

Note the tangible imagery in Qutb's polemics and that of other leading Islamist figures. It is graphic: *Jahaliyyah,* sexy, flirtatious, "lips meeting lips," water pure and polluted, and so on. This is not dry text. The listener is seduced. The heart palpitates. We are at the edge of the precipice. As with compelling theatre, so effective political discourse: the listener sees before he hears, feels before he thinks.[22]

In public conversation there has been much back-and-forth over the meaning of *jihad* in Islam, as used in various communiqués and declarations. Conservatives have noted the more belligerent interpretations. Some liberal academics have suggested the more personal meaning of jihad is dominant in Islamist writings. But in Qutb, the meaning is both political and personal simultaneously: the collective fight against the corrupting influences of the West, and the individual struggle not to be lured into temptation. Emancipated women, at work, in marriage, and in the mingling of the sexes, represent the risk of unveiled, naked attraction—to be seduced in body and, metaphorically, to be seduced by the West.

Qutb's claim that an American woman, sent by the Central Intelligence Agency, attempted to sexually impose herself upon him while he was on a ship vividly captures his sense of the entwined character of jihad.[23] How telling—he sees a woman before him, the air thick with sexual predation. But that body of seduction represents the CIA and as such embodies the West. Sexuality, exploitation, imperialism, corruption, and the West are literally and figuratively embodied in a woman and her conduct.

Tribal Globalists

Qutb resolves the tension between a universal, monotheistic faith and the local tribal patriarchy, first, by seeking a pure Islam—free of the taints of locality, culture, tribe, or nation—while taking tribal patriarchy as the foundation of a global Islam. This made sense for Qutb's reading of the Qur'an. The Prophet himself sought to transcend the warring, fractious tribes of Arabia (although Qutb does note Muhammad's noble tribal lineage).

While the Prophet Muhammad drew away from some of the more egregious patriarchal practices regarding women, such as having a limitless number of wives, patriarchy remained very much in force—including polygamy, if limited to a maximum of four wives. Progressive Muslims interpret the distancing from the most severe gender practices as the critical move. But the "fundamentalists"— the literalists—take the actual circumstances of the time of the Companions of the Prophet as the point of reference. Qutb sincerely believed in his interpretation, but it was also an astute step in the context of the tribal-patriarchal Middle East though he was writing thirteen centuries after the time of the Prophet.

The resolution of the tensions between a universal ideology and patriarchal tribalism takes a different form with the Saudi Wahhabis—even if with similar results. The Wahhabis in effect take one tribe—the Sauds (the only family to have a modern state named after them)—and make that tribe the foundation of "tribal globalists" to which others should join or signify subservience.[24]

The Islamist worldview that Qutb and others propagated demands purity of faith not only for ideological reasons but also as a powerful form of control. The comparison here with Christianity is illuminating: Qutb, for example, has the austere approach of the Puritan Calvinists in rejecting any mediation between soul and Allah—in other words, the believer is alone before Allah. No priest, saintly figures, local superstitions, iconic objects and the like "mediate" the relationship with Allah, directly or symbolically. Only the ideology binds together the faithful.

Qutb, however, also aspires to a universal Islam, akin to the universality of Catholicism—without the centralized church bureaucracy. Radical Islamist universality and transnationalism is represented by ideological and theological purity, without any hierarchical organization. Thus the radical Islamist zeal for Islamic states and for stamping out other Muslim practices (notably of Sufis) that are viewed as *takfir* (apostate): there is no centralized hierarchy such as that represented by the Vatican and the pope. Saints and other icons, such as those of the Sufi Muslims, tend to have a local or regional emphasis.

The supposed universal ideological purity of Qutbism and its fraternal ideologies, together with their *takfiri* view that banished other Muslims as heretics— let alone the gut-felt hatred for Christians, Hindus, and Jews—became, for the so-inclined, a license for murder. The apostate Muslims (that is, most Muslims), Christians, Hindus, Jews, and the various others were *jahili*. This sanctioned the killing of thousands upon thousands, in multiple militant attacks across the globe, with the killers' composed assurance of fulfilling a sacred duty.

The Sirens of Christians and Jews and the Echoes of Marx

It is striking how the wording and the tone of Osama bin Laden's "Letter to the American People" reflects Qutb, down to references to women serving passengers. The parallel continues in Qutb's recounting in *Milestones* of his arguments with Americans during his stay in the United States. Look at capitalism, he says to his American protagonists, "with its monopolies, its usury and whatever else is unjust in it; at this individual freedom, devoid of human sympathy and responsibility for relatives except under the force of law; at this materialistic attitude which deadens the spirit; at this behavior, like animals, which you call 'Free mixing of the sexes'; at this vulgarity which you call 'emancipation of women.'"

Qutb's and Osama bin Laden's attack on the Jews draws from an old anti-Jewish prototype of the West: the Jew as manipulating the system of capitalism—this system of exploitation—from behind the scenes. Indeed, some Islamist attacks go so far as to stress that in the Crusader-Zionist alliance, even the Christians are beholden to and manipulated by the Jews. Zionism has become such a comprehensive ideology, in the words of one such Islamist group, that it has infiltrated all other religions and political systems and now controls them.[25] This attack on Jews or Zionists (the terms are usually used interchangeably) is independent of, and in logic supersedes, the Arab-Israeli conflict in the Middle East. The argument about capitalism echoes Marx, and the anti-Semitic imagery mimics that of certain socialist strains on both the far left and the far right.

Another example of an apparent alliance between the Left and Islamists: Primarily the Left drove the Iranian revolution at first—but they paid dearly for an understanding they thought they had with the Khomeini Islamists. Once the revolution was over, those Islamists routed the forces of the Left. The Khomeinists killed and tortured thousands upon thousands of leftists in the process. This persecution still continues more than thirty years later.[26] Khomeini cared little for class politics except in the tactical sense. But he had been fighting any figment of women's equality—important for the Left—since he had opposed the Shah's "White Revolution," which proposed women's emancipation.

In fact, the Islamist critique of capitalism is moral and religious—unlike Marx's class analysis, which favored economic determinism. Indeed, Qutb assailed socialism and its effects on humanity in much the same way he attacked capitalism. And the moral critique of capitalism is not made in universal, humanist terms, though it may at times be read that way. Rather, it is couched in the language of true Muslims in opposition to infidels and apostates: The enemy is not simply the "owners of the means of production," as Marx would have it, but the full gamut of Western society and other non-Muslims.[27]

The Islamist critique of Judaism, Christianity, and the West generally is much more fundamental than, say, the decolonization struggles after World War II. The colonizers and colonized often shared a vocabulary of a world order built on sovereignty and national self-determination but disagreed on borders and the timing of independence. With the Islamists—especially the militants—there is no meeting point of agreement with the infidel, no shared moral vocabulary.

Furthermore, the struggle is not just "geopolitical." Western imperialism does not have to be solely in terms of physical occupation. Indeed, the most severe trespass is its morally corrupting influences on individuals and society through capitalism, media, pornography, and consumerism.[28] Such an influence is much more pervasive, and more difficult to conquer, than the presence of foreign soldiers.[29]

Martyrdom: The Logic of Suicide Bombing

In fusing tribal patriarchal principles together with a modern-style ideological movement (Islamist networks are not tribes as such), we have a different kind of social project. The Islamist fight, in contrast to the derivative tribal feud, is more impersonal and abstract. As a consequence, the battle then becomes more open-ended, more wide-ranging and potentially without end. As such, it also becomes more extreme: killing thousands, or hundreds of thousands, or millions becomes conceivable and legitimate.

The methods of violence, likewise, become more excessive and the acts more theatrical—drama is central. Violence is a message, an image, and an aesthetic as much as an instrument for an external goal. The targets of extremist violence— the Twin Towers (capitalism), nightclubs (fornication), the Pentagon (imperialism) and other markers of corruption like girls' schools in Pakistan, synagogues, and churches—are clearly chosen for a reason and often represent little tactical value in any standard sense.

This violence is imagined in the sense of Frantz Fanon, a philosopher of revolution from an earlier era of decolonization, in which he proclaimed that revolutionary violence "cleanses" the body politic.[30] More perspicaciously, Leo Tolstoy told a *New York Times* journalist in 1908 that he rejected the path of violent revolution, à la the Bolsheviks, in Russia.[31] Why? Once violence was brought into the assemblage of governing, to draw on the sociologist Saskia Sassen's formulation, it would not go away.[32]

Conventional notions of instrumental rationality, so pervasive in our governments, corporations, and universities, often break down in this arena. This is the case at the levels of the tribe and of Islamist militants alike. Major General Michael Flynn and his colleagues pointed out this problem for U.S. forces in Afghanistan: "The inescapable truth [is that] merely killing insurgents usually serves to multiply enemies rather than subtract them. This counterintuitive dynamic . . . is especially relevant in the revenge-prone Pashtun communities. . . . The Soviets experienced this reality in the 1980s, when despite killing hundreds of thousands of Afghans, they faced a larger insurgency near the end of the war then they did at the beginning."[33]

While some have argued that suicide bombings have served as a useful instrument for political goals in Lebanon and in Sri Lanka (writing before the collapse of the Tamil Tigers in the latter case), suicide bombers have on the whole been limited in their military effectiveness.[34] This, again, points to the theatrics involved, especially among the Islamist groups.

That theatre is involved is not simply an interpretive conceit. The militant leadership has been and is fully aware of this effect. Osama bin Laden noted in a conversation with a man identified only as a Sheik, in the late fall of 2001, referring to the terrorist attacks of September 11 that year: "Those young men said in deeds, in New York and Washington, speeches that overshadowed all other speeches made everywhere else in the world. The speeches are understood by both Arabs and non-Arabs, even by Chinese. . . . This event made people think, which benefited Islam greatly."[35]

The extreme drama, and the employment of images in terrorism reach their apogee in suicide bombing. What is foremost in such acts is the premise that the first imperative of life is defined through the communal good, that we sacrifice and give ourselves as mothers, fathers, men and women to the larger cause of nation, tribe, religion, or class. But here this premise of bodily sacrificing for the larger community is taken to its ultimate conclusion, to the *literal* sacrifice of the body. Militant Islamists are taking tribal principles of martial honor and vengeance to a level that is beyond the ordinary. In so doing they, in their own terms, sanctify the act.

Suicide bombing is not necessarily religious in origin; this endeavor cuts across secular and religious, and Left and Right. Indeed, suicide bombing illustrates that the significance of our relationship to the body is elemental in understanding individuals and societies. Communities that emphasize the notion of the giving of the self cut across the religious-secular divide. And suicide terrorism likewise draws from a range of collective-minded groups, from Marxist and nationalist to religious groups.[36]

But militant Islamists are alone among religious groups today in the systematic use of suicide-murder as a political act, and they frame it in distinct ways. The sacrifice (the word *sacrifice* is rooted in notions of the sacred, as in the biblical Abraham's near-sacrifice of his son Isaac) provides for a particular kind of drama. Insofar as it involves the life and death of the body itself, the sacrifice has an elemental, primordial resonance. The discharge of tribal-like revenge, writ ideological and global, becomes existential: there is no going back, no negotiation, no bridge to cross. The honor so expressed, unlike the Western "corruption" of self-indulgence and self-interest, is absolute. The sacrifice is complete and ultimate, and as such it reveals the imagined purity of the cause.

The notion of honor is such that the act itself is its own motivation: *it is the right thing to do.* What is "right" is ultimately determined extraneously, through family, peers, and communal ties. Honor requires forgetting the ego, the self, or self-interest. Psychologically, people who commit acts of great courage describe themselves as having a "dissociative" state of mind in which they remain lucid in the face of danger.[37] Indeed, suicide bombers—though any even vaguely humanitarian-minded person will not see such an attack on civilians as heroic—share this dissociative quality.

The very act of "altruistic" suicide illustrates the nature of the relationship to the body.[38] It is a transcendent act whereby the suicide fuses himself with a mythic sense of the community. In less extreme forms, where suicide is not the intent, we see this in wartime. Soldiers' sacrifices come to represent the nation.

It is also notable—in all kinds of human situations—how we "feel" the experiences of others with our bodies. Sympathy and empathy are derived in good part from being able to feel the physical state of others, from joy to pain. When people share a "social body," such as a common family, community, nation, or religion, we are more likely to feel the happiness and hurt of kindred souls—or more accurately, we feel the happiness and hurt of kindred bodies. For instance, the 9/11 attack was a shocking event for Americans and those who identify with America's cause. The sight of death and suffering of fellow Americans was a reason for deep national anguish. Conversely, those who identified with the hijackers and with Islamist ideology—or at least with anti-American sentiments—were presumably the ones reported to be dancing in the streets or celebrating in their hearts.

For the Jihadis, they are sanctifying the struggle, avenging past humiliations, and re-establishing the honor of Islam. Indeed, after the 9/11 attacks, the point of departure of Bin Laden's first message was to invoke the humiliation of the collapse of the Ottoman Caliphate, as well as pointing to the presence of American troops in Saudi Arabia—near the holy places.[39]

This is true in the national struggles as well, notably among the Palestinian *shebab*. (*Shebab* means literally "the youth," but it now has a connotation of young fighters, in this case arrayed against the Israeli occupation.) Kinship and affective ties once more play a role. The organization of the *shebab*, from the Palestinian intifada, came to be increasingly based on neighborhood and family ties. The loss of a member of such kin groups generated all the more the desire for vengeance and the splicing together of a political cause and a feud.

This notion of honor cuts across different kinds of religions, but it takes a particular form in tribal patriarchies—one that is martial, male, and based on face-saving. But the underlying premise of "doing what is right," regardless of self-interest, is seen in a broad range of societies. For that matter, most individuals have such points of honor—distinct from strict self-interest—regarding their family, for example. In no way can that sentiment be viewed as "self-interested" or motivated by some extraneous goal. While often laudatory, such a "sense of honor" can also be driven by anti-humanitarian values as well—as when innocents are killed in the name of Allah.

In a real sense, the approach to (or imagination of) self and body gets to the essence of the differences. For Islamists—especially, but not only, the militants—it is through the body that one shows ultimate commitment to the transcendent, in sharp contrast to the modern celebration of the body in the here and now. These different senses of the body implicate, as the sociologist Olivier Grojean puts it, "the way individuals construct their relationship to the world, think of themselves, organize themselves and act in different contexts."[40]

The oft-used expression of militant Islamists across different theatres of conflict, "We love death more than you love life," is not just a form of intimidation. For those Islamists, the violence, and the promise of martyrdom (for most, in theory), is a form of liberation. Across Judaism, Christianity, and Islam we see sects that have rejected the body to attain a transcendent, spiritual being. Monks, especially in the Middle Ages, invited pain (for example, through hairy clothes, sometimes infested with vermin, that irritated the body) as a way of reminding themselves of the corruption of this flesh, of this world. In Christianity, Christ himself gave his body to cleanse humankind of sin. The stigmata of Jesus were sacred evidence of his suffering. Through escape from the body, we have the promise of a transcendent and sacred existence.

Such sacred transcendence also has a role in Islamist suicide bombing. The vital difference is that the change that is sought is political, of this world, a world that in their view will come to embody Sharia. The suicide act, one of jihad, is an act of purification, of a commitment to the living community and an "encounter with Allah more precious than this life." The posthumous honor, vengeance, and prestige are the suicide's legacy, not just to himself but to his family and people. This sacrifice makes them, for their supporters, martyrs or *shuhada*.

"We love death more than you love life" also expresses a view of the West and of others in the West's corrupt, colonialist, and globalizing wake. In Islamists' sacrifice of themselves, and in the celebration of suicide bombers by broader communities of sympathizers, a statement is being made as to the moral superiority of the Islamists vis-à-vis their enemies. In contrast to sacrifice, the West and its emulators are made up of materialists and hedonists, driven by base bodily desires, selfish and immoral. It is the difference between honor and interest. In "loving death," the Islamist militants define and frame the nature of the struggle with the West and its allies.

The suicide himself, however, will attain the joys of Paradise. And there he will enjoy the delights of women who will attend his every need.

The Promised Coda

Curiously, the image of heaven takes on an extraordinarily sexualized and hedonistic quality. The media have at times focused too singularly on the virgins promised to the martyrs after death as a driver for martyrdom, but that motivation is not absent. Saudi cleric Omar Al-Sweilem sermonized on the virgins of Paradise. He describes the moment when the believer encounters the virgins:

> [P]raised be He who created night and day. What hair! What a chest! What a mouth! What cheeks! What a figure! What breasts! What thighs! What legs! What whiteness! What softness! Without any creams—no Nivea, no vaseline. No nothing! He said that faces would be soft that day. Even your own face will be soft without any powder or makeup. You yourself will be soft, so how soft will a black-eyed virgin be, when she comes to you so tall and with her beautiful face, her black hair and white face—praised be He who created night and day. Just feel her palm, Sheik! He said: How soft will a fingertip be, after being softened in paradise for thousands

of years! There is no god but Allah. He told us that if you entered one of the palaces, you would find ten black-eyed virgins sprawled on musk cushions . . . When they see you, they will get up and run to you. Lucky is the one who gets to put her thumb in your hand. When they get hold of you, they will push you onto your back, on the musk cushions. They will push you onto your back, Jamal! Allah Akbar! I wish this on all people present here. He said that one of them would place her mouth on yours. Do whatever you want. Another one would press her cheek against yours, yet another would press her chest against yours, and the others would await their turn. There is no god but Allah. He told us that one black-eyed virgin would give you a glass of wine. Wine in Paradise is a reward for your good deeds. The wine of this world is destructive, but not the wine of the world to come.[41]

It is as if such clerics have to counterbalance, for their male youth, the erotic promise of a globalized Western culture. That promise, however, will only be fulfilled in the world to come.

PART IV

ABROAD AT HOME

European Paradoxes

For those in Western countries, globalization is imagined as a process that ripples outward. But globalization is multidirectional, changing the cultural landscape of "the West" itself. Notably, migratory flows from once-colonized countries are sources of immigrant communities. As globally, so locally, in Western Europe issues of women's status and sexuality engender the sharpest divides. In the chapters that follow, we consider multiculturalism, the struggles of men and the gains of women in patriarchal communities, and the dynamics driving Islamist radicalism. The French and British, offering distinct assimilationist and multicultural models to absorb immigrants, are of special interest. In terms of Muslim women's status, the French do much better.

CHAPTER EIGHT

Europe's Winter of Discontent

A Clash of Traditions and Generations

The casual observer can go for a stroll in neighborhoods like Green Street in London, or Belleville in Paris, or Kreuzberg in Berlin, and observe a picture of multicultural cosmopolitanism. A broad spectrum of humanity is represented—Christians, Jews, and Muslims strolling and shopping together. Furthermore, many Muslims take the mosque as seriously as many Jews take the synagogue or Christians take the church—which is to say, not very seriously at all (though the mosque is better attended than synagogues or churches in Europe).

Of course one can also find less salubrious landscapes in some of the immigrant neighborhoods in Leeds, in Rotterdam, or on the peripheries of Paris and Nice. Still, that is true of many lower-income neighborhoods made up of different ethnic and racial groups. Low-income immigrant neighborhoods are generally removed enough that few native citizens of these countries come across them. In fact, tensions that did exist until the late 1980s and early 1990s were mostly racial.[1]

However, the rainbow picture of multiculturalism started becoming blemished in the wider public imagination with the Salman Rushdie affair. Rushdie, the reader may recall, unintentionally caused the word *fatwa* to become part of the Western world's lexicon. In 1989 the Iranian Ayatollah Khomeini issued a fatwa (legal ruling) against Rushdie for blasphemy for his book *The Satanic Verses*. In condemning to death a citizen of the United Kingdom, Khomeini had extended the law of Islam into the West.[2] The book was burned in Bradford, caused riots and killing in various parts of the world, and was banned in every Muslim majority country but one—Turkey.[3] The commentator Kenan Malik noted: "This was not just a brutally shocking act that forced Rushdie into hiding for almost a decade; it also helped to transform the character of British society. The Rushdie affair was the moment at which a new Islam dramatically announced itself as a political force in the West—and the moment when Britain realized that it was facing a new kind of social conflict."[4] In the same year, France entered into its debate on the wearing of the veil by Muslim schoolgirls in France.

This was the start, at least in the public glare. The cultural cases that hit the headlines and made their way into the courts—honor killings, female genital mutilation, forced marriages, and the array of issues that almost always involved women's status—colored public perceptions about what was happening in immigrant neighborhoods. The foundational idea of multiculturalism—that distinct cultures could peacefully coexist—began to crack. Not all of these cases involved Muslims, though Islam came to be identified with such cases in the public. It was also these court cases that forced the governments across Western Europe—and in North America—to grapple with the issue of the limits of multiculturalism and the integration of immigrants. Judges had to directly mediate on these issues.

So why is there such public unease about the place of Islam and community relations for majority and minority alike? What had "gone wrong"? How much of the unease is driven by real social dynamics in Muslim populations, and how much is it a matter of the lens of the broader public?

In order to get a clearer picture of what is happening, one has to unwind three sets of challenges that European governments (and their respective publics) perceive in immigrant communities—especially Muslim communities. First there is the challenge of traditionalism and patriarchy, which casts a pall in the light of European liberalism on gender and sexual matters. Second, the Europeans are faced with neighborhoods that radiate deep alienation from the "host" societies and on occasion erupt into open violence. Complicating internal communal dynamics, young women in these communities are making much better progress than young men in integrating, as measured in educational gains and, to some extent, in the job market (with national variations). Third, parts of Muslim communities have indeed been radicalized and have voiced Islamist militancy. Of that group, a very small subset has engaged in religiously motivated violence. Given their combative rhetoric and actions, these militants, violent and non-violent, disproportionately define the terms of public debate though they are a minority in immigrant communities.

The patterns of these three challenges vary by country. But across Europe these issues tend to be conflated, which in turn colors Europeans' view of the Muslim communities in Europe. Such a view blurs the real and deep variation across and within communities—a variation that is cultural, generational, and socioeconomic, and that extends even to the degrees of religiosity. But what cuts across these different challenges is women's status and sexuality.

The sharply shifting demographics—with "native" Europeans having fewer children and immigrant populations growing through high birth rates and new influxes of migrants—add to the anxiety of natives. (The term *native* itself is an ironic echo of colonial-era references to indigenous Asians and Africans as "natives"). In this chapter, I turn to the first challenge regarding patriarchy and multiculturalism, and how the courts, in particular, sought to articulate (and limit) multiculturalism in the context of sexually liberal Western societies that also emphasized women's rights.

New Europe, Old Traditions

Leaders and publics across much of Europe progressively soured on the multicultural model as headlines on an almost daily basis appeared regarding culturally motivated attacks—almost all involving women or issues of sexuality—that were in opposition to liberal norms. The cases reported in the media displayed a grim, repetitive quality—a drumbeat going back to the 1980s at least. Perhaps the popular image of multiculturalism once involved different restaurants, dress, and customs. But over time, the sharper edges became a staple of media and popular discussion.

Within parts of immigrant communities, a patriarchal concern was clearly in evidence. First-generation immigrant parents worried about their children, and especially their daughters. Their concerns were, to a degree, the stereotypical concerns of immigrant parents raising children—work ethic and study habits, language skills and familiarity with the parents and families of friends. But for many immigrants, these concerns were compounded by classic patriarchal concerns such as arranged marriages, sexuality, dress, and dating. These reactions generally were within the limits of legal family quarrels.

In the public eye, however, the sharper edge of this backlash tends to be highlighted, as the following examples from the United Kingdom show. In 2002 Abdalla Yones, a Kurd living in London, cut his daughter Heshu's throat, leaving her to bleed to death. This followed months of beatings before he killed her in what was described as a frenzied knife attack. He had disapproved of his 16-year-old daughter's "Western way of life" and her Christian boyfriend. The judge, sentencing Yones to life in prison, stated that the killing was "a tragic story arising out of irreconcilable differences between traditional Kurdish values and those of Western society."[5]

Samaira Nazir sought to elope with her Afghan boyfriend after rejecting Pakistani suitors chosen by her family. She never got the chance: she was killed with eighteen stab wounds inflicted by her brother and cousin at her home in Southall, England, in mid-2005. Violence, of course, does not always involve murder: Girls are reportedly beaten up, for example, for carrying cell phones, which are seen as signs of the modern world. The British government set up an agency in 2006 to help British citizens whose parents are trying to force them to marry partners from overseas. The unit deals with upwards of three hundred cases a year.[6]

So-called honor killings draw more attention in Western Europe than in North America. In the United Kingdom alone, when attacks (not necessarily murder) for the whole range of "honor offenses" are counted, they are estimated in the thousands per year.[7] Such purported offenses include abduction, forced abortion, rape, or victimization—because of relationships with outsiders or sexual orientation. The high suicide rate of first-generation Asian women in Britain also suggested some of the pressures that many face: those aged 15 to 24 commit suicide at about twice the national average of 5.4 per 100,000 women.[8]

Outrage has been expressed across a number of Western countries regarding the cultural practice in which parts or all of a young girl's external genitalia are excised, also known as female genital mutilation or cutting. When the Harborview Medical Center in Seattle agreed in 1996, in order to serve the local Somali community, to perform a symbolic "female circumcision" whereby a small cut would be made to the prepuce (the hood above the clitoris), the hospital was besieged by angry responses from the public and politicians. This was the case even though no tissue would be excised and the children were old enough to understand and consent to the procedure. Harborview consequently retreated from its effort although it was an attempt to prevent local Somalis from taking their daughters to their homeland, where they were at risk of complete removal of the clitoris and labia.[9]

The courts have found themselves increasingly dealing with such cases where "cultural defenses" are made or, as the political theorist Bonnie Honig put it, "my culture made me do it."[10] Examples abound: in Norway, Nadia, a woman of Moroccan ancestry, was kidnapped by her parents, who feared she was rejecting Islam for a Western way of life. They took her, apparently drugged, to Morocco and married her against her will. After their return to Norway, the state prosecuted the parents for holding a person against her will but did not have sufficient evidence for a forced marriage charge. The court found the parents guilty but granted reduced sentences due to Nadia's request for leniency for her parents. The court noted, however, that "traditions cannot supersede Norwegian law." The Norwegian case, which took place in 1998, drew widespread attention.[11]

Courts in the United States as well as Europe found themselves trying to define political boundaries and a multiculturalism that they could live with. A case in Nebraska involved an Iraqi refugee from the first Persian Gulf War who arrived in the United States in 1995. He was ultimately convicted of first-degree assault on a child. The refugee, Latif Al-Hussaini, 34 years old, "married" a 13-year-old girl who had been "given away" by her father on November 9, 1996. After the ceremony, Al-Hussaini took his "bride" to a new home where he engaged in sexual intercourse with her, despite her objections. Al-Hussaini was later arrested. He claimed he did nothing wrong, since arranged marriages with young girls were customary in Iraq and legal under Islamic law. The court nonetheless sentenced him to four to six years' imprisonment.

The Nebraska example is telling, not only in that the rights of the girl negated any cultural claim that subordinated women but also because it illustrates how the legal system edits or reinvents culture through redefining what that culture (or, in this case, religion) is in its purportedly true, authentic form.[12] In Al-Hussaini's appeal in 1998 against the State of Nebraska, the prosecutor for Nebraska argued that "while Al-Hussaini attempts to lessen his culpability by claiming that the acts were sanctioned by religion, there is evidence in the presentence investigation report that such a marriage would not be universally accepted in Iraq and, in fact, was highly unusual and would be considered wrong in the majority of Iraqi communities."[13] The Court of Appeals affirmed the sentence of the lower court, noting "there is really only one victim of this crime and that is the 13-year-old child with whom Al-Hussaini had sexual intercourse without her consent."[14] The court here takes a global perspective, placing itself in the role of an imaginary anthropologist expounding on different world cultures.[15]

The court's role in inventing culture is telling. Defining boundaries—gender boundaries and boundaries on the freedom of association—is more than simply stating a rule. As Robert Cover writes, the judge "becomes constitutive of a world." Such "jurisgenesis" takes place through a cultural form (broadly Western in the cases described here) while transforming another (for example, of one immigrant community). The judge, as in the Al-Hussaini case, adjudicates law as the "social organization of power," but in a real sense, he has to tell a story in order to legitimize the court's judgment. In this regard, it is the "organization of law as meaning." Law here is about the destiny of individuals and nations. "Law must be meaningful," writes Cover, "in the sense that it permits those who live together to express themselves with it and with respect to it."[16] In that regard, when a "foreign" cultural claim fails, the plaintiffs (and by extension, their community) are still invited to express themselves within the cultural framework represented by the state.

The debate around female genital mutilation is perhaps most symbolic and illustrative of the normative and institutional trajectory, in the West at least, of the "women's rights versus culture" clash. I use the term "symbolic" with a specific purpose here. Female genital mutilation has not generated many court cases outside of France. But the cases that have taken place have elicited substantial public attention with the following effect: both judicial and legislative actions to proscribe female genital cutting have privileged a particular cultural form, and thus such mutilation becomes a focal point for a larger "clash of cultures."

Genital mutilation goes to the core issues of women's rights, autonomy, and sexuality (and suppression of women's sexuality, literally), and epitomizes the social struggle on gender. Nearly all the religious and cultural rituals associated with female genital mutilation metaphorically—and, in a sexual sense, bodily—take away a woman's control over her own body in the most fundamental sense. Indeed, the excision of a woman's sexuality through such mutilation has been justified essentially for the sake of domesticating women so they will think of "keep[ing] house" rather than their "own sexual pleasure" (with the interesting presumption that keeping house and a woman's sexual pleasure are mutually exclusive).[17]

This "symbolic" process regarding female genital mutilation, and the role of judicial or quasi-judicial bodies in promoting women's agency, is evidenced in the way the issue arose in the United States and in France. In the United States, it was a judicial asylum case that prompted legislation to ban female genital mutilation. The case was heard before the Board of Immigration Appeals in 1996, and coerced female genital mutilation was found to be grounds for granting asylum. The court noted in its decision the coercive character of applicant Fauziya Kasinga's marriage (into a polygamous union) and how she was pressured to undergo female genital mutilation.[18] Here the judicial body did not hide its abhorrence of the practice, which in this case was associated with the Tchamba-Kunsuntu tribe in Togo. Mutilation of this kind, the Board of Immigration Appeals determined, was persecution under the law, noting that in its extreme forms, the "female genitalia are cut away" and the "vagina is sutured partially closed" and that the operation can cause serious, sometimes life-threatening complications.

The Immigration and Naturalization Service (INS—now called the U.S. Immigration and Customs Enforcement or ICE), fearful of being inundated by asylum claims of this nature, asked to limit such claims when tribal members believed "they were simply performing an important cultural rite that bonds the individual to the society," and to exclude past victims of female genital mutilation if they "at least acquiesced" to the rite. The voluntary quality of the act (implicating the question of individual agency), became the yardstick, even for the INS.[19]

The federal law that criminalized the act of circumcising, excising, or infibulating (sewing together the labia) anyone under the age of 18 years was passed following Kasinga's asylum request (granted in June 1996).[20] It went into effect in March 1997. One section of the law specifically rejected any justification of the law on religious or cultural grounds, such that "no account shall be taken of the effect on the person on whom the operation is performed of any belief . . . [nor] that the operation is to be performed as a matter of custom or ritual." Any cultural defense on the matter is simply negated as a legal option.[21] Federal legislative history on the issue of female genital mutilation pointed to the similar position of the United Nations Children's Fund (UNICEF), the World Health Organization, international human rights groups, and laws in other countries (particularly the United Kingdom).[22]

France was the first Western country to prosecute acts of female genital mutilation within its borders. France has no specific law against female genital mutilation, but the judicial system took action in a series of cases by linking female genital mutilation to the French Penal Code, in particular to Article 312, which concerns violence committed against a child of under 15 years, including "mutilation, amputation . . . or other permanent disability."[23]

Among the French cases that generated public interest was a case in 1990 in which an African father who arranged to have his daughter "circumcised" against his French wife's wishes was given a five-year suspended sentence by the end of the appeal process. The first trial against an "excisor" took place in 1991, and in contrast to the suspended sentences that characterized prior female genital mutilation cases, the court meted out a three-year prison sentence. The first parent to serve time in jail was a Gambian woman who was sentenced to five years in jail, four of them suspended, for "causing the wounding and mutilation" of her two daughters. The French government also ran public campaigns in immigrant communities to warn that female "circumcision" is illegal.

Though France was at the forefront of prosecuting cases of female genital mutilation, it has been criminalized in a number of Western countries, including Sweden, the United Kingdom, Switzerland, Belgium, Canada, Australia, and, with the exception of the mostly symbolic sunnah form of female genital cutting, in the Netherlands.[24] The sunnah form is considered the "mildest"; it involves the removal of the tip of the clitoris and the prepuce—or, alternatively, one of the two.

Also widely noted was a British case where an English mother, described as a non-practicing Christian, opposed the application of her former husband, a non-practicing Muslim of Turkish origin, to have their male child, "J," circumcised. The Official Solicitor supported her. The father appealed, suggesting that the judge had confused the child's religion with the child's upbringing because, under Muslim law, the father's religion determines the child's religion. The Court of Appeal dismissed the appeal in a 1999 judgment, noting that J had a mixed heritage and a secular lifestyle, though the court accepted the father's "passionate" concern for J to be given a Muslim identity. Furthermore, the court endorsed the view that, under United Kingdom law, one parent could not arrange circumcision without consent of the other parent— itself an assertion of individual agency of each parent over patriarchal custom.

Two further comments in the court's judgment in "J" alluded to underlying tensions. First, the court noted, "The fact that the child is recognized as a Muslim under religious law was not and is not an issue [for the court]," a statement that speaks for itself in indicating which law and custom is privileged. Second, the judgment notes, "It is clear that adherents of Islam would regard him as a fellow Muslim and that his father so regards him. There is no reason to suppose the child himself at present perceives himself as a Muslim or as belonging to any faith grouping," suggesting that the question of J's religious identity is to be determined by him, through his own (voluntary) agency, and not through religious and communal fiat.[25]

First Principles of Multiculturalism

The premise of multiculturalism came to be tested in the courts as well as in public opinion. In the West, cultural diversity has been celebrated, but that celebration was and is based on a mostly unstated first principle that rests in the notion that cultural expression resides in the individual, who is sovereign over her or his body. The reality is that many cultural practices—especially patriarchal practices—privilege the family and the community over the individual. Or more specifically, they favor the father, the husband, and the brother over the daughter, the wife, and the sister.

The practice of multiculturalism works well when multiculturalism involves— as it most often does—dress, food, colorful customs, and festivals. The problem arises when that "first principle" is in fact questioned. The question then is this:

How does, or should, the institutional structure (of government, courts, and the police, for example) work? And if anything but individual sovereignty is rejected as the basis of multiculturalism, does the premise underlying multiculturalism—notably that it is universal in import and does not represent a European construct or imposition—implode?

So even if the majority of individuals fit perfectly well into the benign version of multiculturalism, the legal structure of European governments—as well as public opinion—makes it nigh impossible to reconcile the tensions within the multicultural model. Multiculturalism is a more sociologically complex phenomenon than most philosophers, let alone popular discourse, suggest. Academic writing has by and large failed to elicit the complexity of multiculturalism, and many societies entered into multicultural models as essentially a trial-and-error experiment.

Defining social and communal boundaries—inherent in a multicultural society—means designating moral proximity and moral distance, inclusion and exclusion. Social boundaries are forms of "markers": visible signs, as the late sociologist Erving Goffman described them, of a "territory" of some kind. Markers can delineate physical borders, but clothes, architectural designs, an umbrella on a beach, dietary laws like kashrut or halal, and the like are also markers. Markers can be fixed (like state boundaries), transient (space on a beach), or transportable (clothes). "Space" and "social distance" become the elements that, in a sense, define social and political forms.[26]

Community, marriage, friendship, comradeship, kinship, conflict, work, play, and notions of private and public indicate varying forms of association and social spacing. The "social order" is implicitly about spacing, about maintaining the "proper" patterns of interaction. But for this to work, fundamental rules have to be in place, rules that are mutually respected. This characteristic of social order is apparent in the most pedestrian of human circumstances:

> A condition of order at the junction of crowded city thoroughfares implies primarily an absence of collisions between men or vehicles that interfere with one another . . . [Order] does not exist when people are constantly colliding with one another. But when all meet or overtake one another in crowded ways [and] take the time and pains needed to avoid collision, the throng is orderly. Now, at the bottom of the notion of social order lies the same idea. The members of an orderly community do not go out of their way to aggress upon one another. Moreover, whenever their pursuits interfere, they make the adjustments necessary to escape collision and make them according to some conventional rule.[27]

As national borders became less significant as markers of identity, internal domestic boundaries and markers (not necessarily of a geographic kind) became more pronounced. In other words, internal communal distinctions have been increasingly politicized and even internationalized; these communal identities often cut across national borders. Patterns of association and dissociation, and of moral linkages and breaks, are thus shifting in ways that cannot easily be fitted onto a political map. This development reflects a world where diasporic communities are increasingly common and where once-international divisions have been internalized within states. What shape, then, does "politics" take in this setting?

The courts become especially significant. The idiom of judicial (or constitutional) politics is one of "rights." As the role of human and civil rights have grown—ensuring personal protections—so the salience of courts has risen. The judiciary serves as a "traffic cop," imposing social order on a world of potentially conflicting spaces. The traffic-cop role becomes all the more critical as social space—not just territory per se (in the sense of fixed geographic territories permanently delimited from one another)—has to be constantly negotiated.

The judiciary reinforces (or seeks to create) a code of rituals that "respects" social spaces and thus creates or maintains social order. The everyday rules that govern "street traffic"—neutral and demanding no sense of felt commonality—are, when taken to a higher level, a way of adjudicating a society where an overarching sense of community may be fading. Goffman writes, using the street example: "Take, for example, techniques that pedestrians employ in order to avoid bumping into one another. They seem of little significance. However, they are constantly in use and they cast a pattern on street behavior. Street traffic would be a shambles without them."[28]

Where "personal space" is accentuated, the rules of etiquette governing exchanges need to be (for an orderly society) more elaborate, and markers need to be defined. Politeness is the mark of distance. This is all the more heightened in multicultural environments. It is in this context that so-called hate-speech codes and the prohibition of anti-Semitic or racist speech arose—for example, under European national and regional human rights legal codes. Social and communal "markers," being fluid and undefined by fixed geographic space, will necessarily involve more "crossings" or "meetings" than geographic borders.

Shared and mutually respected ground rules are critical in such an environment. There is a perception, at least, that the mutuality of such common rules is insufficiently present in countries such as Britain or the Netherlands for multiculturalism to work.

Territorialities of the Self

Multiculturalism in Europe and the United States has been predicated on the idea of "the territoriality of the self." Any community of culture must rest in individual choice to be truly legitimate in these societies. Indeed, the idea of individual sovereignty was actually reinforced in the European (and American) ideas of multiculturalism. In these visions of multiculturalism, government authority is restrained in shaping the cultural life of the individual citizen. But this most emphatically does not mean that the authority of fathers and patriarchies should be given additional ballast.[29]

Culture in *this* multicultural vision is part of the individual's personal toolbox (as sociologists like to put it), part of her repertoire of identities. She employs her religious, class, ethnic, and other identities as occasions warrant, for emotional or utilitarian effect.

For European publics in countries like the United Kingdom, the Netherlands, and Germany to accept the kind of multiculturalism in which the sovereignty of communities over women's' bodies could supersede a women's control over her own body is a bridge too far. The civil courts are generally not willing to countenance such a move, let alone the broader public.

In the United Kingdom, multiculturalism was also identified with the riots in the north of England, in Oldham and Bradford, and with the terrorism starting with the July 7, 2005, bombings. "Social cohesion" came to be stressed alongside or in lieu of multiculturalism. Significantly, the then-Commissioner for Racial Equality Trevor Philips argued that multiculturalism was "sleep-walking" into segregation. Farrukh Dhondy, who pioneered multicultural broadcasting on British television, wrote of multiculturalism as "a fifth column which must be rooted out" and argued that state funding of multiculturalism should be redirected into a defense of freedom and democracy.[30]

Government policies, however, are not always coherent. British government bodies have also quietly allowed Sharia courts. But this just postpones the day of reckoning, for this development does not resolve the internal institutional contradictions.[31]

It is important to emphasize once again that the issue of patriarchy that comes up in such "cultural defenses" is by no means only Muslim. The religious appellation is highlighted due to the association, in the public mind, of multiculturalism with Islamist radicalism. The importance of women's status and sexuality in these cases make the link to Islam appear plausible to significant numbers of people.

The mutual disdain that ensues places everyone in a cruel cycle. In fact, most Muslims do not belong in these categories of estrangement from the "host" societies. Most British or French citizens do not discriminate. But the institutional and popular tensions are palpable enough to generate fears for the future. In an environment that is unstable—with changing migration patterns, demography, and global politics—those fears will be with us for some time to come. Breaking this vicious circle becomes the primary policy concern. Thus we have a renewed stress on "integration." The attractions of multiculturalism, in this light, dim.

CHAPTER NINE

An Education

Women and Men in Europe's Poorer Neighborhoods

One recent summer in a Parisian café, I talked for some hours with a woman who had been a senior researcher for the French police intelligence. She had played an important role in analyzing the unrest in the French suburbs, the now unfortunately ill-famed *banlieues*.

I was discussing with her an issue that occupies policymakers, the media, and the wider public: What drives the deep discontent in such marginal neighborhoods, not just in France but across Europe? How much of this discontent is, in fact, a function of ethnic and religious factors—or is it broader socioeconomic concerns that cut across ethnicities and religions? Can we connect unrest, as well as general alienation, to Islamist militancy and even terrorism?

The problem in the *banlieues* was not only the riots that made world news in the 1990s and in the early to mid 2000s. It is, in the public's perception, an open sore infected by vandalism, burnt cars, gangs, and harassment of girls and women. Similar stories emanate from comparable neighborhoods in British, Dutch, and Belgian cities as well, though they will also be broadened to a wider array of immigrants, not only Muslims.

The now-retired police researcher said the clearest indicators of violence in France—more than socioeconomic factors as such—had to do with the presence of North African immigrants. (In France, the state is not allowed to collect data on religious affiliation of its citizens and residents, but researchers can extrapolate religiosity from ethnic status. North Africans are overwhelmingly Muslim.) She claimed that similarly poor but mostly non-Muslim areas were less likely to be involved in such social rebellion. But the picture is complicated by external factors, for example by anti-Muslim discrimination.[1] Furthermore, earlier on, in the 1980s, Muslim discourse did not play much of a role. In fact, protesters would hold up French ID cards, claiming their French status was not being respected.[2]

When I described this conversation to French academic colleagues, they responded at times with contempt for her positions. (The retired senior police researcher had complained that the academics had failed to engage the police.) This response is in part a reflection of an institutional and cultural divide between the academy and police, but it also reflects a deeper, more widespread ideological division between liberal and conservative readings of the plight of poorer parts of Muslim and immigrant communities.

Liberals argue that the integration of Muslim immigrants is proceeding relatively smoothly, that the more disturbing developments are rooted in socioeconomic problems unrelated to Islam or are the violent acts of a tiny minority. The communities are faced with discrimination and structural impediments to social and economic advancement. They point to the institutional integration of Muslims, with new mosques and civic institutions, and the close cooperation between governments and Muslim councils.[3]

Conservatives, on the contrary, point to an overwhelming alienation between the Muslim communities and the "host" societies. They cite opinion polls, election results, and controversies over, say, the burqa, to highlight their arguments— or to riots in mostly Muslim neighborhoods of European cities, radicalization of youth, changing shifts in population, and "home-grown" Muslims involved in terrorist incidents. (The riots in Britain in 2011, however, appeared to be equal opportunity events for all hues and creeds.) If liberals point to discrimination and structural factors, conservatives will point to cultural, ideological, and religious causes of social and economic marginalization within such communities themselves.[4]

If these tropes sound familiar, that is because in their essentials they are played out again and again, in different communities, be they minority or immigrant, from Europe, to North America, to Australia. They are arguments about national and social integration and about social and economic upward mobility.

The Right and the Left also diverge in their policy recommendations for issues of socially and economically disadvantaged minorities and immigrant communities. The conservatives push for market solutions, suggesting that policies that generate economic growth in blighted neighborhoods will be the best panacea to marginalization. Liberals argue for anti-discrimination laws and for affirmative action measures.

But where we tend to have consensus across much of the political spectrum is on education. Education is widely seen as the chief mechanism for integrating minorities and marginalized immigrant communities. The premise has and continues to be that education will generate upward mobility in social and economic terms, which in turn will ameliorate the gnawing social and even political divisions. In the Western European context, "Islam" is seen as providing additional challenges in terms of multiculturalism and radicalism. But in terms of the socioeconomic travails of individual communities, from Algerians and Tunisians in France, to Pakistanis and Bangladeshis in the United Kingdom, a common assumption holds that education is essential for at least reducing social gaps.

Prior to becoming the British Prime Minister in 1997, Tony Blair declared his top three priorities for his government to be "education, education, education."[5] His premise (and that of many people) was that if children of all backgrounds had access to a high quality of education, inequality gaps in the British population would be reduced. This was viewed as of special relevance to children of ethnic minority backgrounds—especially overwhelmingly Muslim Bangladeshis and Pakistanis—who had struggled (in the aggregate), and still do, to keep up with most other groups in socioeconomic terms.

Such an approach rested in evidence that suggested that education is a key determinant of life chances—from job prospects to health and even life expectancy. Education helps individuals develop skills and advance both socially and economically. However, one challenge lies in other findings that educational attainment is strongly linked to socioeconomic background.[6]

But while the broad sweep of such pronouncements on the impact of education was correct on an individual level, the communal dynamics can and did play out differently. Surprisingly, the gender dimension and its implications for social and national integration have been, until recently at least, largely ignored. One still reads major contemporary studies on national integration of immigrant groups in which the gender issue is barely addressed.[7]

The truth is not so much between these two pictures, liberal and conservative, as it is more nuanced and more complex.

In a nutshell: Muslim communities in Britain and France in certain respects reflect the greater Middle East writ small. Looking through the prism of educational achievement, by the second immigrant generation women are making great strides as compared to men in ways that generally cut across ethnic and religious communities. Yet women's achievement is not translating into the university level of education—notably in the United Kingdom (though the gender gap is lessening). It appears that patriarchal resistance or desire is driving this drop-off at the post-secondary education level.

The labor market participation rates of women do not reflect the educational trajectories of women in these same communities in France and the United Kingdom—but once again, the lag for the United Kingdom vis-à-vis France is pronounced. Indeed, according to a 2009 study, the average second-generation Pakistani and Bangladeshi female entering working age in the UK has been in full-time education for two less years than her Maghrebi (immigrant communities from North Africa) counterpart in France. These trends carry over into levels of workforce participation, with employment rates of second-generation Maghrebi women France being about 33 percent higher than Pakistani and Bangladeshi women in Britain.[8]

The other side of women's gains is the men left behind or falling further down the social ladder: substantial numbers of non-degreed and often unemployed men from these communities pool at the bottom of the social ladder. What happens to these men? A good degree of alienation, for sure, which impacts these communities through crime and gangs and even in the environment of urban centers more broadly. But this is true for men in other poorer communities, including black Caribbeans, Africans, and whites. These men are at risk of delinquency and, on occasion, outright rioting and looting.

That said, men in poorer Muslim communities are, in the aggregate, distinctive in certain respects. In the United Kingdom, at least, preliminary research suggests second-generation Muslims are more likely to identify first as "Muslim" than black Caribbeans will identify primarily with any single category—Caribbean, black, Christian, British, and the like.[9] The markers of global Islam—for example, conflicts in Palestine, Chechnya, and Afghanistan—can sometimes be triggered in certain contexts of local unrest and conflicts. Islamist invocations of the Ummah or the *kafir* can be part of the discourse, and even used to recruit youth for criminal gangs.[10]

Furthermore, there are some elements (outside the Muslim mainstream) who seek to "Islamicize" public space—through posters proclaiming "sharia zones," defacing advertisements displaying women, chastising women without veils, attacking gays, and the like. Popular culture—notably Muslim rap—is often replete with attacks on the *kafir*. An abstracted "Islam," in other words, can be a trigger for mobilization, even among youth with thin theological knowledge.[11]

But on the whole, the aura of social rebellion is only loosely tied (if at all) to organized militant Islam—aside from limited numbers of individuals who join extremist groups and even commit terrorism. When it comes to the most clearly articulated Islamist militancy and to outright terrorism, then we have a different, counter-intuitive dynamic, as we will see in the next chapter. Poverty as such is a poor explanation for Islamic radicalism and terrorism.

The results of a representative survey we commissioned from the survey company Abt SRBI points to a different dynamic—one in which prosperous respondents are more likely to espouse radical beliefs than their lower-class counterparts.[12] When we consider the survey findings of Muslims in the United Kingdom, France, and Germany collectively, we find the following: while 25 percent of poor respondents would sacrifice personally or engage in violence to defend their faith, 65 percent of prosperous respondents would do so. And while 30 percent of prosperous respondents would sacrifice personally or engage in violence to defend their political beliefs, only 7 percent of working class, lower class, and poor respondents would.[13]

More broadly, we have to re-think what social and national "integration" means when women and men have such different trajectories educationally. Communities cannot necessarily be viewed as organic wholes, moving in lockstep.

Across Europe, we see that Muslims have a significantly younger age structure than non-Muslim Europeans, with roughly half of European Muslims being younger than 30. Furthermore, Muslim European women typically have much higher fertility rates.[14] If we extrapolate these facts to future demographic projections, we see that Muslims will make significant population gains in Europe, both in raw figures and proportionally. So the dynamics within Muslim communities have important implications for the future of Western European societies.

In understanding how immigrants and their children "locate" themselves socially and politically, we have to start by parsing immigrant generation, level of education, socioeconomic status, and, of course, gender. To draw a more precise picture of the dynamics at work, we need to delve more deeply into the data. I begin with the British case, followed by the French instance.

Where Is the Green in the Union Jack?

Over 70 percent of Muslims in Britain are of a South Asian background, with the majority of these coming from Pakistani (40 percent), Bangladeshi (20 percent) and Indian (15 percent) origins.[15] The 2010 figures from the Pew Research Project placed the estimated number of Muslims in the UK at 2,869,000, or 4.6 percent of the population, expected to rise to 5,567,000 or 8.2 percent by 2030.[16]

A 2006 British Office for National Statistics (ONS) report on educational attainment in the UK showed some noticeable trends. The gap in attainment has narrowed between students of an ethnic minority background (especially those of Pakistani and Bangladeshi backgrounds) and white British students. Some ethnic minority background groups are now catching up with the white British population, while some have surpassed white British students. In terms of high school or secondary school grades, the majority of Muslim students in Britain, like the majority of white students, fall in between average Chinese students on the high end, and average black Caribbean students at the lower end of grades.[17]

Perhaps more striking, girls are surpassing boys in educational achievement across all subjects and across all ethnic groups in Britain. Every single ethnic category across the United Kingdom now reflects such a pattern (see, for example, the grade distributions in fig. 9.1).[18]

However, at the university and post-secondary level, Muslims were the least likely religious group in the United Kingdom to have degrees or equivalent qualifications (12 percent) according to a study in 2004. Even more significant is the gender dimension, with girls' success at the high school or secondary school coming to a substantial slowdown at the university level. In terms of university qualifications, in 2005 the number of British Muslim graduates from British universities numbered around 150,000; of these, 61 percent were male and 39 percent

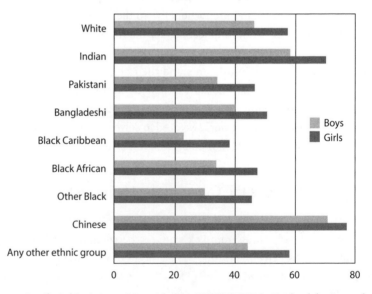

FIG. 9.1. Pupils Achieving 5 or More A*–C at GCSE/GNVQ in England, by Sex and Ethnic Group, 2002. Source: Office of National Statistics, "Focus on Ethnicity and Identity," 2005.

female, although there is evidence that the gender gap in post-secondary enrollment is receding.[19]

Unfortunately, university graduate qualifications do not directly translate
into employment for all British Muslims, particularly women. Only 76 percent of
British Muslim graduates are in work compared to 87 percent for all graduates.[20]

In sum, we see that Pakistani and Bangladeshi girls and young women are
doing much better than boys and young men at the secondary school level (as
with other ethnic groups); that the second generation has made large strides
over their parents' generation; that Bangladeshis and Pakistanis are still lagging
the rest of the population educationally in the aggregate; and that at the university level the participation of Bangladeshi and Pakistani women drops off and is
not as impressive as at the secondary school levels—relative to men.

Girls and women in all groups are making large gains vis-à-vis boys and men.
So what makes the Pakistani and Bangladeshi case stand out in contrast with
other major ethnic groups—and does it have social and political implications? [21]

Perhaps most important are the patriarchal dynamics in which this attainment
of females plays out and how that affects males. Part of those dynamics are influencing the extent to which Pakistani and Bangladeshi women do not continue
on to university and post-secondary education and into the labor market. Furthermore, we need to ask how the patriarchal context affects males of the second
generations and beyond who are falling behind. Those internal community
developments also take place in an environment that can be perceived as discriminatory and at times hostile. It also raises the question of how "Muslim" or
Islam comes to be defined among such men.

The second generation's sense of Islam has evolved in an environment very
distinct from that of their parents. The variety of "Islams" (in terms of different
cultural and theological traditions) they experience generates a more global understanding of their faith. Global media and the Internet reinforce that process.
Islam can be signified in all kinds of social and political ways—indeed, the second
and later generations may well be less theologically sophisticated than the generation that grew up in Pakistan and Bangladesh, and only then immigrated to
the United Kingdom.

The Labor Market in the United Kingdom

When we look at the labor market, especially for British Muslim women, we see
a similar pattern as in the Middle East in recent decades. When we place the

strides of Pakistani and Bangladeshi women educationally against their position in the labor market, a notable dissonance is evident. Discrimination is clearly a factor, but it also appears this dissonance is driven to a significant extent by the patriarchal setting in which many grow up. That setting may be coercive in terms of pressures placed on women by their families and community, and it may reflect the women's own sense of familial obligation.

One of the most recent reports examining the place of Muslim women in the British labor market, published in 2008, found that "British Muslim women are the most disadvantaged faith group . . . with 68 percent defined as inactive in the labor market and only 29 percent in employment."[22] In 2004, the Office for National Statistics (ONS) published data on the labor market, including a breakdown of the data according to both gender and ethnicity (see fig. 9.2). It emerged from the study that in 2004 Pakistani women, at 20 percent, had the highest unemployment rates in Britain. Similarly, when looking at the results for those who were more likely to be inactive in the economy—including those who were disabled, were looking after a family and home or were not available for work, and those not actively looking for work—Muslim women ranked at the top.[23]

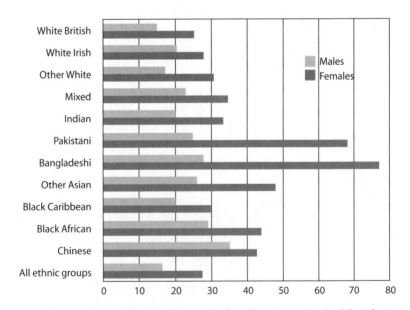

FIG. 9.2. Economic Inactivity Rates for People of Working Age in England, by Ethnic Group and Sex, 2002/03. Source: Office of National Statistics, "Focus on Ethnicity and Identity," 2005.

In 2004, Bangladeshi and Pakistani women had the highest working-age economic inactivity rates in the UK (75% and 69% respectively). These rates were "up to three times the rates for White British, White Irish, and Black Caribbean women (between 25 and 26%)."[24] The term "inactive" can be deceptive; many such "inactive" women are in fact very busy keeping up homes and nurturing the domestic life of families. But the category is telling in terms of the patriarchal constraints or desires of these women relative to other communities.[25]

The inactivity rate for British Muslim women in regard to the economy is higher than for any other religious group in the United Kingdom.[26] Research suggests a complex of factors drives these inactivity rates. Settlement patterns of Pakistanis and Bangladeshis are one consideration. Pakistanis heavily settled in towns that were especially hard hit by the decline of manufacturing. The bulk of Bangladeshis arrived in the United Kingdom at a time of severe economic recession. Human capital or skill-sets, such as English proficiency, are low. However, even when age, education, marital status, and English proficiency are brought into consideration, Pakistani and Bangladeshi inactivity rates of women are still very high. [27]

Women wearing a headscarf, studies suggest, are vulnerable to discrimination by employers. It likely accounts in part for more practicing Muslim women being left out of the workforce. But it is equally clear that many women from these communities give primacy to family life, whether out of choice, pressure, or some combination thereof.[28]

Some employers may be less likely to hire women because of perceptions about Muslim women usually being "temporary" employees in the sense that they are likely to leave the workforce upon marriage or pregnancy and not return.[29] It also appears that a proportion of women make an active decision not to go back to work. As one woman put it, "I think personally, I'd rather do the housewife thing because it's very rewarding actually raising children and teaching them about Islam."[30]

Data in fact suggests that Pakistani and Bangladeshi women do leave the labor market upon having children at far higher rates than women of other ethnic backgrounds. They are also historically much less likely to return to the labor market after their children are of working age, although the story is yet to be written for the younger Pakistani and Bangladeshi women.[31] In the labor market we also see marked differences with other ethnic and religious communities in the United Kingdom. Pakistani and Bangladeshi women are, in the aggregate, 70 to 80 percent economically inactive after age 35 or upon childbearing, with extremely modest job-market reentry even after children become economically independent.[32]

The tensions involved for South Asian women regarding the pursuit of education and their familial and patriarchal pressures and desires can be quite explicit. Some South Asian women speak of higher education and the attainment of a degree as furthering their marital prospects. Yet others say that they are concerned about being "too educated" for potential husbands.[33] When age, education, marital status, and English language proficiency are standardized, Pakistani and Bangladeshi women have lower employment rates than women in other ethnic groups. An official study from 2006 concluded that these women wanted to give priority to family life or were "encouraged" to do so.[34]

In sum, for all the educational gains of British Muslim females, a large pool of them are not following through, for whatever reason, on the same trajectory in the job market that one finds among other groups.[35]

When it came to men in the first decade of the twenty-first century, in the aggregate Indian men were at least on par with white British men to hold higher-status positions. But black Caribbean, Pakistani, and Bangladeshi men were more likely to be unemployed and to be in unskilled jobs compared to white British men. Still, progress was being made from earlier decades, going back to the 1960s.[36]

A footnote to this discussion: if aggregate health statistics reveal the psychological strains of life, as many medical researchers believe they do, the findings of the Office of National Statistics on the health of the British population are revealing. Muslim females have the highest self-reported ill health in Britain (at least as of 2001).[37]

Où est le vert dans le drapeau tricolore?

Today, about 70 percent of France's five to six million Muslims trace their roots to the former French colonies in North Africa: Algeria, Morocco, and Tunisia.[38] The challenge when considering the Muslim population in France is that the French government strictly prohibits state agencies from collecting data concerning religion, so we are left to extrapolate from data concerning ethnicity or nationality. Although this complicates the numbers to some extent, the vast majority of North Africans in France are Muslim, so this proves to be a largely safe extrapolation.

Although most Muslims in France immigrated after World War II, Muslims have resided in France since at least the late nineteenth century. After World War II, however, immigration from North Africa increased dramatically, encouraged by the French government to satisfy industrial and reconstruction labor needs.[39]

Today, Muslims make up about 7.5 percent of the total French population. These numbers are supposed to rise to almost 7 million and make up over 10 percent of the French population in the next couple of decades.[40]

Statistics regarding education and the labor market vary from country to country in the ways they are collected, and this is true across the United Kingdom and France as well. But we find similar patterns when it comes to second-generation immigrants and the success of girls and young women educationally.[41] Similarly, a disproportionate segment of young men are pooling at the lower end of the educational ladder and are unemployed in the labor market. But we observe interesting differences as well.

If one considers the first generation of immigrants, in a survey from France in 2008 we find that men have an advantage educationally across most national groups and across religious affiliations. Data from the *Trajectories et Origines Survey* of those 18 to 50 years old is telling.[42] First-generation North African males hold a 3 to 5 percent advantage in terms of a university degree and completing high school and are less likely to hold no educational certification than are first-generation women.[43]

These disparities reflect a certain patriarchal bias in education, but it is not especially dramatic. One has to keep in mind that North African countries historically had a significant number of secular-minded citizens (especially Tunisia). Secular movements in Algeria and Tunisia pushed women's rights. The civil war in Algeria has reflected a deep secular, centrist Muslim divide vis-à-vis the Islamists.

Immigrants to France improve educationally in their educational attainment over time. Among the immigrants between 18 and 60 years old arriving in France before 1974, 44 percent had no educational certificate; 11 percent had a university degree. For the immigrants of the same age cohort arriving in France after 1998, 25 percent have no educational certification, and 34 percent have a degree from university, demonstrating a dramatic generational context when considering educational attainment.

However, when we turn to the second generation, we begin to see a gender switch that is dramatic, particularly among the North African and Sahelian Muslim populations. (The Sahel is the transitional zone from the desert of North Africa to the savannahs further South, including, among others, the mostly Muslim and francophone Senegal, Mauritania, Niger, and Mali.) While second-generation immigrants make major strides over the first generation, what is most marked is the extent to which girls and young women, in the aggregate, move ahead of boys and young men. Women with descent from Algeria, Morocco,

Tunisia, and the Sahelian Africa are all obtaining university degrees at higher rates than men: a 4 percent advantage for Algerian-descent women, 7 percent for Moroccan- and Tunisian-descent women, and 11 percent for women of Sahelian descent.

If we consider the high school diploma (the General Certificate of Secondary Education), we again see progress overall among the second generation, but with a marked shift in favor of the girls. In the second generation, girls of Algerian descent are 5 percent ahead of boys, girls of Moroccan and Tunisian descent have a 9 percent advantage, and girls of a Sahelian heritage are ahead by 4 percent.

When, among the second generation, we consider the other end—those without any form of educational certification—we see an extraordinary swing from the first to the second generation. And it is a swing that emphatically turns against men. Those from Muslim-majority countries without a school degree of any kind, among the second generation make up a much larger proportion of the popula-

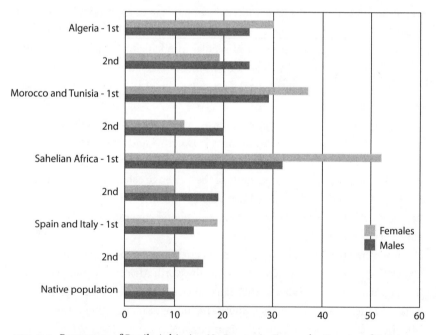

FIG. 9.3. Percentage of Pupils Achieving No Degree in France, by Country of Origin, Generation number, and Gender, 18–50 years old, 2008. Source: Trajectoires et Origines. Survey Ined-INSEE, 2008.

tion than native whites or most other ethnic groups. For men of Algerian descent, 25 percent have no degree, while for women the number drops to 19 percent. For men of Moroccan or Tunisian descent, 20 percent have no degree, while the number is cut almost in half for women to 12 percent. (See fig. 9.3.)

Interestingly, among many non-Muslim second-generation immigrants in France, we also see the women pulling ahead in the attainment of university degrees, but the differences are more nuanced and not as pronounced as with the North African and Sahelian counterparts, nor was there as significant a male-advantage for the first generation in many non-Muslim groups. For example, among immigrants of European descent (except Portuguese) in France, women in the second generation lost ground from the first generation in levels of university degree attainment as compared to their male counterparts, but still hold a slight lead relative to men.[44]

These are compelling figures regarding Muslim North Africans—most notably reflected in the way men are pooling at the bottom of the social-educational ladder relative to women. The contrasts are equally striking among non-Muslim second-generation Central Africans. These imbalances are far more dramatic than among second-generation immigrants from other countries, where the differences between women and men who have no educational certification are more modest.

The Labor Market in France

The French *Trajectories et Origines Survey* also clarifies the situation of immigrants and children of immigrants in the job market.[45] The rate of unemployed immigrants has been particularly high for those originating from North Africa and sub-Saharan Africa—and even higher for their children. The rate of unemployed among North African immigrant populations (in the 18-to-50 cohort) was relatively high in the TeO survey data, which was published in 2008: 16 percent for Algerians and 12 percent for Moroccans and Tunisians (see fig. 9.4).

Where do immigrant women figure in the French labor market? Among Muslim immigrants, less than half of the women are considered part of the "working population"—that is, outside the household. For Algerians, the figure is 48 percent; and for Moroccans and Tunisians, 49 percent. Far higher levels of immigrant women from other European Union countries are considered part of the working population: 76 percent of the Portuguese, 81 percent of the Spanish and Italians, and 71 percent of others from the EU.

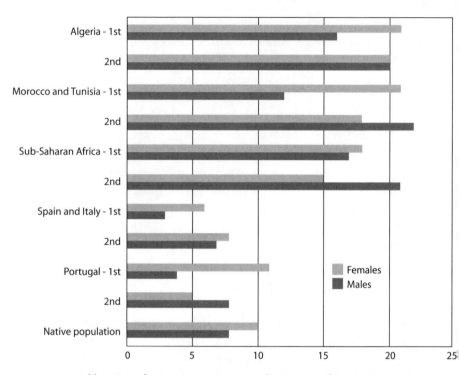

FIG. 9.4. Jobless Rates for Immigrants in France, by Country of Origin, Generation Number, and Gender, 18–50 years old, 2008. Source: Trajectoires et Origines. Survey Ined-INSEE, 2008.

In other words, despite the educational gains of girls and young women with ancestry in Muslim countries, the percentage of those that are committed to a life of working inside their homes (through their own choice or otherwise) remains high, even when compared to immigrant women from other regions. Still, the French data for Muslim women in the work force is more impressive than that of the British.

Patterns of Dissent

Across these British and French cases we see some interesting similarities. Among the Muslim immigrant populations we find patterns of a large swing from first to second generation in the educational attainment of girls and young women. The boys and young men, in turn, are falling behind. Many are gathering at or near the bottom of the social ladder, not just educationally but in the job market as well. While these trends cut across ethnic and religious groups, they are particularly noticeable among Muslim immigrant populations.

But the differences between the countries are equally eye-catching. In France, second-generation Maghribi and Sahelian women are widely outpacing men in terms of both university degrees and General Certificates of Secondary Education. Similarly, far more second-generation Maghribi and Sahelian men are becoming of working age without any qualifications—a dramatic reversal from first generation numbers.[46] From this data, we can infer that while Muslim women are making gains relative to men in both France and the United Kingdom, Muslim women in France are, hitherto at least, progressing educationally at a quicker pace than their British counterparts. We observed the marked differences for women across France and the United Kingdom in pivotal Muslim communities also at the university level (though British Pakistani and Bangladeshi women are making significant strides of late), and the stark differences in the labor market data.

What is one to make of these education and labor market trends for Muslim communities, for women and men, and the French and British political models? Before answering, we need a deeper sense of the political culture and assumptions behind the British and French models. In the next chapter I draw on additional and comparative data from an especially commissioned survey and from collected demographic data of those convicted of terrorism. The patterns that cut across these data are revealing.

But we can note in anticipation the following thread in the emerging picture of the social fabric in these countries: in terms of discontent and occasional unrest in Muslim and immigrant areas in British and French cities, we are seeing a clustering of vectors: the boys and young men are falling behind girls and young women educationally and, in some cases, in work; second and third generations that are increasingly distant from the experiences of their parents; young people in isolated neighborhoods but connected through satellite television and the Internet to the world of Islam. Some will be drawn to the narratives, violent or non-violent, of a more globalized Muslim Ummah—while living among an often suspicious mainstream populace.[47]

Those few who do cross that line to join the ranks of violent Islamists (or even simply articulate a militant Islamist position) include some who come from poorer backgrounds. But most European Islamist militants, based on conviction and survey data, display a different profile—with important implications regarding the French and British models of national and social integration.

One other lesson: in the studies of social and national integration, the tendency is overwhelmingly to view different ethnic and religious communities as organic and almost unitary, with gender as a secondary consideration. We need to reconsider, for in certain ways the differences between males and females can be more important for social dynamics, including social integration, than ethnicity and religion as such—especially when immigrant women integrate better socially and economically, on average, than men. Thinking in these gendered terms demands a distinctly new way of seeing.

CHAPTER TEN

Islamist Tipping Points
Why Think Radically in Europe?

On July 1, 2006, Lance Corporal Jabron Hashmi, a military intelligence specialist in the United Kingdom armed forces, was the first Muslim Briton killed in the "war on terror." He was serving in Helmand province in Afghanistan when the Taliban attacked his base with rocket-propelled grenades. He was killed in the attack along with Corporal Peter Thorpe.

Hashmi was born in Peshawar, Pakistan, some 40 minutes' drive from the Afghan border and had moved with his family to England when he was 12 years old. His older brother, Zeeshan, described him as having wanted to bring peace to the region: "He was doing a job that was worthwhile. These Muslim brothers who are willing to carry out suicide bombings and sell drugs to fellow Muslims, they still think they have the ability to criticize people who want to do things differently." He added pointedly, "With the anniversary of the July 7 [2005] bombings approaching, it is important to try and break down the barriers in society. You can be proud to be Muslim and British—the two don't have to be separate."[1]

But a radical group fronted by extremist preacher Anjem Choudary attacked Hashmi as a "home-grown terrorist." A website run by Al-Ghurabaa, which succeeded the terror movement Al-Muhajiroun, stated that Hashmi, though born Muslim, was a "traitor to Islam and professional terrorist" who "unlike members of Al-Qaida took a salary for his terror."[2]

The story of Jabron Hashmi's death and the reaction captures the polar paths, on a broad spectrum, that British Muslims can take. It illustrates the struggle over Muslim identity within the immigrant communities and from without by government policymakers. It is a fraught process, from individuals to the immigrant communities to the nation as a whole.

In chapters 8 and 9 we considered two challenges facing Western Europe. First, we examined the dynamics of deeply institutionalized patriarchy and traditionalism across significant fractions of immigrant communities. This patriarchal traditionalism is not only Muslim but also mostly, but not only, of the first generation. Second, focusing on Britain and France we analyzed how immigrant men generally are disproportionately (compared to women) stuck at the bottom rungs of the social ladder. Combined with the dynamics of patriarchy, discrimination, and religious politics, this state of affairs has an alienating effect on poorer second- and third-generation Muslim men.

In this chapter I ask why a significant proportion, though a distinct minority, of Muslims are adopting a radical Islamist stance. Those who do so are mostly among the second generation of immigrant Muslims, unevenly across the different Muslim communities. Often such an Islamist perspective is accompanied by a disdain for their European countries of birth. And a small number of these Islamists will turn to actual terrorism.

I also ask how the more multicultural model of the United Kingdom and the republican, secular, and assimilationist French model compare in terms of their respective effects on Islamist radicalism and, in particular, on the militant and violent Islamist fringe. The differences are striking. Upwardly mobile and middle-class French Muslims are less likely to adopt radical positions than British Muslims of similar status. It appears that the French secular and assimilationist model is largely working, in terms of the professional and middle classes, to a greater extent than in the United Kingdom.

This divergence between the French Muslims and British Muslims is of particular note when it comes to those who have been convicted of terrorism-related crimes. An important caveat with the French case is that while French Muslims who are middle class or upwardly mobile appear to generally think of themselves as French to an extent greater than British Muslims think of themselves as British, the native French are less accepting of this population as, indeed, French in identity. This tension may well be problematic in the future and could conceivably shift the identification of some middle-class French Muslims.

To analyze these issues, I draw on the survey I directed in France and the United Kingdom, among other countries. To analyze the profiles of those Islamists who have been convicted for terrorism-related crimes, I use data collected for that purpose.[3] I also use the Tribal Patriarchy Index, discussed in chapter 6 of this book.

Why some individuals turn to radicalism is a complex process. We can point to a cluster of factors at work, though some influences (especially in cases of outright terrorism) will be case-specific. Still, we can discern a number of sociological parameters that correlate to radicalism more broadly, and to violent militancy specifically.

But in order to map the way ahead, we begin first with a discussion of the alternative British and French political cultures and their modes of integration of immigrant populations.

Which Is Prettier? French and British Models

Of late, a burgeoning debate has taken place on the French and British models for addressing the role of religion in public life.[4] This is more important than it may first seem, since the Western societies—especially in Western Europe—grapple with the increasing prominence of Islam. Indeed, the future shape and form of citizenship—the cornerstone of the modern, democratic state—may well rest on the outcome of these debates. Criticizing the French model has become something of a cottage industry for academics in the Anglo-American world, following French bans on the hijab, niqab, and burqa from public schools to public space in general.[5]

Much of this discussion among academics has been philosophical: What makes for a better and more just democracy? But the issue is also sociological: What are the outcomes of these models for addressing the challenges of diverse societies? Another, perhaps more pretentious, way one could put it is that much of the academic discussion has been *deontological*—focusing on the rightness or wrongness of the respective models themselves, regardless of outcomes on the ground. Academics have discussed less the arguably more important issue: What are the *consequences* of the models for the integrity and democracy of these societies?

When it comes to models for the coexistence of church and state, or on the relationship of religion and politics, the two most prominent are what are called the Anglo-American model and the French model.

The first model (involving most notably the United Kingdom and the United States) is traced to political theorists such as John Locke. The French model is credited to Jean-Jacques Rousseau. For Locke, the concrete individual, rather than the state, is endowed with rights and freedom of conscience; but for Rousseau, individual liberties can only be achieved through the state. The anthropologist John Bowen writes: "Here Rousseau stands against Locke, freedom through the state against freedom from the state, society as a 'coming together' and 'living together' against society as isolated rights-bearing individuals or (worse) as isolated communities defined by religion, race or ethnicity. In the Anglo-[American] mirror image of France, agents of the state display their separateness in their turbans or their headscarves, and the people follow suit."[6]

The Constitution of the Fifth Republic, enacted in 1958, defined France as an "indivisible, secular, democratic, and social republic," where the state *protects* individuals from the claims of religion. French citizenship is not only protected from religion but is seen in contrast to it. French secularism means the separation of "church and state through the state's protection of individuals from the claims of religion." In contrast, in the United States, secularism "connotes the protection of religions from interference by the state."[7]

Remember, in the French Revolution—and in historical memory—the forces of autocracy are the twinned repressions of the monarchy and the Catholic Church. Religion was (and in much of France's public mind is) the enemy of freedom. In America, Protestant dissenters, intensely religious, were the backbone of the Revolution of 1776. In Britain, the picture is more ambiguous. The republicans of Oliver Cromwell were religious zealots, liberators for some and oppressors for others. Out of this ambiguity, and over time, arose the Great Compromise, establishing the Church of England as the state church yet openly tolerating dissenting Protestant sects. Catholics and Jews came to be accepted as well, if with a certain ambivalence.

French national self-understanding is of a nation based on individuality, indivisibility, and universalism, and assimilation to a singular culture. Religion accommodates itself to the state and the secular nation, not vice-versa. Belief, in the French tradition, should be highly privatized both in mind and in geography.

In the Anglo-American model, the state is conceived "as a place in which all religions have an equal right to manifest themselves in public and freedom of religion is a constitutionally protected right."[8] Separation of church and state in the United States denies supremacy to any one denomination, and it protects religions from the state. Here the citizen has a freedom of religion and conscience enforced by the state. Federal (and state) governments promise neutrality of the public sphere with respect to religion. Wear your cross, hijab, kippah, and whatever other religious symbolism you can muster—in public, in school and wherever else—with pride.

But in fact, the story on the ground in contemporary Europe regarding Muslims is much more complicated. The notion of a pluralist society without assimilation into a singular identity is, in the French view, inherently fraught. In the writing of political scientists Alvin Rabushka and Kenneth Shepsle,

In a homogeneous society, the purchase of a cathedral provides an indivisible "public good," i.e., every citizen may benefit from its construction. In the plural society, however, the erection of a Chinese temple constitutes a "public bad" for Muslims; in a similar manner, Muslim mosques provide few or no benefits for Chinese. Therefore, in the plural society social demands often result in public expenditures with benefits for one community and opportunity costs for the others. The plural society thus isolates the demands of its separate communities, and fails to aggregate . . . common social demand. . . . In the absence of national consensus (a common social will), economic competition among the separate communities is the only feasible mutual activity.[9]

The noted philosopher John Rawls asked, "How is it possible that there may exist over time a stable and just society of free and equal citizens profoundly divided by reasonable religious, philosophical, and moral doctrines?"[10] The French answer is clear: the multicultural model is too burdened with too many structural stresses to maintain the individual freedoms of citizens in the long term.

In France the burqa, niqab, and even the hijab are viewed as a violation of the neutrality of the public sphere. It represents a threat to the Republic and to the assimilation with a universal culture as a prerequisite of French identity. Furthermore, such customary dress and practices are viewed as violating enlightenment values and threatening a regression to antediluvian times.

In fact, France has made compromises in its strict republicanism—recognizing, for example, Muslim councils. Local governments have also leaned to more "communitarian" (meaning multicultural) policies than the central government.[11] But equally clearly, France has taken a much more assimilationist approach than the United Kingdom, at least until the ascension of David Cameron to 10 Downing Street.

I subtitled this discussion—with a wink—by asking which model is prettier. But aesthetics are indeed an important part of the debate. Vivid French descriptions of the burqa—in the spirit of "a coffin that kills individual liberties"—or British effusions about the many hues of multiculturalism replacing a gray, monochromatic England are indicative of the role of beauty in the eye of the citizen.

The Nation's Two Bodies

In the book *The King's Two Bodies*, considered a classic of historical writing, the author Ernst Kantorowicz illustrated the basis of late medieval political thinking.

The two bodies are the body spiritual and the body natural. The king's natural body was vulnerable and frail, and would decay and pass on. But the king's spiritual body is transcendent and immortal, and represents the divine grace of the king. The intermingling of the two bodies made possible the continuity of the monarchy, as expressed in the archetypal saying, "The king is dead. Long live the king."[12]

Less articulated, but clearly implicit is the nation-state equivalent of this duality. We take it for granted, but the nation-state has been bestowed with a corporeal character and a "personality." Indeed, in certain ways this was a revolutionary response to the king's body spiritual in the early establishment of nation-states. This personality is expressed in the language of national *self*-determination, right of *self*-defense, and other similar terms. Personality is also implied in reportage along the lines of "Paris announced that it regrets Washington did not adopt a more multilateralist position."

The body natural in the nation-state is the citizen herself. The nation-state's two bodies are mutually constitutive and reinforcing (as are the king's two bodies). Historically, the emergence of more central states and individual rights grew in tandem. Central governments had an interest in breaking down the power of feudal and other authorities. Guilds, the aristocracy, tribes, and locally autonomous authorities limited state power. Centering the rights of individuals in the state itself benefited both states and the favored individuals.

From the modern emergence of citizenship—for example, in the American and French revolutions—this relationship was fully institutionalized. The idea of the "citizen" describes not just the individual but also that individual's association with the state. He (and it was he, to start) is the source of the state's authority. The state is the source of *his* authority, his right to vote, and, over time, his expanding civic rights. Similarly, democracy inheres in this relationship epitomized by the citizen. The citizen's control over his own body—his self-determination—is inherently a part of national self-determination of the state. And so, it came to be understood, the reverse is equally true.[13]

In the French approach, if we break apart this relationship of the body natural and the body spiritual that is bundled into *le citoyen*, we put individual and republican liberties at risk. It is revealing indeed that Marianne is the symbol of France. She is always presented as a woman of beauty. A different "model" is chosen periodically as the official Marianne for a time—not just beautiful but frequently radiating an unabashed sexual allure, as in the celebrated choice of Brigitte Bardot.

Why, in the French context, does rupturing this relationship of the body natu-ral and the body spiritual (or, more explicitly, the body politic) threaten liberties? Take the hadith that the Ummah is likened to the human body: if one part is in pain, the whole body suffers. In other words, if one part of the Muslim commu-nity, of the Ummah, is in distress, the whole Ummah should feel its concern. It is critical to emphasize this is generally a *social* concept—that is, it can be an empathy that does not necessarily take on political import. In fact, this sense of a communal body is shared broadly. Thus, when Haitian Americans respond to a devastating earthquake in Haiti, for example, no one questions that sense of obli-gation. Nor is it viewed as having political implications within the United States.

But among most if not all Islamists, the Ummah as the body spiritual does take on a political connotation. The sense of the body personal elides almost seamlessly into the body spiritual. And, in certain circumstances, the body spiritual *is* the body politic. What are those circumstances? Sometimes this is clear, as in the nation-state or for a monarch in medieval Europe. Sometimes there is a constructive— or destructive—ambiguity.

France—the public and the government—concluded, in banning the public display of the burqa and the niqab, that such dress is political. That is, the gov-ernment sees the hijab (equivocally) and the niqab and burqa (unequivocally) as representing an approach to the body politic (as well as the body itself), both of the French nation-state and of the Ummah.

For France, in the most palpable sense, this dress represents oppression of women. As such, it represents a negation of the citizen and the promotion of an alternative cultural authority. Even if some women voluntarily dress themselves in these ways, all they are doing is veiling—metaphorically—the cultural oppres-sors. In this way, the sartorial can be perceived as a tangible threat to the future of democracy and republicanism. From the French perspective, multiculturalism— to the extent that it generates different bodies spiritual and politic among large populations—cannot stand.

The French case appears as something of a paradox, especially when viewed through the lens of British and American political traditions of church and state. As the political philosopher Seyla Benhabib puts it, in France "we encounter public officials and institutions who supposedly champion women's emancipa-tion from [their] communities by suppressing the practice of veiling. . . . [Yet] some women resisted the state not to affirm their religious and sexual subordi-nation as much as to assert a quasi-personal identity independent of the domi-nant French culture."[14]

After Multiculturalism?

France sees a destructive ambiguity in multiculturalism—but in practice has allowed elements of "communitarianism," as they call multiculturalism, to take hold. Britain, initially at least, saw a constructive ambiguity in its multicultural experiment. But it became clear by 2010 that Europe—that is, the public and policymakers in government—was turning against the multicultural model, at least in its more robust forms. This was reflected in public referendums across Europe on restricting dress or on the building of mosques or on the height of minarets. Such public sentiment was echoed in speeches by Chancellor Angela Merkel of Germany, President Nicolas Sarkozy of France, and Prime Minister David Cameron, where they stated bluntly that multiculturalism "had failed." Instead, they called for more defined and singular national identities. David Cameron, in a major speech in Munich in 2011, called for a more "muscular liberalism."[15]

The challenge in Europe regarding approaches to European Muslims has been, in part, that three distinct issues have been conflated into a single optic: multiculturalism, the plight and anger of poorer immigrant and Muslim neighborhoods, and Islamist extremism.

In terms of Islamist radicalism, is the perception that multiculturalism is feeding into extremism correct? To analyze this question, let's consider this issue in two parts. First, what do we see in terms of general political identification among Muslim immigrant populations? Second, in terms of actual Islamist militancy and violence, what evidence do we have? For both questions I compare the British and the French in the light of their different models.

Surveying the Political Landscape

So how do British and French Muslims, in the aggregate, break down in their political orientations to their respective home countries and to the West more broadly? And what do these orientations say about their respective political models and the place of women? Drawing from the commissioned survey, a number of differences in the British and French cases are readily apparent from the survey respondents.

French Muslims are generally more liberal on issues of women's status than British Muslims. While France has been roundly condemned on its positions limited or banning the public display of what is identified (sometimes problematically) as Muslim dress, French Muslims actually are largely in accordance with broader French mores.

For example, while 71 percent of French Muslims felt that a woman could shake hands with men who are not related, only 30 percent of British Muslims felt this was appropriate. Only 13 percent of French Muslim respondents felt that a woman should cover their faces with a niqab, while 44 percent of British Muslims felt this was desirable. British Muslims who were born in Britain were more liberal about the niqab, compared to the first-generation, foreign-born British Muslims. The numbers of those supporting the niqab shifted from 51 percent to 29 percent from the first- to second-generation immigrants. However, British-born Muslims were still significantly more conservative than French-born Muslims, of which 17 percent supported wearing the niqab.[16]

British Muslims are more likely to feel that their government is "hostile to Islam"—results that may be surprising, given that the French have incurred international censure for their handling of its approach to issues like the ban on wearing the burqa in public. Some 40 percent of French Muslims strongly disagreed that the French government is hostile to Islam, while 22 percent of British Muslims have that sentiment, based on the survey.[17]

Remarkably, 46 percent of French Muslim *women* strongly disagree that the French government is hostile to Islam, compared to 34 percent of French Muslim men. In contrast, the percentage of British Muslim women who strongly disagreed that the British government is hostile to Islam, 23 percent, is very close to the figure for men in the same category 19 percent.

The survey also shows a pattern of misgiving among British Muslims regarding the West in general, a pattern that is sharply different in France. At least 70 percent of French Muslims "strongly" agree that Western countries are essential to economic development, help expand democracy, and advance women's rights in the Muslim world. Only half as many British Muslims, proportionately, feel this way. While 55 percent of French Muslims disagree that Western countries lower moral standards in the Muslim world, only 20 percent of British Muslims share this perspective (table 10.1)

The survey asked, "Would you sacrifice personally or engage in violence to defend your faith?" The "Yes" response is indicative of a more activist or even militant approach to faith, whereas a "No" response indicates a more benign and even pacific view of religion. The differences between British and French Muslims were striking. Two-thirds of British Muslims indicated a positive response to the question, while only 25 percent of French Muslims answered affirmatively to the use of violence or personal sacrifice to defend the faith. Class differences play different roles in France than they do in the UK. We broke down responses to the questions in self-described economic classes. The results show a series of

TABLE 10.1
Opinions of British and French Muslims on the Impact
of Western Countries on the Muslim World

Respondents	Help expand democracy		Help advance women's rights		Are essential for economic development		Lower moral standards	
	No.	%	No.	%	No.	%	No.	%
British Muslims								
Strongly agree	139	37	134	36	131	34	138	38
Somewhat agree	151	41	160	43	175	46	151	42
Disagree	82	22	82	22	74	19	72	20
Total	372		376		380		361	
French Muslims								
Strongly agree	263	70	266	71	269	72	111	29
Somewhat agree	48	13	58	15	56	15	58	15
Disagree	64	17	52	14	51	14	208	55
Total	375		376		376		377	

clear patterns. More prosperity is associated with greater activism or militancy in the UK, while in France class differences have only a mild impact on attitudes on the issue (table 10.2).

These findings, collectively, speak to a larger trend of British Muslims to be more conservative on gender and sexuality issues, more uneasy with the mores of the surrounding society and of the West in general, and more supportive of personal sacrifice and even violence to support the faith than French Muslims.

What shall we make of this picture? The results are quite revealing both in terms of the impact of the political models of the British and the French. But surveys provide only one slice, and it is best to consider different kinds of data sources in combination. Expanding on the issue of violence, let us consider the demographics of those Islamists convicted for terrorism in Britain and France.

Islamist Terrorism

When we examine the profiles of Islamists convicted since the 1990s for terrorism-related offenses, the patterns differentiating Britain from France are clear. Indeed, the French are in part correct: British multiculturalism, for all its many positive qualities, has opened a social space for the growth of militant and violent Islamism. Conversely, in contrast to the British case, the upwardly mobile

TABLE 10.2
*Readiness of British and French Muslims to Personally Sacrifice or Engage
in Violence to Defend the Faith*

	Prosperous or living very comfortably				Living reasonably comfortably				Just getting along or poor				Total			
	No		Yes		No		Yes		No		Yes		No		Yes	
ɔondents	No.	%	No.	%	No.	%	No.	%	No.	%	No.	%	No.	%	No.	%
ish Muslims	61	26	171	74	56	43	75	57	15	50	15	50	132	34	261	66
nch Muslims	64	82	14	18	197	73	72	27	41	76	13	24	302	75	99	25
al	125	40	185	60	253	63	147	37	56	67	28	33	434	55	360	45

and middle class among French Muslims are more likely to consider themselves French and less likely to engage in militant and violent Islamist activities.

The French had been furious with the British from the mid-1990s for their lax policies regarding asylum for Islamist radicals in London, giving the capital city the sobriquet of "Londonistan," a title provided by French officials.[18] But the different attitudes toward harboring such militants revealed distinct approaches to immigrant populations more broadly, and this came out in the patterns even (or especially) of native-born Islamists. (British law enforcement did, however, take a more firm approach to radicals in their midst following the September 11, 2001, terrorist attacks.)

The class differences between the two countries are revealed in that the British militants have been well educated. Of those for whom data is available, almost 60 percent have attended university. Many of the French Islamist militants, in contrast, involved individuals without any experience in higher education; moreover, a large number of the French convicted Islamist militants lacked even basic high school qualifications. The militancy is derived precisely from that group that is experiencing a status inconsistency in the context of British multiculturalism—economically successful and highly articulate, but seeking to locate themselves in the world "Islamically." In France this middle-class Islamist is less evident (though not absent).

Additionally, not only are the convicted Islamists in France tending to come from working or "underclass" backgrounds, but many have also been involved in petty crime and serious criminal and gang-related involvement to extent greater than have the UK militants. Furthermore, in the case of the French Islamists convicted for terrorism, there appears to be a much more consistent and long-term involvement in criminal activity prior to their known involvement in terrorism—especially petty crimes, thievery, narcotics dealing, and common thuggery.[19]

While criminal activity is also present in the British cases, they are of a distinctly different nature than those in France. In the British case, criminal activity seemed shorter in length and involved less violent crimes such as fraud and web-based criminal activity. (It must be noted that there remain some gaps in the available biographic data.) This pattern of British middle-class, university-educated militants matches the survey data, which points to radicalism and support for violence to defend the faith as going up with socioeconomic class.

Among the British Islamists convicted for terrorism, those of Pakistani descent stand out disproportionately in the conviction numbers. Furthermore, they are notably British-born and second-generation. Many have actually had trips to the "homeland," Pakistan, in their youth (independent of their terrorism-related activities). From Omar Sheikh, believed to have killed the American journalist Daniel Pearl, to the two suicide bombers in a Tel Aviv pub, the 7/7 suicide bombings in London, and the attempt to blow up planes over the Atlantic in 2006, second-generation Pakistanis were centrally involved.[20] (Though those of Pakistani descent stand out among those convicted for Islamist terrorism, it is important to emphasize the numbers of British Pakistanis convicted for terrorism is still a tiny number relative to the British Pakistani community as a whole.)

About 70 percent of Pakistanis have their origins in the rural, impoverished Mirpur region of Pakistani Kashmir. Some suggest that the Kashmiri connection is significant. British Pakistani youth who went to fight in Kashmir felt, the researcher Alison Pargeter writes, that they were upholding the honor of their communities. One journalist described meeting a group of British Pakistani Islamists in Lahore: "They loathed everything about the West. The values of the kufr, the infidels, were sick, corrupt, and empty, they said. Pornography, alcohol, exploitation . . . they couldn't see anything in British society that was positive."[21]

When the Tribal Patriarchy Index is applied, we find a significant relationship of tribal patriarchy and religiously motivated violence, even though the protagonists of violence may be two or even three generations away from the "homeland."[22] As Pargeter points out, while the second- and third-generation Pakistanis have a unique experience growing up in the United Kingdom and their Islam can be expressed in more politicized terms, that does not mean a proportion of them do not share the patriarchal values of many of the first-generation parents.

The role of patriarchy is also telling in the disproportionate numbers of Somalis convicted in the United Kingdom for terrorism offenses. Somalia is perhaps an expression par excellence of a tribal patriarchal society. The Somali case is different from the Pakistani, in that of those arrested, many are first-generation immigrants or residents. But that in turn reflects both the more recent surge of migration of Somalis (compared to the South Asian immigrant communities) and the upswing of Islamist and tribal violence in Somalia itself.

Not only is the profile of Islamist militants distinct, overall, in France vis-à-vis Britain, but the character of the terrorism itself is different. A spate of deadly bomb attacks in the mid-1990s in France quickly caught the attention of Europe and the world. But those attacks were widely understood to be a spillover of the vicious war taking place in Algeria itself. In fact, militant-minded Islamists living in France showed little interest of starting a francophone version of global jihad. Rather, the competing Algerian extremist groups tended to use France as a symbol of internecine struggles—a proclamation as to who is the real representative of Algeria against the former colonial overlord.[23]

The Armed Islamic Group (GIA or *Groupe Islamique Armé*) sought to use French Muslims of Algerian origin to shape the prism of the war in Algeria. But their efforts failed in mobilizing French Algerians to their cause in the French mainland. Furthermore, many efforts by French Islamists were amateurish, involving efforts to blow up automatic teller machines or deploying crude bombs. In other words, the French Algerian groups seemed at best to make inroads with criminal elements, and the main focus remained on Algeria itself. Tellingly—with the possible exception of a planned bombing during the French-based World Cup in 2002—suicide bombing, with its potent symbolism, did not reach the level of British Islamist extremism.[24]

We do witness, however, an emergence of some global jihadis of French origin, who after 9/11 went abroad to engage the struggle of Muslims in Chechnya, Bosnia, and elsewhere. The terrorist attacks in Toulouse in 2012 on a Jewish school and on off-duty French paratroopers by Mohammed Merah, who had travelled to Afghanistan, is a notable case. Some jihadis are more educated. For instance, Zacarias Moussaoui, suspected to be the twentieth man of the 9/11 terrorist attacks, has several diplomas.[25]

The question confronting French policymakers by the second decade of the twenty-first century was about the long-term durability of the pattern of French Muslims as generally identifying themselves as, indeed, French. In such a context, the Counselor on Immigration and Integration to President Sarkozy expressed to me in a conversation at the Élysée Palace in 2010, the security authorities feel they are well in control of extremist elements in France. But, he added, would extremism remain contained, or would it grow in the future? One can further ask if the hostility of many native French to Islam, crystallized around issues of woman's status, will affect the pattern of francophone identification of French Muslims?

Universal Islam

In the discussions on Muslims in Britain, the media ask if Muslims generally identify as Muslims first or as Britons first. If someone feels "Muslim first," that does not suggest that he or she is veering toward an extremist direction, though media coverage seems to imply that it does. (Research suggests that coverage of Muslim issues in the UK press is over 90 percent negative.)[26] Still, clearly radicals feel their religious identity trumps any other affiliation, including that of their nation of birth.

The sociologist Dan Nilsson DeHanas approached this issue of identification in a more nuanced way. Working with second-generation Bangladeshi Muslims of both sexes, he handed them a series of cards, each indicating an identity: Bangladeshi, English, Muslim, Londoner, and the like. He did the same with Jamaicans, also second-generation of both sexes. He asked these individuals—about thirty in each community—to place the cards in order of priority. If being British, for example, was the most important to a particular interlocutor, she would note first "British." If being Bangladeshi or Jamaican was what counted most highly next, that would be the second card, and so it went.[27]

The Bangladeshis, DeHanas found, responded overwhelmingly as "Muslim" first. By contrast, the Jamaicans had no particular pattern, and certainly did not almost uniformly call themselves first "Christian" or "Jamaican." Unlocking why "Muslim" is so prominent for this second generation of Muslims is critical to understanding the dynamics of communal relations at work. These findings for Bangladeshis are likely true for Pakistanis in the United Kingdom as well.

The second generation, in part, "globalizes" Islam, in an immigrant environment where they come across many "Islams." Furthermore, the Internet reinforces a world with alternative scales of identification—a geographic respacialization of identity—to that of the nation-state. The collective "body" is not that of the nation but of the Ummah. This is reinforced by an alienation from European society due to its permissiveness and its discriminatory practices. It is in this context that part of this generation becomes highly ideological, and furthermore, it radicalizes.[28]

However, global Islam can be defined in a variety of ways—and in ways that are not necessarily Islamist, let alone violent.[29] For example, the Tablighi Jamaat movement is a global religious movement that seeks a spiritual reformation. It stresses personal missionizing, almost akin to evangelical Protestant groups. It has traditionally been avowedly apolitical.[30]

Moreover, Islamists in Europe, as elsewhere, are not all in sympathy with the idea that violence should be in their repertoire as activists. More broadly, many Salafis are detached from the European societies around them and even other-worldly. But Islamist and Salafi orientations do indicate a profound alienation from Western values, notably in issues of women and sexuality.[31]

Still, one can see how the dynamics of British multiculturalism, while working reasonably well for the great majority of individuals of all faiths and hues, generates social spaces for detached alienation—or radicalism and, in a few cases, militant violence.

Vive le Modèle Français?

The different forms of data, disparate in their sources, show a remarkable convergance that lead to a clear conclusion that the French model works better than the British—in terms of Muslim women's status, education attainment, and labor market particpation; in the relationship between French Muslims and their government, at least for the middle class and upwardly mobile; in the lower levels of alienation of French Muslims; and in patterns of radicalism and terrorism.

The findings also suggest that, perhaps counter-intuitively, the British form of multiculturalism generates a greater sense of disenchantment from the surrounding society, in contrast to the French stress on assimilation, among the respective Muslim populations.

French republicanism is working—in that the upwardly mobile and middle-class Muslims of immigrant roots do generally feel that they are French. Native French may not accept the francophone quality of such citizens, and that may not bode well for the future. Nevertheless, this national self-identification is less true for middle-class and upwardly mobile British Muslims. Again, the dynamics of British multiculturalism appear to have played a role in this difference.

This is ironic, given the ongoing fusillade of criticism France faces from North American and British academics and media figures, mostly for France's approach on issues of what is understood as Muslim women's dress. Part of the difficulty of the issue is assessing whether, on the face of it, patriarchal dress reflects the wearer's choice or is a function of pressure and coercion. The question remains open—though it is clear the answer is not exclusively one or the other.

It is surely revealing, however, that 57 percent of French Muslim women strongly or somewhat disagree that the French government is hostile to Islam. In contrast, 39 percent of British Muslim women strongly or somewhat disagree that the British government is hostile to Islam. In that light, the arguments attacking the French government for its supposed oppression of French Muslim women (while being, implicitly at least, supportive of British multiculturalism) are simplistic.

French Muslim women have been doing better than British Muslim women, on average, across a number of diverse measures. This means at the very least that the French approach of privatizing religion, of suppressing the symbols of patriarchy in public (and even in private life), rejecting (unlike the British government) religious or Sharia courts, and largely seeking the privatization of religious practice demands a more nuanced analysis than we have seen of late in the media and academy.

The criticism of the French case has, by and large, kept a single focus on sartorial concerns and the secular character of the French state, without considering other issues—notably, the broader impacts on women's status. If women's status and sexuality is a major fracture point in Europe as in the world, and what we see in Britain and France are two "experiments" in countering that patriarchy, then the French model appears to be more effective in promoting liberal democratic values.

One can argue that the price of the French model is too high. The French position demands that cultures and religions—the believers—accommodate themselves to the state. In the British model, the state has—more so than the French at least—accommodated different religions and cultures. But we have to ask what ultimately it is that we value and follow up with a better understanding of the dynamics at play in countries like Britain and France.

Does the heritage of the sending countries of the first-generation immigrants account for these differences—in South Asia in the case of the United Kingdom, and in North Africa in the case of France? It does not appear so. The Tribal Patriarchy scores for the main sending countries—Pakistan and Bangladesh in the first case, and Algeria, Morocco, and Tunisia in the second—are in the aggregate similar. But perhaps more importantly, these countries were colonies of Britain and France respectively. So the institutional dynamics we see in, say, post-colonial education, reflect the influence of the British and French models at the source, as it were. The British as colonizers had, by and large, an approach of "indirect rule," relatively respecting local tradition. France sought a francophone and more secular education in its colonies as far as possible. These colonial approaches directly reflect, or are analogues of, multiculturalism and republican assimilationism in Britain and France respectively.

Body Symbolism

The symbolic role of the body has played an extraordinary role in the evolution of Islam in Europe. From the hijab and the burqa to—in the extreme case—suicide bombing, we witness a struggle over the body. As such, the image of women plays an especially significant role. And it is not just how the body natural is defined, but the definitions of the body spiritual and the body politic.

We must not lose sight of a broader development at the raw edges of discontent among both immigrant and native communities. Second- and third-generation Muslims, as the French sociologist Jocelyne Cesari observes, are mostly seeking an Islam that is not just a function of birth but one of individual choice.[32] Much rests on how the give-and-take between ascribed and chosen identities is resolved—and whether the answer lies in a more privatized, apolitical direction, or in a more Islamist, political direction. European governments are desperately trying to shape that answer.

Conclusion

We are witnessing an extraordinary turn in our present moment, a turn that is historically unique—at least on this geographic scope. It is not only the way women have been a *casus beli* for the conflict we have observed in this book. It is how women are making extraordinary strides vis-à-vis men or threatening to do so—a major factor in the patriarchal and Islamist backlash. But its implications loom larger than that. For the first time, women on a broad scale have, or conceivably could, change gender hierarchies in important institutions of society, from education to sectors of the economy, in various parts of the world. This is perhaps the core issue that we need to address from scholarship to policy—and out of sheer intellectual curiosity—since it will cause dramatic shifts throughout societies and communities, affecting work, ideas of citizenship, courtship and marriage, and the very sense of self.

Our institutions, from universities, national governments, and innumerable non-government organizations to the United Nations, address inequities for women. And that is a good thing since inequities remain, and in parts of the world those inequities are harsh and even brutal. However, as we look forward, we will need to broaden the sphere that concerns sexual and gender relations. Men are, across different cultures, falling behind in a variety of ways. At the beginning of the twenty-first century we were seeing patterns such as the following: women are almost twice as likely as men to leave the economically depressed Eastern Germany for the more dynamic Western Germany; in China a massive surplus of men are unable to marry, following the one-child policy and the subsequent infanticide and selective abortion targeting girls; in Russia men's life-longevity is falling, while their rates of alcoholism and drug abuse have climbed; and from Bangladesh to Ghana, microloans are limited to women.[1] Women repay their loans at greater rates and are more likely to use them for the stated purpose.[2] Across parts of the world, women are surpassing men in education. The travail of men, and what that means for women, has slipped into the lore of popular culture.[3] The struggles of men will invariably weigh on societies as a whole, from the marriage market to the threat of extremist ideologies.

Historically unique, on this level, is that in tandem with the strides women have made we have what some have called a growing "crisis of masculinity." In a curious way, as the very term "women's status" has indicated a challenge across humanity, we may have to engage the issue of "men's status" and sexuality, albeit with a very different lens than that of women's status. The implications—social, cultural, political, and international—of these shifts for women and men alike need to be worked out. Given the core importance of sexuality and the body to the well-being of individuals and societies as a whole, these social changes need to be engaged with some urgency.

Globalization is a deeply sexualized and gendered process. We have not fully come to grips with the centrality of sexuality and gender in the way the world has become a single space—economically, culturally, and through media and the Internet. This does not mean global agreement or consensus, but rather that now our struggles are global, not just national or local. Issues of sexuality have become a central gauge for defining the future. Struggles over sexual mores are contests over the evolving shape of our societies, including that of democracy itself.

Issues of gender and sexuality are expressed in myriad ways, not only in the big sociological categories of changing job markets, marriage and divorce, and the way people engage through the Internet but also in innumerable individual ways. Google searches for "sex" in 2004, when such search patterns can be first ascertained, are most marked in highly patriarchal societies. New worlds are being opened up in the most parochial corners. Even Viagra has become an international currency. American military intelligence veterans of the second Iraq war told me that informants demanded "payment" in Viagra tablets and pornography.

Globalization does not only affect gender relations, of course. India illustrates the varying dynamics, such as globalization's effect on the caste system. The prolonged economic boom in India aided millions of India's poorest, including many Dalits, or "untouchables," the lowest rung of India's caste hierarchy. Those who have successfully taken advantages of new economic opportunities have risked deadly responses from those in higher castes. Higher-caste communities act out of a sense of a violated social order, interlaced with economic competition and jealousy.[4]

For millennia, shifting modes of economic production and technological changes have altered the relative fortunes of different groups and in turn caused political jockeying and conflict. Yet the case of women is different from the conflicts that rile castes or ethnic groups. Women are not likely to disengage from their communities, let alone their families, because of "gender conflicts." Some women, for example, play active roles in the Muslim Brotherhood. But what is different here is that unlike transformations of past history, these changes cause us to turn inward. Because of the highly intricate and, as I have argued, elemental aspects of gender and sexuality, these global social changes are generating a deeply personal response. That response goes to profoundly felt issues of identity and the experience of the body.

The backlash against the growing engagement of women in social and economic life outside the family is more commonly personal and cultural than political and ideological. To go back to India, there has been a volatile clash as growing cities, enmeshed in the global economy, encroach on nearby patriarchal villages. Young educated women, free to work outside the household in a way rare even a decade ago, are increasingly harassed, physically attacked, and raped. The accused are almost always poorly educated men, dropouts from close-by villages. They see these women, educated and career driven, as of loose morals—and thus deserving of attack. "If these girls roam around openly like this, then the boys will make mistakes," said a mother of two men who had been accused of rape.[5]

The geography of attacks mirrors the patterns of patriarchy, with most attacks taking place in the more patriarchal and tribal North, especially around New Delhi. Compared to cities further South and East, the rate of reported rape in New Delhi is nearly triple that of Mumbai and is ten times as high as in Kolkata, according to government records. A survey indicated that 80 percent of women were verbally harassed in the Delhi area. Nearly half of the women reported being stalked. Women will often not press charges, even for rape. "The police will not be able to restore my honor," one rape victim responded to a police inquiry.[6]

In other words, the challenges in the wake of globalization regarding gender and society are not only political, military, or even economic. These challenges are deeply social and cultural. Indeed, even the Islamist movements, though politically oriented, have seen their most important objectives as cultural, as reversing the supposed Western corruption of a particular Muslim way of life.

Tribal Citizenship

The French have a phrase, *cherchez la femme,* or "look for the woman." Its meaning is parallel to the term "follow the money." In untying the motivations in the acts of men, follow the money or *cherchez la femme.* Both terms have a core truth in their respective worlds.[7]

Following the money suggests a view of humans as essentially driven rationally by their material interests. Our story is more in line with *cherchez la femme.* It is a story that, by its nature, is not necessarily "rational" in the sense of being coolly calculating. When it comes to gender and sexuality, it is an intricate web that we humans weave. Nearly all of us experience that drunkenness that is love and love lost.

But when being female or male is the very hinge of status, when it determines the individual's life chances, and when the distinction is the basis of social order, as in tribal patriarchal societies, there is a certain level of predictability to such a social structure. It is a structure that is explainable, even if it seems exotic to many in the West. Tribal patriarchy is not an opaque mystery. That is not to say tribal societies do not or will not change. But one should not understate the durability of such tribal and patriarchal institutions, especially those that have marked the Middle East for millennia.

The dilemma of Islamist movements for the West is that the Islamists have successfully provided a bridge between deep-seated tribalism and the contemporary world. Islamism fuses the most parochial, local society to a global movement—it creates *one* form of global Islam. Islamism provides the "cultural material" available in such societies—notably around issues of patriarchy, honor, and religion—that allows for a "natural" transition from the local to the national and indeed to the global scales. Islamism bridges tribalistic communities to national societies and to a global Islam in an almost seamless way. At the same time, the internal social distinctions of clan and tribe can, in the right circumstances, reemerge as a fractionalizing force.

In Western countries, notably in the United Kingdom, Islamism becomes for many Muslims the means for engaging domestic as well as global politics. Finding a "civic Islam," as distinct from Islamist or quietest (apolitical) Islam, is an ongoing challenge from Western Europe to the Middle East. The alternative paradigm, which we see in the French model, is to strip public life of all religion, especially where religion can be a point of contention.

Some have argued that moderate Islamists are akin to the Christian Democrats in, for example, Germany. What would this mean? Such a "civic Islam" would involve a party or a movement whose objective would be mobilizing Muslims who are informed by Muslim ethics to engage broadly in civic issues—from civil rights to the family—while not seeking recognition of Islam as such in public life. This is in essence the mainstream of Christian Democrats. They represent a constituency ostensibly informed by Christian ethics, while precluding the introduction of "Christianity" into the public sphere.

Such a move demands an acceptance of secular law as the only source of the law of the land.[8] In this light, religious law is only a moral guide. This is a benchmark that Christian Democrats, in the main, have crossed for some time. Clearly, in European countries many individual Muslims do just that—engage civically, while informed by their understandings of Muslim ethics—much as Christians and Jews may do. But it is less clear that Islamist groups have, to a significant degree, reached such a point.[9]

When Islamist movements take on a militant form, this creates a potent and dangerous force, as we know only too well. Opposition to Islamist movements within Islam tends to be local—women's groups in Indonesia, for example. For a more liberal and tolerant future in areas where such Islamist groups operate, two developments are necessary. One is a more rigorous assertion of alternative, civically minded "global Islams," which already exist but tend to be apolitical and overshadowed by the militants. The other is a more promising civic future for the Middle East, the symbolic center of Islam, both Sunni and Shia, even though only some one-fifth of Muslims actually live there.

Seasoning the Arab Spring

We know a moment is filled with hope when the world thinks as a collective "we." From men landing on the moon to the rescue attempt of Chilean miners stuck deep in the earth, we are witness to global media events that beam a shared sense of being human. These are flickering moments when we belong, not just to a particular national body politic, but to the "body of humanity," universally sensing the same joys, fears, hopes, and aches. And so it came to pass, in late 2010, when popular and civically minded demonstrations skipped across the Arab world. In a hopeful echo of the earlier sprouting of democracy in Eastern Europe, the Arab Spring was so named (though some later renamed it the "Arab Uprising").

A certain optimism was not unfounded. Under the authoritarian, corrupt, and nepotistic states of the Arab world, there has been a growing civic society. It grew out of an increasingly educated citizenry and a growing middle class—individuals with a modicum of income, a growing sophistication about civil rights, a more cosmopolitan and consumer driven worldliness—and a thorough acquaintance with the social media that these days goes with such a worldliness. This group included women and men committed to women's rights. In the first flowering of the Arab Spring, these more liberal-minded citizens were very evident in its most visible site: Cairo's Tahrir Square. This moment was met with exuberant expectation by the world at large.

Western audiences were also, however, soon introduced to the deep tribalism at work in the region, from the vicious battles in Libya to the bloody rearguard actions by Assad and his Alawite clan in Syria. Given the role of grievances and vendettas in such tribal societies, it is difficult for a tribe or a clan that has ruled ruthlessly for decades to give up power. The accumulated resentments are considerable; the risk of a sweeping acts of revenge by newly unfettered clans too great. Writing in the fourteenth century, Ibn Khaldun, the Muslim historian, said of the authoritarians of his day, "Exaggerated harshness is harmful to royal authority and in most cases causes its destruction." As with much that Khaldun wrote on tribal and urban life in the Middle East, his proposition is proving correct some seven hundred years after he wrote it.[10]

In addition, in the period after the early demonstrations, groups from liberal democrats to Christian Copts found themselves under threat and sometimes physical attack. Women, or at least women who were not connected to the Islamists, receded from the forefront of the uprising. Sexual harassment, assault, and rape reached epidemic proportions at the geographic and symbolic center of the Egyptian uprising, on Tahrir Square. (It took brutal attacks on Western women, most notably on the CBS reporter Lara Logan, to bring Western attention to the pervasiveness of sexual harassment and assault in Egypt.)[11]

Patriarchy and tribalized identities are evidently still deeply rooted in the region, and that has to be brought into account when evaluating social change. When tribal societies like Libya collapse in that environment, what can an aspiring national leadership appeal to? Civic concepts (including women's equality) will appeal mostly to a small, albeit growing middle class, professionals, and others with university education. Even then, this group will include those who will turn to family, clan, and political Islam. Indeed, political Islam may especially appeal to a class that has been nurtured through national and international universities and yet feels excluded by the apparently false promises of the West.

The commentator David Ignatius noted how Westerners like to think that the Arab Spring was a sign that Osama bin Laden and Al Qaeda had failed in that the Muslim world had apparently rejected jihadi tactics. This was especially the case as Muslims were the primary victims of militant Islamist terrorism. But, Ignatius writes, "in terms of bin Laden's broader goal of moving the Islamic world away from Western influence, he has done better than we might like to think." He further notes that "his movement is largely destroyed, but his passion for a purer and more Islamic government in the Arab world is partly succeeding. In that sense, the West shouldn't be too quick to claim victory. . . . So, a year on, it's a time to think about bin Laden's failures but also about the ways his fellow Islamists have morphed toward a political movement more successful than even bin Laden could have dreamed." These Islamist movements draw on inspirational roots common to Al Qaeda, notably Sayyid Qutb.[12]

Others, writing at the same moment as Ignatius in mid-2012, were more hopeful. The scholar Olivier Roy argued that we were witnessing a pivotal turn among some Islamists, where individual choice is a guiding factor in defining politics and religiosity. This is crucial, since it suggests a fundamental shift in the sense of identity and the body. "When the uprisings began," Roy argues, "two-thirds of the Arab world's 300 million people were under the age of 30. They are better educated and more connected with the outside world than any previous generation. Many speak or understand a foreign language. The females are often as ambitious as their male counterparts. Both genders eagerly question and debate. Most are able to identify and even shrug off propaganda." The shift, Roy suggests, does not mean this new generation is more liberal or secular but that in their religion they emphasize direct relations with God, self-realization, and self-esteem—which sounds like much of Western religiosity. He further argues that the debate over whether Islam and democracy are compatible has reached a "stunning" turning point. Rather, with the Arab uprisings that began in late 2010, political Islam and democracy are "increasingly interdependent." Political Islam and democracy in the Arab world, he claims, cannot survive without each other.[13]

What are we to make of such disparate interpretations? Focusing on rapidly moving events is like looking through a kaleidoscope, with a changing sequence of objects and elements in constant motion. It is tempting for scholars and commentators to highlight those elements that confirm their predispositions and theories, especially where empirical evidence is partial. Trends are often mistaken for prediction, when it is the social ruptures that can be most critical. Changes are also, in good part, organic. That is, they are unique to the events in question and not always reducible to the categories and variables in use in the social sciences. The role of tribalism, for example, has been consistently underrated in the political analysis of the Middle East.

Kaleidoscopes however, do have their focal points, the points from which the sequence of objects and elements appear to alternately meet and disperse. That focal point is women's status and sexuality. We will elicit much through the lens of gender, not just about women as such, but about attitudes toward civic tolerance and governance more broadly. Women's rights will necessarily be implicated in highlighting alternative models of global Islam and in a more civically oriented Middle East. But it is a complex dynamic since, as we have seen, the improvement in women's status can generate a reactionary backlash. Realistically, however, for all the dramatic changes for women in large parts of the world, improving the status of women in the greater Middle East remains a gradual project, though individual countries may well show significant strides.

The Stigmata of Humanity

The contentions about women tell their own particular stories, with their own gathering of human drama, discord, suffering, and violence. They are stories that tear at individuals and families and divide nations and the world itself. Yet such contentions are symptomatic of deeper torments and conflicts across the body of humanity. The body of humanity and of the body politic is ultimately located in the body natural. Our figurations and metaphors, our very language, are extrapolated from the bodies we inhabit, that we *are*.

So in turn each of us, literally and figuratively, embodies that humanity—its historical evolution, its cultural complexity, its moments of compassion and love, and its pains and decline. Women symbolically transcend that mortality through birth and rebirth, especially for more traditional communities. In this sense, the struggle over and by women can be viscerally felt to be primordial—"from the beginning of and to the end of time."

Researching and writing this book have been arduous and exhausting but also, I dare say, engaging and deeply stimulating. To explain how arduous is also to explain why so stimulating. To wit, the investigations went from biblical stories to trends in fashion, from theological writings to ideological polemics, from directing an international survey to consolidating numerous statistical data-sets, from linguistics to art history, from gathering data on social trends to analyzing criminal verdicts, and from studying historical writings to coming up with new measures to make manifest patterns in human life.

The research also involved numerous interviews and conversations, all of which were enlightening indeed. I engaged, in different countries, with scholars, foreign affairs officials, members of non-government groups, counter-terrorism officials, and members of the intelligence community. The interviews ranged from a former leading Islamist militant who had direct contact with Osama bin Laden and Ayman al-Zawahiri, to the Counselor of Immigration and Integration to the French President. Those that I acknowledge have a variety of views on the issues I address here. So I emphasize that they do not necessarily share the analysis or perspectives that are expressed in this book. Some will have views very different from mine on the issues I engage here. Yet all, including many I do not mention, willingly devoted their time, knowledge, and intellect on these critical issues.

I am grateful to Seyla Benhabib and Judith Resnick, who, through an invitation to a workshop on gender and migration at Yale University, sparked my thinking on issues of women's status. The chapter on multiculturalism is derived from work in that workshop.

I was fortunate to a be a member of a multi-university and global team of scholars examining social and political patterns and trends within Muslim communities across nine countries in Western Europe, West Africa, and Southeast Asia. That project was funded out of a competitive Minerva initiative of the Office of the Secretary of Defense and involved ethnography, Web studies, and survey research. I directed the survey, which involved seven countries. In particular, I have to note a debt to two scholars on that project, Sani Umar and Mark Woodward. I benefited from their extraordinary knowledge in Islamic studies. I draw on the survey results of the project, and part of my research support came through that funding. I should note that I am solely responsible for the contents and analysis in this book.

I am grateful for periods as a visiting researcher at Sciences Po in Paris and as a non-resident fellow at the University of Exeter. I benefited from presentations I made at, among other places, the University of Heidelberg, University of Bath, Princeton University, CERI-Sciences Po, Graduate Center at CUNY, University of Florida, University of British Columbia, and Columbia University.

I hope the scholars I note here, many of them good friends, will forgive me for being all too brief in my mentions. They do not do justice to the often lengthy conversations, in some cases over several years. I am, in fact, indebted beyond words to (in no particular order), Subrata Mitra, Saskia Sassen, Samir Khalaf, Roseanne Khalaf, Catherine Hakim, John Meyer, Robin Simcox, Jonathan Githens-Mazer, Bob Lambert, Alyas Karmani, Catherine de Wenden, Abdoulaye Sounaye, Mohammed-Ali Adraoui, Daniel Levy, David Abraham, John Torpey, Galya Lahav, Terri Givens, Tim Scott, Galya Ruffer, Diane Wolfthal, Jocelyn Wogan-Browne, Juliann Vitullo, Rosalynn Voaden, Jim Hollifield, Bertrand Badie, Patrick Weil, Phil Kasinitz, Ariel Colonomos, Ali Amin, Hwa Ji Shin, Jason Ackelson, Mark Jurgensmeyer, Muhammad Velji, Antje Wiener, Ning Wang, David Pijawka, Emmanuel Dupuy, Daniel Nilsson DeHanas, Mariani Yahya, Cinzia Solari, Andre Grjebine, James Mayall, Laurence Louer, Karoline Postel-Vinay, Lisa Caviglia, Steve Corman, Diana Coleman, Didier Chaudet, Steven Grosby, Kenton Sparks, Jacob Wright, Fiona Adamson, John Barnshaw, Dietrich Thranhardt, Katherine Meyer, Jonathan Laurence, and Bill Tupman.

I do want to mention in particular Subhro Guhathakurta and Bernardo Arevalo, who have been founts of scholarly and worldly wisdom, and wonderful friends.

Thank you to John Roberts for his kind support. He is an individual of utter integrity, and unquestioning loyalty to his friends.

My thanks also to Martin Steele, Jason Epperson, and Howard Clark, and to the many individuals across numerous government agencies and non-government organizations on both sides of the Atlantic for their gracious help and lengthy exchanges on topics related to this book.

Given the scope and complexity of the topic covered in this book, I could not have managed without a stellar group of research assistants. I am especially indebted to Natalie Delia Deckard. She came to me as a graduate student but proved to be in equal part a teacher and friend. Natalie was deeply involved in the development of the Tribal Patriarchy Index, from database consolidation through to the iterative construction of the index itself. I also relied on her prodigious statistical skills. Rafael Serrano undertook close analysis of patterns of violent conflict. I benefited from his rich in-country experience from Central Asia to the Middle East.

Zacharias Pieri undertook research work for me in the United Kingdom, and Leyla Arslan did the same in France. Jennifer Earles researched the literature in women's studies. Azka Tanveer Mahmood proved an insightful researcher on issues of fashion. I learned from Joanna Rozpedowski's essays on citizenship. I am grateful to Intan Suwandi for her research on Indonesia. Gregory Mills helped me, through numerous drafts, on education and labor market data. Barbara Smith was a graceful editorial reader. Sean Currie generated background research. I also profited from exchanges with Charlie Tafoya, Amanda Confer, and Nicole Rennell.

I am fortunate to have a group of supportive colleagues at my university. My dean, Eric Eisenberg, brings an unusual combination of intellectual acuity and organizational skills to his position. I am grateful for our many fruitful conversations. Thank you also to Linda Whiteford, Roger Ariew, Stephen Turner, Sara Green, and Jim Cavendish. In particular, I am grateful to the staff at the center I direct, including Samantha Haylock, Gina Bingham, and Leslie Trinkle.

To say my editor, Suzanne Flinchbaugh, went beyond the call of her vocation is an understatement. I always looked forward to her thoughtful comments and guidance, from beginning to end.

My wife, Sharon, and our children were sympathetic fellow travelers in the writing of this book. I cannot imagine any journey without them.

Introduction

1. The fascination of those in the West with the sexual mores of the Tahitians has not ceased since Samuel Wallis's "discovery" and has fed the Western imagination to this day, not least in Hollywood. It is an interesting contrast, in terms of gender, to contemporary conflicts with Islamists. This telling of Wallis's engagement with the Tahitians is recounted in (among other journals of the time) *The London Magazine or Gentlemen's Intelligencer*, vol. 37 (June 1768): 328. This recounting is contested by Nicholas Thomas, *Cook: The Extraordinary Voyages of Captain James Cook* (New York: Walker & Co., 2003), 20. The Master of the *Dolphin*, George Robertson, told a somewhat different story in his diary; however, the essential details are the same. After some initial encounters between the sailors and the Tahitians, Robertson describes how among the Tahitians that came to the waterside to observe these exotic Europeans were a "good many fine young Girls," which attracted "our men's fance a good dale." A day later, on June 23, 1767, Robertson described the following scene:

> At sun rise about three hundred canoes came off and lay round the ship . . . by Eight oclock their [*sic*] was upwards of five hundred canoes round the ship, and at a Moderate Computation there was near four thousand men—the most . . . had a fair young Girl in Each Canoe, who playd a great many droll wanton tricks, which drew all our people upon the Gunwells to see them, when they seemd to be most merry and friendly some of our people observd great numbers of stones in every canoe, this created a little little suspition in several of our people, but the most of us could not think they hade any Bade Intention against us. . . . [They] behaved freindly untill a large double canoe came off from the shore, with several of the Principle Inhabitance in her. This canoe . . . was observed to hoist some signal by some of our men, the very instant that this signall was made all trade broke up, and in a few secants of time all our Decks was full of Great and small stones, and several of our men cut and Bruisd this was so sudden and unexpected by the most of us, that we was some time before we could find out the caus, therefor orderd the sentrys to fire amongst them, in hopes that would frighten them, but this hade not the desired Effect, they all gave another shout and powerd in the stones lyke hail amongst us which hurt a great many of our men, we then found lenity would not

do, therefor applyed to the Great Guns and gave them a few round and Grape shot, which struck such terror amongst the poor unhapy croad that it would require the pen of Milton to describe, therfor too mutch for mine.

The spelling and grammar in these quotations are as they appear in the original. See George Robertson, *The Discovery of Tahiti: A Journal of the Second Voyage of H.M.S. Dolphin Round the World under the Command of Captain Wallis, R.N., in the Years 1766, 1767 and 1768.* Issued by the Hakluyt Society, Second Series, No. XCVIII (London, 1948), 154.

2. See Iris Chang, *The Rape of Nanking: The Forgotten Holocaust of World War II* (New York: Basic Books, 1997). The Rape of Nanking is not just a figure of speech, since tens of thousands of women were in fact raped.

3. On Somalia, see Jeffrey Gittelman, "For Somali Women, Pain of Being a Spoil of War," *New York Times*, 28 December 2011, A1. Estimates of human rights groups indicate that at least thousands of women have been raped in Somalia. Gittelman, reporting of the abhorrent circumstances facing these Somali women, writes that "Shabab fighters had even paired up with thin little girls as young as 12, who are left torn and incontinent afterward. If a girl refuses, [Sheik Mohamed Farah Ali, a former Shabab commander] said, 'she's killed by stones or bullets.'"

4. The divisions in public opinion in Western countries and predominantly Muslim countries regarding women's rights and sexuality issues more broadly was strikingly revealed in two waves of the World Values Survey (WVS) conducted in 1995–96 and 2000–2002, with some supporting evidence in subsequent surveys from the Gallup World Poll to the Pew Global Attitudes Project. Ronald Inglehart and Pippa Norris reported on the WVS surveys in "The True Clash of Civilizations" (*Foreign Policy*, March/April 2003) that across the world, including the Muslim world, democracy is viewed as the best form of government—countering Samuel Huntington's clash of civilizations thesis on a core tenet. However, on gender equality and sexual liberalization, the gaps between Muslim and Western countries is a "chasm." On women's rights and opportunities for women, Western and Muslim countries score 82% and 55%, respectively. Public opinion in predominantly Muslim countries is much less welcoming of homosexuality, abortion, and divorce. However, what Inglehart and Norris do not bring out sufficiently is that Muslim countries outside of the Middle East and North Africa are more supportive of gender equality in the same surveys, relatively speaking, and more akin to Eastern European countries. Furthermore, non-Muslim countries such as Georgia, Belarus, Armenia, and Moldova are as hostile to gender equality as Jordan, Egypt, and Iran. As our story develops in this book, the role of patriarchy, and the particular role of the Islamist movement, will become increasingly evident.

5. See Nicola Woodstock, "Islamist gang 'plotted to bomb biggest nightclub in London,'" *The Times* (London), 26 May 2006, at www.timesonline.co.uk/tol/incomingFeeds/article726406.ece.

6. Mohammed Atta's will, dated April 11, 1996, was published by *Der Spiegel* in October 2001 and translated into English by ABC News; see "Suspected Hijacker's Will Found," 4 October 2001, on http://abcnews.go.com/US/story?id=92367.

7. Qutb recounted the story of the attack by a drunken, semi-naked woman, allegedly sent by the CIA to his biographer, Salah 'Abd al-Fattah, and re-told in Jonathan

Raban, *My Holy War: Dispatches from the Home Front* (New York: New York Review Books, 2006), 26.

8. Quoted in Kamal Abdel-Malek, *America in an Arab Mirror: Images of America in Arabic Travel Literature* (New York: Palgrave Macmillan, 2000), 22. See also Sayyid Qutb, "Amrika allati ra'ayt: fi mizan al-insaniyya" [The America I Have Seen], *Al-Risala* 959 (1951): 1301–6.

9. The term "Greater Middle East" has been questioned on the grounds that the region is too diverse for such an appellation or that the term was created by the United States and other Western powers as a rubric for regional reform or even "regime change." I use the term simply as a geographic reference and because that region can be generally characterized in terms of a high level of tribal patriarchy. I discuss this concept of tribal patriarchy at different points in the book and in particular in chapter 6 regarding the "Tribal Patriarchy Index."

10. Patriarchy can be presented in positive ways. The Tablighi Muslim perspective, as reflected in the book *Heavenly Ornaments*, written by the major Islamic scholar Maulana Ashraf Ali Thanwi, for example, equates women to jewels. Women are so precious and important that they must be protected at all costs. From this ideology, however, stems the desire of having them fully covered and supervised by father, brother, or husband at all times outside of the house.

11. On the varied gender impacts of the recession beginning in 2008, see Floyd Norris, "In This Recession, More Men Are Losing Jobs," *New York Times*, 14 March 2009, A1.

12. These observations come from a trip I took in Ghana in the summer of 2008.

13. The term "adventure of the self" is used in a different context in Gilles Lipovetsky, *The Empire of Fashion*, translated by Catherine Porter (Princeton, NJ: Princeton University Press, 1994), 155.

14. See Afshin Valinejed, "Islamic Barbie Iran Creates Culturally Correct Dolls," *Milwaukee-Wisconsin Sentinel* (Associated Press wire report), 3 November 1996, 1. As one of my students, a Pakistani, drily put it, Barbie herself is the *kufur* Barbie—that is, the unbeliever or heathen Barbie.

15. Curtis Rush, "Cop apologizes for 'sluts' remark at law school," *thestar.com*, 18 February 2011; www.thestar.com/news/article/940665. On India, see Sonakshi Babbar, "Now India Gears Up For a 'Slut Walk,' " *Hindustan Times*, 4 June 2011. Aparna Sharma, a student of Delhi University, is quoted as saying: "Finally, something liberating for women of this highly harassed city! I have already selected the skimpiest clothing from my wardrobe; it's an opportunity to prove to the prudes that a woman's integrity is in her heart and not in what she wears. A woman should be able to do exactly what she wants to do to feel emancipated, it's her body, her choice."

16. Virginia Woolf's oft-repeated comment on December 1910 was made in her 1924 essay "Mr. Bennett and Mrs. Brown."

17. Anne Judith Penny, *An Introduction to the Study of Jacob Boehme's Writings* (New York: [s.n.], 1901), 10.

18. We do find a rich and copious literature on women and war from myriad angles. The role of patriarchy looms large, though patriarchy here is usually defined in much more generic terms than I do in this book. I focus mostly, though not wholly, on the more severe forms of patriarchy. Sometimes the term *patriarchy* is used insofar as to indicate that patriarchy underlies both American imperialism and its Middle Eastern protagonists

with little to differentiate the forms of patriarchy. But more usefully, scholars have illustrated the intricate influences of war and the military on the very concept of gender and on society more broadly. See, for example, Cynthia Enloe, *Globalization and Militarism: Feminists Make the Link* (Lanham, MD: Rowman & Littlefield, 2007); Nahla Abdo-Zubi and Ronit Lentin, eds., *Women and the Politics of Military Confrontation: Palestinian and Israeli Gendered Narratives of Dislocation* (Oxford: Berghahn Books, 2002); and Radhika Coomaraswamy, "A Question of Honour: Women, Ethnicity, and Armed Conflict," in *Feminists under Fire: Exchanges across War Zones*, ed. Wenona Giles, Malathi de Alwis, Edith Klein, and Neluka Silva (Toronto: Between the Lines, 2003).

19. The Descartes scholar Roger Ariew points out that the sense of Descartes' separating the mind from the body, even of the sovereignty of the mind, is better expressed as a second-order proposition—that is, it represents the popular understanding of Descartes rather than a first-order proposition about his philosophy. The joining of mind and body, Descartes thought, is very tight:

> By means of these sensations of pain, hunger, thirst and so on, nature also teaches that I am present to my body not merely in the way a sailor is present in a ship, but that I am most tightly joined and, so to speak, commingled with it, so much so that I and the body constitute one single thing. For if this were not the case, then I, who am only a thinking thing, would not sense pain when the body is injured; rather, I would perceive the wound by means of the pure intellect, just as a sailor perceives by sight whether anything in his ship is broken.

See René Descartes, *Philosophical Essays and Correspondence*, edited by Roger Ariew (Indianapolis: Hackett Publishing, 2000), 136. I also benefited from a lengthy exchange with Professor Ariew on June 13, 2011.

20. For an absorbing discussion of the mind-body problem, on accumulating neuroscience research, and a philosophical argument on the importance of the body, see Mark Johnson, *The Meaning of the Body: Aesthetics of Human Understanding* (Chicago: University of Chicago Press, 2007).

21. What of the body and political theory since the seventeenth century? For Hobbes, freedom was constrained when an external agency interferes with the *body* such that the individual is physically unable to act as he wishes. Physical force is of the essence here. But for Hobbes one's freedom is not implicated if one's *will* is coerced. John Locke suggested, on the contrary, that freedom of will is essential to liberty. Note that this brings up the distinction between physical and moral repression. Thus, for example, if moral pressure is imposed and, say, a student feels uneasy about expressing an opinion that goes against the opinion of her professor and fellow students, for Locke this is a problem (but not necessarily for Hobbes). This is explicit in the thought of John Stuart Mill. The yoke of laws has become lighter, he suggested, but the yoke of opinion has become heavier.

Relatively recent theorists, starting with Marx, suggest that so-called consumer freedom is to yoke oneself to bourgeois customs. We become tethered to our possessions, turn into tools of management, and consequently are alienated and in a state of "false consciousness" regarding our supposed freedom. (As we shall see, there is an Islamist echo of this position.) The contemporary theorist Charles Taylor suggested that freedom is not about "opportunity" but about the *exercise* of self-realization. In Hannah Arendt's terms, freedom is realized through civic politics. Quentin Skinner seeks to close the circle: the slave lives solely at the mercy of someone else. He self-censors. He seeks to avoid the rage of the master. Freedom, for Skinner, is the absence of dependence on arbitrary power. For an overview, see Quentin Skinner, *Reason and Rhetoric in the Philosophy of Hobbes* (Cambridge: Cambridge University Press, 1996).

Yet I suggest that thinking in terms of control—or sovereignty—over one's body gives us a better prism to life as lived than traditional political theory. First, some of the conflicts we are facing today regard not political autocracy primarily, but issues of culture. The body and its control are central in this regard. Second, thinking of who controls one's body—the self or an external "body"—captures the literally *visceral* quality of the human condition. For example, we can comprehend—and in a palpable way experience—consumerism, changing sexual mores, and fashion much more readily from a body-centric perspective than from political theory per se. If I control my own self, how does this shape me consequently? The scaffold of politics and of political theory then becomes derivative of those concerns.

22. David Le Breton, *The Sociology of the Body* (Paris: Presse Universitaire, 2004). See also Lee F. Monaghan, "Corporeal Indeterminacy: The Value of Embodied, Interpretive Sociology," in *Body/Embodiment: Symbolic Interaction and the Sociology of the Body*, ed. Dennis Waskul and Phillip Vannini (Aldershot: Ashgate, 2006), 125–40; Sara J. Crawley, Lara J. Foley, and Constance L. Shehan, *Gendering Bodies* (Lanham, MD: Rowman & Littlefield, 2008); and Carol Wolkowitz, *Bodies at Work* (London: Sage, 2006).

23. See Judith Butler, *Bodies that Matter: On the Discursive Limits of 'Sex'* (New York: Routledge, 1993); *Gender Trouble: Feminism and the Subversion of Identity* (New York: Routledge, 1990); and "Imitation and Gender Subordination," in *The Second Wave: A Feminist Reader*, ed. Linda Nicholson (New York: Routledge, 1991). Regarding Foucault, see Michel Foucault, *Discipline and Punish* (New York: Vintage Books, 1979), and *The History of Sexuality* (New York: Vintage Books, 1983).

24. Nor, notes Nussbaum, are women's rights served by this approach: "Even where sex difference is concerned, it is surely too simple to write it all off as culture; nor should feminists be eager to make such a sweeping gesture. Women who run or play basketball, for example, were right to welcome the demolition of myths about women's athletic performance. . . . [They] were also right to demand the specialized research on women's bodies that has fostered a better understanding of women's training needs. . . . Butler's abstract pronouncements, floating high above all matter, give us none of what we need." See Martha Nussbaum, "The Professor of Parody—the Hip Defeatism of Judith Butler," *New Republic*, 22 February 1999, 37–45.

25. Considering extreme events as symptomatic of broader social structural considerations is akin to the sociological study of suicide. For example, Protestants historically had much higher suicide rates than Catholics. But the higher rates of suicide reflected social organizational and structural differences between, in this case, Protestantism and Catholicism. Catholicism historically exhibited greater social solidarity than the more individually minded Protestant congregations. See Emile Durkheim, *Suicide: A Study in Sociology* (New York: Free Press, 1997), first published at the turn of the twentieth century. Likewise, Islamist militancy reveals structural tensions in different ways around gender in patriarchal communities (though not necessarily in Islam more broadly).

Chapter 1 · The Honor of Virgins

1. For the story of David, I draw on Robert Alter's graceful translation as well as his commentary; see Robert Alter, *The David Story: A Translation with Commentary of 1 and 2 Samuel* (New York: W. W. Norton, 1999). This comment is on p. ix. Other biblical quotations are from the King James Version unless otherwise noted.

2. Alter, *David Story*, 269–70.

3. An outstanding set of discussions on virginity in biblical society can be found in Victor H. Matthews, Bernard M. Levinson, and Tikva Frymer-Kensky, eds., *Gender and Law in the Hebrew Bible and the Ancient Near East* (Sheffield: Sheffield Academic Press, 1998). See in particular the chapters by Frymer-Kensley, Matthews, and Washington, which inform my discussion. The story of Sara and Hager, in which Sara exerted some influence over Abraham, represents cases of women having influence over their husbands. Ruth and Esther are also examples of powerful women in the Bible. The lengthy biblical period is patriarchal as a rule, but some social circumstances permitted women to play roles in shaping social life. (Kenton Sparks, personal communication, April 17, 2012.)

4. See discussion in Harold C. Washington, " 'Lest He Die in the Battle and Another Man Take[s] Her': Violence and the Construction of Gender in the Laws of Deuteronomy 20–22," in Matthews et al., *Gender and Law*, 198–99.

5. Rupert Brooke, "The Soldier," *The Collected Poems of Rupert Brooke* (New York: John Lane Company, 1915), 115.

6. Regarding the critical role of family and community to the survival of individuals in traditional societies, historian Joseph Strayer discusses the distinction between life in medieval communities and the modern state in *On the Medieval Origins of Modern States* (Princeton, NJ: Princeton University Press, 1970). The import of his observations goes beyond the period and geography of his study.

7. Johan Huizinga, *The Autumn of the Middle Ages*, trans. Rodney Payton and Ulrich Mammitzsch (Chicago: University of Chicago Press, 1996). I draw on Huizinga in capturing the experience—the accentuated texture and contrasts of daily life—of medieval and (in this book) of traditional societies.

8. Unni Wikan, *Behind the Veil in Arabia: Women in Oman* (Chicago: University of Chicago Press, 1982), 35–36.

9. Ibid., 51–72. As Wikan notes, these customs existed before Islam's rise. In addition, like in any society, norms are not always followed. Most, but not all, follow honor codes. For example, some brides are not virgins as they may be purported to be. Segregation of women may indeed be worse in the contemporary Middle East compared to the biblical period, but biblical and other sources do point to some segregation. For example, the city elders, who sat at the gate assembly-style and made legal decisions in the Bible and ancient world, excluded women. The broader Ancient Near East had harems. But the Bible also does portray women and men interacting freely. (Kenton Sparks and Jacob Wright, personal communications, April 17, 2012.)

10. A wealth of material is available on Catherine of Siena. On her writings, see Vida Dutton Scudder, ed. and trans., *Saint Catherine of Siena as Seen by Her Letters* (London, New York: J. M. Dent and E. P. Dutton, 1905), the source of quotations here. See also Raymond of Capua, *The Life of Catherine of Siena*, trans. George Lamb (Rockford, IL: Tan

Books, 2003), and an excellent entry on Saint Catherine of Siena in Kevin Knight, ed., *Catholic Encyclopedia* (Denver, CO: New Advent, 2009), and accessible at http://www .newadvent.org/cathen/03447a.htm.

11. The quotations on virginity are from literary scholar William Shullenberger, "The Profession of Virginity in 'A Maske Presented at Ludlow Castle,'" in Catherine Gimelli Martin, ed., *Milton and Gender* (Cambridge: Cambridge University Press, 2004), 77–94. He writes of virginity in the context of the work of John Milton, the seventeenth-century English poet, but his observations capture the significance of virginity more broadly. See also Bella Millett and Jocelyn Wogan-Browne, eds., *Medieval English Prose for Women* (Oxford: Clarendon Press, 1990), 2–43, on the *Hali Meiðhad* ("Holy Maidenhood"), which aims to persuade young women to stay virgin in order to avoid the perils of marriage. Jane Tibbetts Schulenberg, *Forgetful of their Sex: Female Sanctity and Society, 500–1100* (Chicago: University of Chicago Press, 1998), 127–75, discusses women who went so far as to mutilate themselves in order to preserve their virginity.

12. For a very different approach to political economy of gender and sex informed by Marxist thinking, see Gayle Rubin, "The Traffic in Women," in *Literary Theory: An Anthology*, 2nd ed., ed. Julie Rivkin and Michael Ryan (Malden, MA: Blackwell, 2004), 770–94.

13. Scudder, *Saint Catherine of Siena*, 106.

14. See also Raymond of Capua, *Life of Catherine of Siena*.

15. Scudder, *Saint Catherine of Siena*, 105.

16. Raymond of Capua, *Life of Catherine of Siena*, 22–65, describes Catherine's extreme efforts to make herself unattractive.

17. Scudder, *Saint Catherine of Siena*, 251–52.

18. See Piero Camporesi, *The Incorruptible Flesh: Bodily Mutation and Mortification in Religion and Folklore* (New York: Cambridge University Press, 1988).

19. On the image of the body in the Middle Ages, the sense of the naked body and of bathing, and sex differences and dress, see the highly readable Georges Duby, ed., *A History of Private Life: Revelations of the Medieval World* (Cambridge, MA: Belknap Press of Harvard University Press, 1988). See in particular the chapter by Georges Duby and Philippe Braunstein, "The Emergence of the Individual."

20. Katherine Crawford's *European Sexualities 1400–1800* (Cambridge: Cambridge University Press, 2007) is an informative survey of the subject and helped inform the discussion here on Christianity and the body and on New Testament sources. See also the discussion in Millett and Wogan-Browne, eds., *Medieval English Prose for Women*, on the *Hali Meiðhad*.

21. See Elaine Pagels, *Adam, Eve, and the Serpent* (New York: Random House, 1988), 133.

22. Peter Brown, *The Body and Society: Men, Women, and Sexual Renunciation in Early Christianity* (New York: Columbia University Press, 1990), 54.

23. On women's sexuality and marriage, including the discussions about St. Clement of Alexandria and of St. Jerome (and the quotations noted here), Diane Wothol provides an enlightening survey in *In and Out of the Marital Bed: Seeing Sex in Late Medieval and Early Modern Art* (New Haven, CT: Yale University Press, 2010). She discusses how, in terms of medieval Catholic doctrine, passion was to be kept out of the marital bed. See also her "Women in the Window: Licit and Illicit Sexual Desire in Renaissance Italy," in

Sex Acts: Practice, Performance, and Perversion in Early Modern Italy, ed. Allison Levy (London: Ashgate, 2008).

24. *The Kreutzer Sonata* (London: Penguin, 1985), 59.

25. See Mary Carruthers, "The Wife of Bath and the Painting of Lions," *PMLA* (1979), 209–22, for discussion on the Wife of Bath. She notes, by the standards of the day, the middle-class background of "the wife" and how this may color her outlook.

26. "Sermon at Major Mosque in Vienna: Jewish and Christian Women Are Prostitutes,"AlWatanVoice.com, posted 4 January 2007; translated by the Middle East Media Research Institute, www.thememriblog.org/blog_personal/en/294.htm.

27. On Mao, see Li Zhisui, *The Private Life of Chairman Mao* (New York: Random House, 1996). I also draw from discussion with the Sinologist Stephen West.

28. I benefited from lengthy discussions with professors of medieval studies Juliann Vitullo and Giacomo Todeschini regarding civic concepts and the images of the Jews and Muslims.

29. Frantz Fanon referred to the cleansing quality of violence in *The Wretched of the Earth,* first published in 1961 and available in many editions and languages. Khomeini is quoted as speaking in a similar vein in Geraldine Brooks, *Nine Parts of Desire: The Hidden World of Islamic Women* (New York: Anchor Books, 1995).

30. Benjamin Barber's well-known book, *Jihad vs. McWorld* (New York: Times Books, 1995), provides a different perspective on the conflict of "mirror opposites" that I refer to.

Chapter 2 · A Pirouette in Europe

1. The Protestant destruction of those images—statues, tapestries, paintings, and the like—is discussed in Johan Huizinga, *The Waning of the Middle Ages* (Mineola, NY: Dover, 1999), where he wrote of the precursor to that destruction: "Piety had depleted itself in the image, the legend, the office. All contents had been so completely expressed that mystic awe had evaporated," 159.

2. The various self-compounds, and the etymology of *self* as a prefix, are noted in the full Oxford English Dictionary.

3. Norbert Elias, *The Civilizing Process* (Oxford: Blackwell, 2000), 48.

4. On the background on autobiography and speaking in the third person (including the quotation of Maximilian I), see *A History of Private Life,* ed. Philippe Ariès and Georges Duby (Cambridge, MA: Belknap Press of Harvard University Press, 1987), 4:540–42.

5. Katrin Unterreiner, *Emperor Franz Joseph, 1830–1916: Myth and Truth* (Ann Arbor: University of Michigan Press, 2006), 87.

6. Max Weber's *The Protestant Ethic and the Spirit of Capitalism* is available in numerous editions and languages.

7. More recently, mannequins dressed with designer clothing have replaced some of the windows once featuring prostitutes. See Marlise Simons, "Amsterdam Tries Upscale Fix for Red-Light District Crime," *New York Times,* 2 February 2008. http://www.nytimes .com/2008/02/24/world/europe/24amsterdam.html.

8. This may have been daring in the day. Now that standards have changed more broadly in Europe, the Dutch are still claiming the vanguard: Dutch council officials announced they will permit public sex in Amsterdam's Vondelpark, the Netherlands best-

known public park. The park's rose garden had become well known for gay men looking for brief trysts. The city council did indicate that there would be rules: "Condoms must always be cleared away, [sex] must never take place in the neighborhood of children's playgrounds, and the sex must be restricted to the evening and night-time," one alderman indicated. Bruno Waterfield, "Dutch to Legalise Gay Sex in Public Park," *Daily Telegraph*, 13 March 2008: http://www.telegraph.co.uk/news/worldnews/1581598/Dutch-to-legalise-gay-sex-in-public-park.html.

9. In the United States, by contrast, women were generally not allowed in taverns prior to Prohibition. Alcohol (as well as tobacco) was often associated with masculinity since only men could drink in taverns. John C. Burnham, *Bad Habits: Drinking, Smoking, Taking Drugs, Gambling, Sexual Misbehavior, and Swearing in American History* (New York: New York University Press, 1993).

10. Marijke Spies, *Rhetoric, Rethoricians, and Poets: Studies in Renaissance Poetry and Poetics* (Amsterdam: Amsterdam University Press, 1999), 115.

11. For discussion on Dutch women in the sixteenth and seventeenth centuries, see Marijke Spies, "Women and Seventeenth Century Dutch Literature," in ibid., 109–24; and Klaske Muizelaar and Derek Phillips, *Picturing Men and Women in the Dutch Golden Age: Paintings and People in Historical Perspective* (New Haven, CT: Yale University Press, 2003). See also Simon Schama, *An Embarrassment of Riches: An Interpretation of Dutch Culture in the Golden Age* (Vintage Books, 1997). The extracts from Lodovico Guicciardini, Jacob Cats, and Janus Secundus appear in Spies' article.

12. The discussion of Thomas of Chobham on prostitutes and usurers relative qualities is discussed in Jacques La Goff, *Your Money or Your Life: Economy and Religion in the Middle Ages* (New York: Zone Books, 1988), 50.

13. Regarding the Dutch and the Golden Age, see Schama's *An Embarrassment of Riches*. The quotations of Aglionby and Mandeville are on pages 290–98. See also Lisa Jardine's detailed study, *Worldly Goods* (London: Macmillan, 1996), where she stresses the conspicuous consumption in capitalism's roots, which she places in the Renaissance.

14. Edward L. Deci and Richard M. Ryan, eds., *Handbook of Self-Determination Research* (Rochester, NY: University of Rochester Press, 2002).

15. Dan Ariely's discussion of the predictably irrational is his book of the same name, *Predictably Irrational: The Hidden Forces that Shape Our Decisions* (New York: Harper-Collins, 2008).

16. Adam Smith, *An Inquiry into the Nature and Causes of the Wealth of Nations* (Chicago: University of Chicago Press, 1977), 140.

17. Albert O. Hirschman, *The Passions and the Interests* (Princeton, NJ: Princeton University Press, 1977). The quotations of Hume and Spinoza that follow come from that book (pp. 55 and 24, respectively).

18. Ibid., 40.

19. Ibid., 39.

20. On manners and etiquette, see Elias, *The Civilizing Process*. Elias is perhaps the most creative thinker on issues of self-restraint, the study of advice books that advised on manners and etiquette, and the linkage of such psychological issues to the rise of the modern state and civil society. Yet a larger audience discovered him rather late. His most renowned book on the civilizing process was first published in 1939 in German, but it only drew widespread scholarly attention in the 1970s (after the first English translation).

A leading figure in the German Jewish youth movement, he fled Germany before the war, spent the war years at the London School of Economics, and later taught at the University of Ghana.

21. Pat Conroy, "Death of a Marriage," *Reader's Digest* 131 (October 1987): 107–10.

22. François M. A. de Voltaire, *Philosophical Dictionary from the French of M. de Voltaire* (London: J. & H. L. Hunt, 1824), 23.

23. On divorce history in Europe, see Roderick Phillips, *Putting Asunder: A History of Divorce in Western Society* (Cambridge: Cambridge University Press, 1988). On divorce and the variants of Protestant doctrine, see especially chapter 2.

24. That roughly two-thirds of divorces are initiated by women in the United States (in recent history) is noted in National Center for Health Statistics, *Advance Report of Final Divorce Statistics, 1988,* Washington, DC, 1991. This report is the most recent federal study available on this question.

25. The seventeenth-century timing, the Dutch and English beginnings, and the long-term trends of violence are discussed in Manuel Eisner, "Modernization, Self-Control, and Lethal Violence: The Long Term Dynamics of European Homicide Rates in Theoretical Perspective," *British Journal of Criminology* 41 (2001): 618–38. Eisner cites Elias's *Civilizing Process*, noted above. Steven Pinker builds on Eisner's and Elias's analysis in *The Better Angels of Our Nature: Why Violence Has Declined* (New York: Viking, 2011).

26. Norman Davies, *Europe: A History* (New York: Oxford University Press, 1996), also quoted in Pinker, *Better Angels of Our Nature,* 145.

27. Christian Lacroix is quoted in Terry Jones and Susie Rushton, *Fashion Now 2* (Cologne: Taschen, 2005), 156.

28. Valerie Steele, "Abstraction and the Avant Garde," in *Fashion, Body, Cult,* ed. Elke Bippus and Dorothea Mink (Stuttgart: Arnoldsche Art Publishers, 2007), 24–28.

29. See Joanne Entwistle, *The Fashioned Body: Fashion, Dress, and Modern Social Theory* (Cambridge: Polity Press, 2000).

30. An excellent set of chapters on the history and sociology of fashion is found in Bippus and Mink, *Fashion, Body, Cult.* On fashion as an "intimate architecture," see the chapter by Valerie Steele, "Abstraction and the Avant-garde," 24–28; on fashion as an individual and group phenomenon, the "I" and the "we," and as the "construction site of the self," see Elena Esposito, "The Imitation of Originality in Fashion," 200–207, and Dorothea Mink, "Fashion the Language of the Self," 268–25; on the shift from class to gender in fashion, see Barbara Straumann, "Aristocratic Cult Bodies," 122–43.

31. Russell Jenkins, "Jack Straw Calls on Muslim Women to Lift Their Veils," *Sunday Times,* 5 October 2006, www.timesonline.co.uk/tol/news/uk/article662160.ece.

32. As one nineteenth-century writer put it, subjectivity is when the "much greater portion of man's life and interest . . . is occupied in observation of his own thoughts, feelings, and actions" (William G. Ward, *The Ideal of the Christian Church* [London: James Toovey, 1844]). Interestingly, Ward, an English writer, was a convert to Catholicism and a strenuous supporter of papal authority.

33. On the symbolic meanings of material goods, see the illuminating (if dry) book, Mary Douglas and Baron Isherwood, *The World of Goods* (New York: Basic Books, 1979).

34. Michel de Montaigne, Charles Cotton, and William Carew Hazlitt, *The Essays of Michel de Montaigne* (New York: G. Bell, 1905), 1:102.

35. Ibid., 1:103.

36. See Simone de Beauvoir, *The Second Sex* (New York: Knopf, 1952). She argued that woman could not have true subjectivity while she is the "other."

37. See, for example, David Riesman, Nathan Glaser, and Reuel Denney, *The Lonely Crowd: A Study of the Changing American Character* (New Haven, CT: Yale University Press, 2001), and Robert Putnam, *Bowling Alone: The Collapse and Revival of American Community* (New York: Simon and Schuster, 2000).

38. On extreme self-awareness, see Dennis Smith, "The *Civilizing Process* and the History of Sexuality: Comparing Norbert Elias and Michel Foucault," *Theory and Society* 28 (1999):79–100.

39. Dr. Phil's comments can be found at www.drphil.com/articles/article/73.

40. Marcel Proust, *In Search of Lost Time: Swann's Way*, trans. C. K. Scott Moncrieff and Terence Kilmartin (New York: Random House, 1998), 60.

41. Katherine Crawford notes the relatively recent emergence of "sexual identities," as opposed to practices, in her *European Sexualities 1400–1800*, cited above. See also Michel Foucault, who makes this observation from a very different trajectory in *The History of Sexuality* (New York: Vintage, 1990). Jill Dolan has argued for saying, "I have lesbian sex" rather than "I am a lesbian." She suggests that gay and lesbian relationships have been desexualized so as to fit into the mainstream and to make straight people feel more comfortable. See her *Presence and Desire: Essays on Gender, Sexuality, Performance* (Ann Arbor: University of Michigan Press, 1993).

42. See the concluding chapter in Uday Singh Mehta, *The Anxiety of Freedom: Imagination and Individuality in Locke's Political Thought* (Ithaca, NY: Cornell University Press, 1992).

43. Ariely, *Predictably Irrational*, 76–114, 135.

44. Ayaan Hirsi Ali's book, the source of the quotation, is *Infidel* (New York: Free Press, 2007).

45. On using the body as such for making statements, see Maud Ellman, *The Hunger Artists: Starving, Writing, and Imprisonment* (Cambridge, MA: Harvard University Press, 1993). Ellman explores the use of hunger strikes as a means of protest and how this practice gives "agency" to the body.

Chapter 3 · Jerusalem, Rome, Mecca

1. Sudarsan Raghavan, " 'In the Land of the Blood Feuds': South of Baghdad, U.S. Troops Navigate Fault Lines of Sect and Tribe," *Washington Post*, 10 August 2007.

2. Hisham Sharabi, *Neopatriarchy: A Theory of Distorted Change in Arab Society* (New York: Oxford University Press, 1988).

3. Personal communication from Professor Mark Woodward, February 15, 2010.

4. The Sufis are often idealized in the West: they are not *necessarily* committed to "peace," nor do they all object in principle to the use of violence for political goals. They generally do not have any special love for the West. But they do hate the Wahhabis and other Islamists—who have crushed Sufis at every opportunity—so they can indirectly act as a counter-radicalizing force. On Sufis, I have benefited from discussion with Azka Tanveer Mahmood.

5. The current Indonesian Islamists are rooted in Middle Eastern Muslim Brotherhood and Salafi sources. But we do historically have some exceptions to the rule; for example,

the Negara Islam Indonesia group is homegrown, and has been engaged in a struggle for an Islamic state sporadically from the late 1940s. But the overall pattern is clear. As I discuss further in chapter 6, the gains of Islamist parties in elections in Arab countries following the Arab Spring vary in percentages from the low 40s in Tunisia to the mid-60s in Egypt. In Indonesia, in contrast, the Islamist parties have hitherto gained in the mid-teens.

6. See Marshall G. S. Hodgson, *The Venture of Islam: Conscience and History in a World Civilization*, Vol. 1 (Chicago: University of Chicago Press, 1974).

7. Ibid., and Phillip Salzman, *Culture and Conflict in the Middle East* (Amherst, NY: Humanity Books, 2008).

8. Lila Abu-Lughod notes of the Bedouin that "females are defined by their associations with reproduction, not so much in its social aspect of motherhood, but in its natural aspects of menstruation, procreation, and sexuality." See Abu-Lughod, *Veiled Sentiments: Honor and Poetry in a Bedouin Society* (Berkeley: University of California Press, 1986), 124.

9. See Deniz Kandiyoti, "Bargaining with Patriarchy," *Gender and Society* 2, no. 3 (1988): 274–90, and Valentine Moghadam, "Patriarchy in Transition: Women and the Changing Family in the Middle East," *Journal of Comparative Family Studies* 35, no. 2 (2002): 137–62. See also the documentary on the British Broadcasting Corporation (BBC) about a British Yemeni boy who goes back to Yemen to visit his family. He is shocked that when the father goes out for extended periods, the youngest male (a boy of about 10 years old) is in charge of the household, including his mother and sisters. The documentary, *A Dangerous Place to Meet My Family*, was broadcast on BBC Three, on 5 April 2011.

10. Salzman, *Culture and Conflict in the Middle East*, 11.

11. Ibid., 11 and 32. The idea of the Ummah as a whole being part of the balanced opposition to, for example, the West has been more in the way of ideological expression than in actual social mobilization across the Islamic world. Muslim anti-colonial rhetoric in the late nineteenth and early twentieth centuries was framed in this way by major figures like Jamal-al Din al-Afghani. For anti-colonial "modernists" like al-Afghani, Islam was referenced as a "social body" rather than in terms of its theological details. See Vali Nasr, *Shia Revival: How Conflicts within Islam Will Shape the Future* (New York: W. W. Norton, 2006).

12. See Ibn-Khaldun, *The Muqaddimah: An Introduction to History*, translated from Arabic by Franz Rosenthal (New York: Pantheon Books, 1958); and Norbert Elias, *The Civilizing Process, Sociogenetic and Psychogenetic Investigations* (Oxford: Blackwell, 2000), 232.

13. Mike Donkin, "Eyewitness: Albania's Blood Feuds," *BBC News:* http://news.bbc.co .uk/2/hi/europe/1964397.stm.

14. See Albert O. Hirschman, *Exit, Voice, and Loyalty: Responses to Decline in Firms, Organizations, and States* (Cambridge, MA: Harvard University Press, 1970); and Salzman, *Culture and Conflict in the Middle East*, 13.

15. Salzman, *Culture and Conflict in the Middle East*, 79–80, 92–98.

16. Ibid., 197–203; Khaldun, *The Muqaddimah;* and Ernest Gellner, *Muslim Society* (Cambridge: Cambridge University Press, 1981). A former Islamist militant, originally from Libya, told me that he thought one problem in the Arab world was that modern Arab leaders (until the Arab Spring at least) had seen themselves as "conquering warriors" in the tribal mode rather than identifying with any civic imagery.

17. Salzman, *Culture and Conflict in the Middle East*, 98.

18. Hodgson, *Venture of Islam*, 72–73.

19. Ibid., 163–64. The Qur'an's imagery of the Last Day (LXXXI, 1–14) is quoted on p. 163.

20. Ibid., 181. Many find ways around inheritance law such as distributing one's estate before death.

21. Ibid., 182.

22. Ibid., 340–43.

23. See John L. Esposito, *Women in Muslim Family Law* (Syracuse, NY: Syracuse University Press, 1982).

24. Clifford Geertz, *Islam Observed: Religious Developments in Morocco and Indonesia* (Chicago: University of Chicago Press, 1968).

25. Hodgson, *Venture of Islam*, 392–96.

26. Annemarie Schimmel, *Mystical Dimensions of Islam* (Chapel Hill: University of North Carolina Press, 1975), 26–27.

27. Hodgson, *Venture of Islam*, 407–9. See also Louis Massignon, *Hallaj: Mystic and Martyr*, trans. and abridged by Herbert Mason (Princeton, NJ: Princeton University Press, 1994).

28. Rābi'ah al-'Adawīyah and Charles Upton, *Doorkeeper of the Heart: Versions of Rabi'a* (Putney, VT: Threshold Books, 1988), 36, emphasis added.

29. Schimmel, *Mystical Dimensions of Islam*, 40–41. However, one should not overstate the role of women among the Sufis. Their greater role is relative to the more conservative or "orthodox" Muslims. For example, women have been limited in their leadership roles in Sufi orders.

30. See Olivier Roy, *Holy Ignorance: When Religion and Culture Part Ways*, trans. Ros Schwartz (New York: Columbia University Press, 2010). Salafis themselves would not phrase it this way, claiming they find their authenticity in scriptures that uphold the supremacy of the Qur'an and Sunnah over all local customs, including Arabian customs. Wahhabi Salafis waged relentless campaigns—military and intellectual—against Arabian traditions. The analysis here is more sociological, of how patriarchal norms that existed in Arabian tribes were in part universalized (in ethical terms) through Islam. See Hodgson, *Venture of Islam*.

31. Bernard Lewis, *Faith and Power: Religion and Politics in the Middle East* (New York: Oxford University Press, 2010), 54.

32. Johan Huizinga, *The Waning of the Middle Ages* (Mineola, NY: Dover Publications, 1999), 204. This book of Huizinga came out in a new translation with the title *The Autumn of the Middle Ages*, trans. Rodney Payton and Ulrich Mammitzsch (Chicago: University of Chicago Press, 1996).

33. Trinitarianism may be found in several books of the Bible, one of the most cited passages being Matthew 28:19: "Go therefore and make disciples of all nations, baptizing them in the name of the Father and of the Son and of the Holy Spirit."

34. The Five Pillars of Islam are: Shahadah (belief), Salat (worship), Sawm (fasting), Zakat (almsgiving), and Hajj (pilgrimage).

35. Bernard Lewis, *The Political Language of Islam* (Chicago: University of Chicago Press, 1988), 92.

36. In addition to Shia Iran, majorities in Iraq, Azerbaijan, and Bahrain are also Shia, as well as large minorities in Kuwait, Yemen, and Lebanon.

37. Gilles Kepel, *Jihad: The Political Trail of Islam*, trans. Anthony F. Roberts (Cambridge, MA: Belknap Press of Harvard University Press, 2002), 106–35.

38. From my days growing up in Apartheid South Africa, that word still turns my stomach.

39. In the same century the expansion of Islam into Europe was halted after a series of brutal battles. The most remembered is that of Vienna in 1683 where, after a siege of some two months by the Ottoman forces, the Christian Holy League defeated the Turks. This battle is seen as the pivotal point in ending Ottoman expansion into Europe after a 300-year struggle. See John Stoye, *The Siege of Vienna: The Last Great Trial Between Cross & Crescent* (New York: Pegasus Books, 2006).

40. Quintan Wiktorowicz, "Anatomy of the Salafi Movement," *Studies in Conflict and Terrorism* 29 (2006): 207–39.

41. See Bernard Lewis, *The Crisis of Islam: Holy War and Unholy Terror* (New York: Modern Library, 2003).

42. Lewis, *Political Language of Islam*.

43. Hodgson, *Venture of Islam*.

44. Shmuel N. Eisenstadt, *Revolution and the Transformation of Societies: A Comparative Study of Civilizations* (New York: Free Press, 1977).

45. Bernard Lewis, *What Went Wrong? Western Impact and Middle Eastern Response* (Oxford: Oxford University Press, 2002), 113–14.

46. See Bernard Lewis, *The Multiple Identities of the Middle East* (New York: Schocken Books, 1999), 18–19, and *What Went Wrong* (2002), 90–91, 109–11.

47. It is important to note a particular nuance here. In Islamic law there are strict rules that do not allow state authorities, for example, to intrude into homes to investigate mere suspicion of crimes. So in this regard we can say there is a notion of the "private" (personal communication from Muhammad Sani Umar, January 5, 2012). Rather, the absence of the public-private distinction noted here is in terms of how public and private is defined in a civic polity, where individuals collectively form and shape their political community. In the civic polity, the "church" is a discrete, separate institution. In classical Islam, and in other communities such as Orthodox Jews, the "ecclesiastical" cannot in principle be separated out. Private actions represent communal obligations that do not recognize any public-private distinction. The relationships are much more organic. One is a member of the (religious) community in every capacity, at least in principle.

48. Bernard Lewis, *Political Language of Islam*, 32.

49. See Vincent J. Cornell, *Voices of Islam: Voices of Change* (Westport, CT: Praeger, 2007), viii–xix.

Chapter 4 · Global Markets

1. Alexandra Hrcak, "Women as Migrants on the Margins of the European Union," in *Mapping Difference: The Many Faces of Women in Contemporary Ukraine*, ed. Marian Rubchak (Oxford: Berghahn Books, 2010), 47–63. The author notes that anti-trafficking groups have fueled "sensationalist claims in the Western press and . . . among human rights groups, that 400 thousand Ukrainian women have disappeared as the result of trafficking into 'sex slavery.' Were this estimate accurate, then *all* of the women who

migrated abroad for work from Ukraine in the 1990s were trafficked into involuntary sex work" [italics in the original]. In fact, the Ukrainian Parliamentary Ombudsman for Human Rights concluded, Hrcak notes, that Ukrainian women tend to work as caregivers, cleaners, or domestics.

2. On sociology and anthropology of culture, see Jeffrey Alexander, *The Meanings of Social Life: A Cultural Sociology* (New York: Oxford University Press, 2005); Clifford Geertz, *The Interpretation of Cultures: Selected Essays* (New York: Basic Books, 1973); Roland Robertson, *Globalization: Social Theory and Global Culture* (London: Sage, 1992); Ann Swidler, "Culture in Action: Symbols and Strategies," *American Sociological Review* 51 (1986): 273–86; Robert Wuthnow, *Meaning and Moral Order* (Berkeley: University of California Press, 1987); and Robert Wuthnow, James Davison Hunter, Albert Bergesen, and Edith Kurzweil, *Cultural Analysis: The Work of Peter L. Berger, Mary Douglas, Michel Foucault, and Jürgen Habermas* (London: Routledge and Kegan Paul, 1984).

3. Note that culture is experienced in multifaceted ways and contexts. "Culture" is not one seamless web that binds all society. At the same time it is clear that overarching ideas are significant—tribe, nation, and religion, for example.

4. Language, like culture more generally, gives us a repertoire of ideas and concepts that enable us to act in this world; culture also limits us by the limits of the choices of those same repertoires, as with language more specifically.

5. In some respects the body precedes language. This is not just chronologically—we are born without language—but also experientially, in our "sense" of the world. Babies can smile at their mothers, expressing a "sensation" of happiness. And even later in life language has its limits in the face of bodily experience. The way romantic physical love is experienced is extraordinarily difficult to convey in text except to a limited extent by allusion and poetry. There is a reason that the British *Literary Review* gives a "Bad Sex in Fiction Award" annually. Our best literary figures, from John Updike to Jonathan Franzen, get nominated.

6. See Charles Miller, *The Lunatic Express: An Entertainment in Imperialism* (New York: Macmillan, 1971).

7. See Peter Rogers, "The British and the Kikuyu 1890–1905: A Reassessment," *Journal of African History* 20 (1979): 255–69.

8. See James C. Scott, *Seeing Like a State: How Certain Schemes to Improve the Human Condition Have Failed* (New Haven, CT: Yale University Press, 1998).

9. Foucault saw the modern state treating the "body as machine" through "technologies of power." But this could be stated that the body is a machine, *mutatis mutandis*, for all "societies." Islamists, for example, fight over issues of family planning in the Muslim world and see family planning as a Western conspiracy but wish to control bodies (especially of women) to different ends. See Michel Foucault, *Discipline and Punish: The Birth of the Prison*, trans. A. M. Sheriden Smith (New York: Vintage Books, 1995).

10. On thinking through the "body as bridge," I benefited from conversations with Alexander Henn, October 10, 2010.

11. "Europe, US Probe Serb Rape Allegations," *BBC Online Network*, 9 April 1999. http://news.bbc.co.uk/1/hi/world/europe/315460.stm. This use of rape by multiple parties was conveyed to me in a conversation, on January 3, 2012, with Lieutenant-General

Martin Steele, of the US Marine Corps, now retired. He was sent by the U.S. government to Croatia during the war to observe the humanitarian situation.

12. The following discussion and literary sources on Cuba and prostitution has benefited from the work of Angelica Nieves as well as conversations I had with her in the fall of 2009.

13. Julie Marie Bunck, "Women and Post-War Socialism: The Cases of Cuba and Vietnam," in *Cuba and Transition: Papers and Proceedings of the Seventh Annual Meeting of the Association for the Study of the Cuban Economy,* ASCE (1997): 31.

14. Fidel Castro, "Castro Speaks on 'Economic Reality' at ANPP," National Assembly of the People's Government," ANPP, Havana Convention Center, July 11, 1992. Transmitted by *Havana Tele Rebelde and Cuba Vision Networks,* 12 July 1992 and translated in FBIS daily report FBIS-LAT-92-136 of the same date.

15. Elisa Facio, "Jineterismo During the Special Period," *Global Development Studies,* 1, 3–4 (Winter 1998–Spring 1999): 57–78.

16. Nancy A. Wonders, "Bodies, Borders, and Sex Tourism in a Globalized World: A Tale of Two Cities—Amsterdam and Havana," *Social Problems* 48, no. 4 (2001): 562. For the salary data, Wonders cites Raymond Michalowski, "Market Spaces and Socialist Places: Cubans Talk about Life in the Post-Soviet World," unpublished paper presented at the Latin American Studies Association, Chicago, 1998.

17. Julia O'Connell Davidson, "Sex Tourism in Cuba," *Race and Class* 38, no. 1 (1996): 39–48.

18. See Barbara Bush, *Slave Women in Caribbean Society: 1650–1838* (Bloomington: Indiana University Press, 1990); Marietta Morrissey, *Slave Women in the New World: Gender Stratification in the Caribbean* (Lawrence: University Press of Kansas, 1989); Rhoda Reddock, *Women, Labour and Politics in Trinidad and Tobago* (London: Zed Press, 1994); and Vera M. Kutzinski, *Sugar's Secrets: Race and the Erotics of Cuban Nationalism* (Charlottesville: University Press of Virginia, 1993).

19. Angelica Nieves, "Globalization, Sex Tourism and 'Jinteras': The Incursion of Capitalism in Cuba," unpublished paper, University of South Florida, Tampa, 2009.

20. Ibid.

21. Kevin O' Rourke and Jeffrey Williamson, "When Did Globalisation Begin?" *European Review of Economic History* 6, no. 1 (2002): 23–50.

22. Klas Ronnback, "Integration of Global Commodity Markets in the Early Modern Era," *European Review of Economic History* 13 (2009): 95–120.

23. Bank for International Settlements, *66th Annual Report,* 1st April 1995–31st March 1996, Basel, 10 June 1996, 96.

24. United Nations Conference on Trade and Development, *World Investment Report, 1994: Transnational Corporations, Employment and the Workplace* (Geneva: United Nations, 1994), 128.

25. The complexity of this financial globalization contributed significantly to the Great Recession beginning in 2008; important financial instruments such as "collateralized debt obligations," or CDOs, became increasingly opaque and difficult to manage.

26. See Paul Krugman, *The Return of Depression Economics and the Crisis of 2008* (New York: W. W. Norton, 2009).

27. See the following: United Nations Department of Economic and Social Affairs, "Women's Control over Economic Resources and Access to Financial Resources, includ-

ing Microfinance," *2009 World Survey on the Role of Women in Development* (New York: United Nations, 2009), 13–14; Stephan Klasen and Francesca Lamanna, "The Impact of Gender Inequality in Education and Employment on Economic Growth: New Evidence for a Panel of Countries," *Feminist Economics* 15 (2009): 91–132; Stephen Knowles, Paula K. Lorgelly, and P. Dorian Owen, "Are Educational Gender Gaps a Brake on Economic Development? Some Cross-Country Empirical Evidence," *Oxford Economic Papers* 54, 2010: 118–49; Mayra Buvinic and Elizabeth M. King, "Smart Economics," *Finance and Development: A Quarterly Magazine of the IMF* 44 (2007).

28. See Teri L. Carraway, *Assembling Women: The Feminization of Global Manufacturing* (Ithaca, NY: Cornell University Press, 2007).

29. See the seminal work in this area, including the migration dimension, in Saskia Sassen, *The Mobility of Labor and Capital: A Study in International Investment and Labor Flow* (Cambridge: Cambridge University Press, 1988).

30. Ricardo Hausmann, Laura D. Tyson, and Saadia Zahidi, *The Global Gender Gap Report 2011*, World Economic Forum, Geneva, 2011. In the discussion that follows, I also draw from *The Global Gender Gap Report 2010* by the same authors. The gender gap in each country is measured by a specific methodology and analysis that is based on three underlying concepts. First, the Gender Gap Index is measured independently from each country's level of development. This means that the focus of the measurement is on the access to resources and opportunities rather than on the actual levels of the available resources and opportunities. Second, the Gender Gap Index evaluates each country based on outcome variables rather than input measures. Third, the Index does not focus on whether or not women have outperformed men. Its main aim is to demonstrate whether the gap between women and men in particular areas have declined. The Index measures the gender gap in, *inter alia*, the following: (1) *Economic participation and opportunity*, which includes the participation gap, the remuneration gap, and the advancement gap; (2) *Educational attainment*, which measures the gap between women's and men's access to all three levels of education (primary, secondary, and tertiary); and (3) *Political empowerment*, which measures the gap between men's and women's participation in political decision making at the highest levels (minister-level, parliamentary, and executive-level).

31. In the fourth category, health and survival, the Middle East and North Africa are fourth out of the six regions. But in this category the differences between the regions are the least marked (96% of the health gap for women had been closed by 2011) compared to the other three categories regarding economic opportunity, education attainment, and political empowerment.

32. Ricardo Hausmann, Laura D. Tyson, and Saadia Zahidi, *The Global Gender Gap Report 2010*, World Economic Forum, Geneva, 2010, 30.

33. See Clifford Geertz, *Islam Observed: Religious Development in Morocco and Indonesia* (Chicago: University of Chicago Press, 1968).

34. Caraway, *Assembling Women*.

35. In addition to Carraway, I draw on the following for this discussion: *International Financial Statistics July 2007* (CD ROM), International Monetary Fund; *Yearbook of Labor Statistics 1988*, Geneva, International Labour Organization; *Yearbook of Labor Statistics 1991*, Geneva, International Labour Organization; *Yearbook of Labor Statistics 1998*, Geneva, International Labour Organization; *Yearbook of Labor Statistics 2008*, Geneva, International Labour Organization. Two sources cited by Carraway are also relevant here: Indonesia's

Bureau of Statistics, *Statistik Industri Besar dan Sedang 1973* and *1998* (Jakarta: Biro Pusat Statistik); and Indonesia's Department of Manpower, *Departemen Tenaga Kerja, Subdit Informasi Pasar Kerja, Dit Penyaluran Tenaga Kerja 1983–1996,* Jakarta. See also Diane Wolf's interesting discussion, *Factory Daughters: Gender, Household Dynamics, and Rural Industrialization in Java* (Berkeley: University of California Press, 1992).

36. *International Financial Statistics July 2007.*

37. International Labor Office (ILO), *Women in Labour Markets: Measuring Progress and Identifying Challenges,* Geneva, 2010, 17. Between 1980 and 2008, the rate of female labor force participation increased from 50.2% to 51.7%, while the male rate decreased slightly from 82.0% to 77.7%. Thus the gender gap in labor force participation rates has narrowed slightly from 32% to 26% in that period. The ILO notes in its report that in countries where participation rates in 1980 were below the world median, the increases were much more dramatic. This means that there has been a general increase in female economic participation and a reduction in the distance between countries on the low and high levels of participation (ILO, x).

Chapter 5 · Fashioning Herself

1. Lebanese Broadcasting Corporation, "Saudi Women Stripping in Internet Chat Rooms," www.youtube.com/watch?v=FzKlAPbmd_w.

2. For one of the limited books on this subject, see *Sexuality in the Arab World,* ed. Samir Khalaf and John Gagnon (Beirut: Saqi Books, 2006).

3. Valarie Cumming, *Understanding Fashion History* (London: Batsford Books, 2004), 130.

4. Catherine Hakim, *Erotic Capital: The Power of Attractiveness in the Boardroom and the Bedroom* (New York: Basic Books, 2011).

5. The actress Hedy Lamarr complained, "My face has been my misfortune . . . a mask I cannot remove. I must live with it. I curse it." Her beauty, ironically, overshadowed her brilliance as an inventor, and inevitably she suffered from the jealousy of others. See Ruth Barton, *Hedy Lamarr: The Most Beautiful Woman in Film* (Lexington: University Press of Kentucky, 2010). Lamarr is an extreme example of a more common problem that has on occasion been a topic in women's magazines, e.g., Rebecca Mead, "Hating the Beautiful," *Allure,* December 2011, 172–78.

6. Hakim, *Erotic Capital.* The discussion that follows on erotic capital draws from Hakim's book.

7. See Judith Butler, *Gender Trouble: Feminism and the Subversion of Identity* (New York: Routledge, 1990).

8. Andrea Dworkin, *Intercourse* (New York: Basic Books, 1987).

9. Naomi Wolf, *The Beauty Myth: How Images of Beauty Are Used Against Women* (New York: W. Morrow, 1991); see also discussion in Hakim, *Erotic Capital,* and Butler, *Gender Trouble.*

10. But not all of academic feminism. For an interesting discussion on "anti-pornography feminists" and "feminist sex radicals," see Amy Allen, "Pornography and Power," *Journal of Social Philosophy* 32 (2001): 512–31.

11. Elaine Scarry, *On Beauty and Being Just* (Princeton, NJ: Princeton University Press, 1999), 5–24.

12. "Tell them dear, that if eyes were made for seeing, / Then beauty is its own excuse for being" (Ralph Waldo Emerson, *The Rhodora*).

13. Ibn-Khaldun, *The Muqaddimah: An Introduction to History*, translated from Arabic by Franz Rosenthal (New York: Pantheon Books, 1958), 2:377.

14. Social scientists who emphasize external behavioral markers are uncomfortable with a notion like "feel," deeming it too subjective and thus too difficult to measure. But on another level "feel" is commonsense—we all experience it. Furthermore, it is not necessarily subjective in the sense of being a uniquely felt sense. Overwhelmingly, what we "feel" will be shared by others—it is intersubjective. For example, we all have the experience of encountering a hitherto unknown word that describes something we have had a prior "feeling" (a sense) for but were unable to articulate. For instance, few of us know the word *petrichor*. What is its definition? "The smell of rain on dry earth." Aha! That is palpable. I can feel it. I can smell it now (even if I am far from such moist earth)—the scent fills my very nostrils. Not just mine, but just about everyone who reads that definition. Yet before I had that word, all I had was a feeling, a sensation, an experience. But it turns out that many others, numbering probably in the millions, do too.

15. See the discussion in Lindsay Waters, "Literary Aesthetics: The Very Idea," *Chronicle of Higher Education*, 16 December 2005, which is also the source of the quotes from Sontag.

16. Ibid.

17. This is why exceptional novelists and writers—for instance, George Orwell—can richly inform social science when they portray life in a nuanced way, as it is experienced. In a sense, such writers capture what German philosophers called the *lebenswelt*, the life-world that is "self-evident" (in the literal sense of self-evident, i.e., as evident to the subject herself), and the world as it is lived by a shared group of people. See Edmund Husserl, who introduced the concept of the life-world, in his *Crisis of European Sciences* (Evanston, IL: Northwestern University Press, 1970).

18. From Azka Mahmood, "Muslim Fashionistas," unpublished manuscript University of South Florida, Tampa, 2010. Also see Anne Meneley, "Fashions and Fundamentalisms in Fin-De-Sicle Yemen: Chador Barbie and Islamic Socks," *Cultural Anthropology* 22 (2007): 214–43.

19. See Afshin Valinejed, "Islamic Barbie Iran Creates Culturally Correct Dolls," *Milwaukee-Wisconsin Sentinel* (Associated Press), 3 November 1996, 1.

20. Katherine Zoepf, "Bestseller in the Mideast: Barbie with a Prayer Mat," *New York Times*, 22 September 2005; and DPA, "Fulla—the Arab World's Barbie," *Khaleej Times*, 25 November 2005.

21. See the commercial website "fullashop.eu" and the webpage www.fullashop.eu/blog/fulla-articles/fulla-the-doll-with-values/.

22. Douglas Jehl, "Cairo Journal: It's Barbie vs. Laila and Sara in Mideast Culture War," *New York Times*, 2 June 1999.

23. See the website for ordering such dolls at http://lamamandismael.com/2010/06/12/la-maman-dismael-les-poupees-dune-musulmane-pour-tous-les-enfants/#comments.

24. Arlene Elowe Macleod, *Accommodating Protest: Working Women, the New Veiling, and Change in Cairo* (New York: Columbia University Press, 1991).

25. Annelies Moors, "Fashionable Muslims: Notions of Self, Religion, and Society in San'a," *Fashion Theory: The Journal of Dress, Body, and Culture* 11 (2007): 319–46, 338–40.

26. As noted in N. Smith Hefner, "Javanese Women and the Veil in Post-Suharto Indonesia," *Journal of Asian Studies* 66 (2007): 389–420; and by Mona Abaza in "Shifting Landscapes of Fashion in Contemporary Egypt," *Fashion Theory* 11: 281–98.

27. Moors, "Fashionable Muslims," 319–46.

28. I am grateful to Azka Tanveer Mahmood for this observation. Philosophers and feminist scholars have engaged in a lengthy debate over the extent of "agency"—the expression of free choice—of women who wear covering dress, from hijabs to burqas. This is a debate driven often by the politics of France's ban on the burqa and general French unease with what is understood as Muslim dress. But for all the intricate theory on this matter, the question is really an empirical one. If the dress is expressive of a woman's agency—including the desire to wear a hijab—the likelihood is that voluntary expression will be evident in individual use of cloth, color, style, and fashioning of such dress. If communal or ideological norms are being strictly enacted, this is likely evident in the uniformity of the dress in color, style, and the like. On this debate, see for example, Lila Abu-Lughod, "Do Muslim Women Really Need Saving? Anthropological Reflections on Cultural Relativism and Its Others," *American Anthropologist* 104, no. 3 (2002): 783–90; Talal Asad, *Formations of the Secular: Christianity, Islam, Modernity* (Stanford, CA: Stanford University Press, 2003); Bonnie Honig, *Democracy and the Foreigner* (Princeton, NJ: Princeton University Press, 2001); Saba Mahmood, *Politics of Piety: The Islamic Revival and the Feminist Subject* (Princeton, NJ: Princeton University Press, 2005); Peggy Phelan, *Unmarked: The Politics of Performance* (London: Routledge, 1993); and Joan Wallach Scott, *The Politics of the Veil* (Princeton, NJ: Princeton University Press, 2007).

29. Personal communication from Mark Woodward, January 18, 2011.

30. Quoted in Moors, "Fashionable Muslims," 327.

31. Ibid., 334.

32. See Gilles Lipovetsky, *The Empire of Fashion*, trans. Catherine Porter (Princeton, NJ: Princeton University Press, 1994), 155.

33. Mahmood, "Muslim Fashionistas."

34. Carla Jones, "Fashion and Faith in Indonesia," *Fashion Theory* 11 (2007): 211–32.

35. Muhammad Velji, "Seductive Piety: Faith and Fashion through Lipovetsky and Heidegger," *Comparative Studies of South Asia, Africa and the Middle East* 32, no. 1 (2012).

36. As argued in Lipovetsky, *Empire of Fashion*.

37. Moors, "Fashionable Muslims," 332.

38. Elke Bippus and Dorothea Mink, eds., *Fashion, Body, Cult* (Stuttgart: Arnoldsche Art Publishers, 2007), 192. For Chalayan, "Veils are uncodified, intractable and forbidding, while at the same time dramatic, exotic and even enchanted." See Caroline Evans, Suzy Menkes, Ted Polhemus, and Bradley Quinn with contributions by Hussein Chalayan, *Hussein Chayalan* (Rotterdam: NAI Publishers, 2005), 1858.

39. Lipovetsky, *Empire of Fashion*, 29.

40. See Charles Taylor's *A Secular Age* (Cambridge, MA: Belknap Press of Harvard University Press, 2007), 481, and Richard Sennet's *The Fall of Public Man* (New York: Knopf, 1976).

41. Muhammad Velji, "Fashionable Religiosity: Consumer Culture, Secularization, and Changes in Religious Practice," unpublished manuscript, University of South Florida, 2010.

42. Quoted in Ann Treneman, "One Glance Took Away My Freedom," *The Times* (London), 7 October 2006.

Chapter 6 · *Loathing the Feminist Mystique*

1. The Armed Islamic Group (*al-Jama'ah al-Islamiyah al-Musallaha*). The acronym GIA is from the French *Groupe Islamique Armé*.

2. Personal communication from Selma Belaala, September 21, 2010. Dr. Belaala, a French Algerian sociologist, spoke with the general in 1998–99.

3. Selma Belaala, "The Cultural Aspects of Counter-Radicalization in the Case of Algerian Women," unpublished paper, Institut d'Etudes Politiques de Paris, 2010.

4. These challenges regarding women's status in the Middle East have had broad public airing. In particular, see the *United Nations Arab Development Program's Human Development Report 2009*, accessible at http://hdr.undp.org/en/reports/regional/featured regionalreport/ahdr2009e.pdf; and the same agency's *Human Development Report* for 2011, accessible at http://hdr.undp.org/en/reports/global/hdr2011/download/; and, for a more detailed view of the question of gender, see the World Economic Forum's 2011 *Global Gender Gap Report* at www.weforum.org/reports/global-gender-gap-report-2011.

5. This problematic position of most women in the greater Middle East—a position that has in cases been exported across parts of the world through migration—is one we are constantly confronted with in the media. Explanations for this status of women generally rest in mistaken attributions to an abstracted and generic Islam (which is actually rather diverse in terms of family structure) by many in the West. Or there is denial of a general problem for women specific to the greater Middle East. This denial, or looking the other way, is especially true of those academics who claim, for example, that patriarchy in the West is little different. Or there is uneasiness, in a post-colonial world, about engaging the issue at all, feeling that Westerners have little authority in judging foreign cultures. On the conflict as one of dueling patriarchies, see Valentine M. Moghadam, "Confronting 'Empire': The New Imperialism, Islamism, and Feminism," *Political Power and Social Theory* 20 (2009): 201–26.

6. See the following: Angie Boy and Andrzej Kulczycki, "What We Know About Intimate Partner Violence in the Middle East and North Africa," *Violence Against Women* 14 (2008): 53–70; Yunus Kaya and Kimberly Cook, "A Cross-National Analysis of Physical Intimate Partner Violence Against Women," *International Journal of Comparative Sociology* 51 (2010): 423–44; S. Kishor and K. Johnson. *Profiling Domestic Violence: A Multi-Country Study* (Calverton, MD: ORC Macro, 2004); and C. Watts and C. Zimmerman, "Violence Against Women: Global Scope and Magnitude," *The Lancet*, 359 (2002):1232–37.

7. Zoltan Grossman, "The Global War on Tribes," *Counterpunch*, 13 April 2010.

8. On the differences in rates of violence between stateless societies, including tribes, vis-à-vis nation-states and other centralized states, see Steven Pinker, *The Better Angels of Our Nature: Why Violence Has Declined* (New York: Viking, 2011).

9. The sociological comparison across different religions is still significant, even if it refers to conduct that characterizes small minorities of individuals, as I noted earlier on the case of suicide statistics across religious groups.

10. Robert Pringle, "Indonesia's Moment," *Wilson Quarterly* 35 (2011): 26–33. Also see Clifford Geertz, *The Interpretation of Cultures* (New York: Basic Books, 1973).

11. The background and additional detail of developing the index and the analysis is available on www.OfVirginsandMartyrs.com.

12. Extensive research has been undertaken on "failed states." The premise has been that failed states, by failing to secure citizens' lives or property, obstruct development, breed poverty and resentment, and provide havens for terrorist groups. This is partially true. But the failed-states paradigm obscures analysis as well, because failed states are a partial proxy for what is more critical—namely, the patriarchal tribalism that by definition undermines the ability of states to succeed. The conditions of failed states often reflect the power of tribes—as in Somalia or Afghanistan—and it is the tribalism that we must first and foremost consider. See Jean-Germain Gros, "Toward a Taxonomy of Failed States in the New World Order: Decaying Somalia, Liberia, Rwanda, and Haiti," *Third World Quarterly* 17 (1996): 455–71; Gerald Helman and Steven Ratner, "Saving Failed States," *Foreign Policy* 89 (1992–93): 3–20; and Anna Simons and David Tucker, "The Misleading Problem of Failed States: A 'Socio-Geography' of Terrorism in the Post-9/11 Era," *Third World Quarterly* 28 (2007): 387–401.

13. The Tribalism Index formula is as follows:

$$\frac{Y_{TI}}{k} = X_1 + .5(X_2) + .5(X_3) + 2(X_4) + X_5$$

where X_1 is the Corruption Perceptions Index, X_2 is the Ethno-Linguistic Fractionalization Index, X_3 is the Indigenous Population as a Percentage of Total Population Data, X_4 is Gender Gap Data, and X_5 is Group Grievance Data.

Since the internal reliability of the scale is high, shifting the weightings of specific variables within the index does not significantly change the rankings of individual nations or meaningfully alter its ability to predict religiously motivated violence. Additional details on the Tribalism Index can be found on www.OfVirginsandMartyrs.com. The website also provides for the reader's interactive operation of the Index, together with visualization capabilities.

14. For this purpose, the Tribal Patriarchy Index makes use of the Gender Gap Index published annually by the World Economic Forum. Unlike other measures of gender inequality, the Gender Gap Index is not influenced by a nation's overall wealth. Although GDI, or the Gender Development Index, is a more-cited measurement of women's status, it uses overall human development to establish its rankings—that is, measures of overall poverty are merged with gender-related variables—and is therefore not appropriate for our purposes. The Gender Gap Index does, however, carefully quantify the disparate health outcomes, educational attainment rates, and representation of women in parliamentary bodies, among other variables, giving a good indication of women's position in the larger society. See World Economic Forum, *Global Gender Gap Report*, 2011.

15. The source for the corruption measures is Transparency International. This organization compiles an index that asks third parties as well as internal stakeholders about corruption within each government. Rather than focusing on how much objective corruption goes on—which would require separating nepotism from coincidence in state hiring, and contract outsourcing from cronyism in the distribution of state funds, for example—this index focuses on to what extent the state is perceived to be merely a mechanism for individuals and different parties to extort money and privilege.

16. Detailed information regarding the compilation of the group grievance variable may be accessed at the *Foreign Policy* magazine website devoted to the Failed State Index at http://www.foreignpolicy.com/failedstates. In a tribal society, we expect to see equilibrium of balanced opposition between tribes. However, when these tribes are combined within a single state with no consideration for the tribal dynamics within the national boundaries, one tribe is generally over-represented within the government. Power will thus be utilized primarily for sectarian (tribal) interests. The "state," which is essentially the bureaucracy surrounding the modernized dominant tribe, will be associated with acts of violence against sub-groups within the national boundaries— generating a high measurement on the group grievance portion of the Failed States Index.

17. The fractionalization statistical measure derives from work done by Alberto Alesina, Arnaud Devleeschauwer, William Easterly, Sergio Kurlat, and Romain Wacziarg; see Alberto Alesina et al., "Fractionalization," *Journal of Economic Growth* 8, no. 2 (2003): 155–94. The Index includes, as noted, the percentage of the country's population that is made up of peoples indigenous to that country's territory. The larger the proportion of indigenous peoples present will, in this context, add modestly to levels of tribalism. This measure complements the fractionalization component and was derived from a variety of reference sources, such as the *CIA World Factbook*.

18. In statistical terms, we control for levels of patriarchal tribalism and allow the statistical model to simulate the effects between countries as though they had the same level of patriarchy.

19. In the determination of violence exportation, individual incidences of religious terrorism in the NCTC database from 2005 to 2010 were aggregated first by nationality of perpetrator or perpetrating group. An additional sub-total level was added within these groups, aggregating the number of incidences committed outside of national borders. The latter number was then divided by the former, giving a percent of incidences exported.

20. Richard N. Haass, "The Restoration Doctrine," *American Interest*, January/February, 2012, www.the-american-interest.com/article.cfm?piece=1164.

21. Mounira Charrad, *States and Women's Rights: The Making of Postcolonial Tunisia, Algeria, and Morocco* (Berkeley: University of California Press, 2001).

22. Peter G. Mandaville, *Global Political Islam* (London: Routledge, 2007), 260 n 6.

23. See Ernest Gellner, "The Tribal Society and Its Enemies," in *The Conflict of Tribe and State in Iran and Afghanistan,* ed. Richard Tapper (London: Croom Helm, 1983), 437.

24. Jess Bravin, "U.S. Witness Doesn't Link Bin Laden Driver to Attacks," *Wall Street Journal,* 24 July 2008, A4.

25. Noor Huda Ismail, "The Role of Kinship in Indonesia's Jemaah Islamiya," *Terrorism Monitor* 4:11, 2 June 2006. www.jamestown.org/single/?no_cache=1&tx_ttnews[tt_news]=791.

26. Ibid.

27. Mandaville, *Global Political Islam,* 259; Gamal Moursi Badr, "Islamic Law: Its Relation to Other Legal Systems," *American Journal of Comparative Law* 26 (1978): 187–98; and Nikos Passas, "Demystifying Hawala: A Look into its Social Organization and Mechanics," *Journal of Scandinavian Studies in Criminology and Crime Prevention* 7 (2006): 46–62.

28. See Michael Hastings, "The Runaway General," *Rolling Stone,* 22 June 2010.

29. Stanley A. McChrystal, "It Takes a Network: The New Frontline of Modern Warfare," *Foreign Policy,* March/April 2011.

30. See chapter 9 in Sayyid Qutb, *Milestones* (Indianapolis, IN: American Trust, 1990).

31. I am grateful to Didier Chaudet for this information from his research in Pakistan. See also Norman Cigar, *Al-Qaida, the Tribes, and the Government: Lessons and Prospects for Iraq's Unstable Triangle,* Middle East Studies Occasional Papers, No. 2 (Quantico, VA: Marine Corps University Press, 2011).

32. Charles Levinson and Margaret Coker, "Al Qaeda's Deep Tribal Ties Make Yemen a Terror Hub," *Wall Street Journal,* 22 January 2010, A1. Levinson and Coker note how Al Qaeda also included the Yemeni tribes in their propaganda. In an audio tape released on February 22, 2009, Ayman Al Zawahiri, Osama bin Laden's deputy, asked the Yemeni tribes to protect Al Qaeda operatives just as tribes in Pakistan and Afghanistan had done: "I call on the noble and defiant tribes of the Yemen and tell them: 'Don't be less than your brothers in the defiant Pashtun and Baluch tribes,'" Mr. Zawahiri said in the recording. Marriages were highlighted. In August 2009, *Sada al-Malahim,* Al Qaeda's online newsletter in Yemen, announced the marriage of one of Al Qaeda's leaders, Mohammed al-Umda, to a local tribeswoman.

Chapter 7 · Thoughts and Consequences

1. Quoted in Peter Mandaville, *Global Political Islam* (New York: Routledge, 2007), 237.

2. Reuven Paz, "Debates within the Family: Jihadi-Salafi Debates on Strategy, Takfir, Extremism, Suicide Bombings, and the Sense of the Apocalypse," in *Global Salafism: Islam's New Religious Movement,* ed. Roel Meijer (New York: Columbia University Press, 2009), 235–48.

3. Mandaville, *Global Political Islam,* and Mandaville, *Transnational Muslim Politics: Re-Imagining the Umma* (New York: Routledge, 2001).

4. Mandaville, *Global Political Islam.*

5. See Alexi Vasilliev, *The History of Saudi Arabia* (New York: New York University Press, 2000).

6. Mandaville, *Global Political Islam.*

7. On the Muslim Brotherhood, see Gilles Kepel, *Jihad: The Trail of Political Islam,* trans. Anthony F. Roberts (Cambridge, MA: Belknap Press of Harvard University Press, 2002).

8. Mandaville, *Transnational Muslim Politics,* 66–68.

9. Ibid.

10. See "Bin Laden's 'Letter to America'," *The Guardian,* 24 November 2002.

11. Quoted from: Sayyid Qutb, *Milestones* (Islamic Book Services—SIME, 2005), 3–4.

12. Ibid., 4.

13. Ibid., 1.

14. Ibid., 16.

15. Ibid., 23.

16. Ibid., 60.

17. Ibid., 67–68.

18. Kamal Abdel-Malek, ed., *America in an Arab Mirror: Images of America in Arabic Travel Literature: An Anthology, 1895–1995* (New York: St. Martin's Press 2000), 20. The original source is Sayyid Qutb ash- Shaheed, *The America I Have Seen*, Kashf ul Shubu-hat Publications, [no place of publication noted], 1951.

19. Ibid., 22–23.

20. Quoted from Jonathan Raban, *My Holy War: Dispatches from the Home Front* (New York: New York Review of Books, 2006), 25.

21. Ibid., and in Sayyid Qutb, *In the Shade of the Qur'ān*, translated from the Arabic and edited by Adil Salahi (Markfield: Islamic Foundation, 2005).

22. The listener is also clearly, in the imaginary of such polemics of Qutb, male.

23. Qutb recounted the story of the attack by a drunken, semi-naked woman, alleg-edly sent by the Central Intelligence Agency, to his biographer Salah 'Abd al-Fattah, and it is re-told in Jonathan Raban, *My Holy War*, 2006.

24. For more on tribal globalism, see Hassan Mneimneh, "The Lessons of the Jihad-ist Insurgency in Saudi Arabia," in *Conflict and Insurgency in the Contemporary Middle East*, ed. Barry Rubin (New York: Routledge, 2009), 71–82.

25. Mark Woodward, "Tropes of the Crusades in Indonesian Muslim Discourse," *Contemporary Islam* 4 (2010): 311–30. Woodward writes, "Denunciations of Jews and Zion-ists, who are said to dominate the world economy and dictate US foreign policy, are often coupled with demands for an end to paper money. . . . There are perhaps thirty Jews [living] in Indonesia. When I first visited the country [in 1978], no one thought or wrote much about Jews. Today anti-Semitism is rampant. . . . Many Indonesians accept [the] scandal-ous forgery [the *Protocols of the Elders of Zion*] as an accurate account of the world eco-nomic order."

26. Kepel, *Jihad: The Trail of Political Islam*, 40.

27. For a full reading of the Marxist political economy approach, see Karl Marx, *Capi-tal*, vol. 1, ed. Frederick Engels, trans. Samuel Moore and Edward Aveling (New York: Appleton and Company, 1889).

28. For Qutb, "British Imperialism was characterized as merely one aspect of a more wide-ranging and sinister form of collective enmity—that of the secular materialist, in-dividualist and capitalist West." See Charles Tripp, "Sayid Qutb: The Political Vision," in *Pioneers of Islamic Revival*, ed. A. Rahnema (London: Zed Books, 1994), 158, quoted in Mandaville, *Global Political Islam*, 77.

29. Mandaville, *Global Political Islam*.

30. Frantz Fanon, *Damnés de la Terre* (New York: Grove Press, 1963).

31. Herman Bernstein, "As Tolstoy Views the World at Eighty Years: Reform of Social Conditions, He Believes, Cannot Be Accomplished through Violent Means, But Only by Spreading Vital Ideas." *New York Times*, 9 August 1908, SM6.

32. Saskia Sassen, *Territory, Authority, Rights: From Medieval to Global Assemblages* (Princeton, NJ: Princeton University Press, 2008).

33. Michael T. Flynn, Matt Pottinger, and Paul D. Batchelor, *Fixing Intel: A Blueprint for Making Intelligence Relevant in Afghanistan*, Center for a New American Security, Washington, DC, January 2010.

34. Diego Gambetta, "Can We Make Sense of Suicide Missions?" in *Making Sense of Suicide Missions*, ed. Gambetta (Oxford: Oxford University Press, 2005), 263. See also Robert A. Pape, "The Strategic Logic of Suicide Terrorism," *American Political Science*

Review 97 (2003): 343–61; and Ariel Merari, "Social, Organizational, and Psychological Factors in Suicide Terrorism," in *Root Causes of Terrorism: Myths, Reality, and Ways Forward*, ed. Tore Bjørgo (London: Routledge 2005), 70–86; cited in Gambetta, *Making Sense of Suicide Missions.*

35. Gambetta, *Making Sense of Suicide Missions*, 263

36. Though much discussion emerged regarding Muslim women suicide bombers such as the Chechen "black widows," the great majority have been men. However, in principle, women who undertake such acts can share the same symbolism of sacrifice, purity, and restored honor. On women suicide bombers, see Mia Bloom, "Female Suicide Bombers: A Global Trend," *Daedalus* 136 (2007): 94–102; Debra D. Zedalis, *Female Suicide Bombers* (Carlisle, PA: Strategic Studies Institute, U.S. Army War College, 2004); and Cindy D. Ness, *Female Terrorism and Militancy: Agency, Utility, and Organization* (New York: Routledge, 2008).

37. Gambetta, *Making Sense of Suicide Missions.*

38. Emile Durkheim, *Suicide: A Study in Sociology*, New York: Free Press, 1997.

39. Osama Bin Laden, "Warning," *BBC News*, 7 October 2001.

40. Olivier Grojean, "The Violence Against the Self: The Case of Kurdish Non-Islamist Group," in *The Enigma of Islamist Violence*, ed. A. Bucaille, Laetitia Blom, and Luis Martinez (New York: Columbia University Press, 2007), 107.

41. "Saudi Cleric Omar al-Sweilem Extols the Breasts and Thighs of the Black-Eyed Virgins of Paradise," www.youtube.com/watch?v=6okEEdkWgzE.

Chapter 8 · Europe's Winter of Discontent

1. Many conservatives had been critical of multiculturalism though many came around to it. Infamously, the Member of Parliament Eliot Powell delivered his "rivers of blood" speech warning against further immigration from Commonwealth countries in 1968. (The phrase "rivers of blood" does not appear in the speech, but it does include the line, "As I look ahead, I am filled with foreboding; like the Roman, I seem to see 'the River Tiber foaming with much blood.'") However, the speech, which caused his dismissal from Edward Heath's shadow government, concerned race rather than religion. (Heath was Prime Minister from 1970 to 1974.)

2. Although a fatwa is generally a ruling regarding proper Islamic practice, the fact that it has come to mean the imposition of a death sentence in the Western mind shows how deeply ingrained this episode is in the Western collective mentality.

3. Gilles Kepel, *Jihad: The Trail of Political Islam*, trans. Anthony F. Roberts (Cambridge, MA: The Belknap Press of Harvard University Press, 2002), 9.

4. Kennan Malik, "Salman Rushdie: The Book Burning that Changed Britain Forever," *The Times* (London), 1 February 2009.

5. Sue Clough and Sean O'Neill, "Muslim Cut[s] his Daughter's Throat for Taking a Christian Boyfriend," *Daily Telegraph*, 30 September 2003. See also Sandra Laville, "Tide of 'Culture Clash' Violence Worries Police," *Daily Telegraph*, 30 September 2003, and "Police to Target Wave of Murders in the Name of Family Honor," *Daily Telegraph*, 10 March 2003. The section that follows draws in part from my chapter, "Multiculturalism, Gender, and Rights," in *Migrations and Mobilities*, ed. Seyla Benhabib and Judith Resnik (New York: New York University Press, 2009), 304–32.

6. Caroline Alexander and Charles Goldsmith, "U.K. 'Honor Killings,' Cloaked in Family Silence, Stymie Police," *Bloomberg.Com*, 16 January 2007.

7. Statistics for the United Kingdom obtained under the Freedom of Information Act in 2011 by the Iranian and Kurdish Women's Rights Organization (Ikwro), for the 39 police forces that gave Ikwro figures, show 2,823 honor crimes in 2010. Police forces in 13 areas did not provide data. Such recorded violence—which can include murder, abduction, acid attacks, beatings, forced marriage, and mutilation—is likely only the "tip of the iceberg," Ikwro campaigners say, since many incidents go unreported because of victims' fears of recriminations. See Rachel Williams, "Honour Crimes against Women in UK Rising Rapidly, Figures Show," *Guardian*, 2 December 2011.

8. Ibid. Veena Raleigh, from the University of Surrey, is cited in the article for the suicide statistics.

9. Doriane Lambelet Coleman, "The Seattle Compromise: Multicultural Sensitivity and Americanization," *Duke Law Journal* 47 (1998): 717–84.

10. Bonnie, Honig, "My Culture Made Me Do It," in *Is Multiculturalism Bad for Women?* ed. Joshua Cohen, Matthew Howard, and Martha Nussbaum (Princeton, NJ: Princeton University Press, 1999), 35–40.

11. Alison Dundes Renteln, "Cross-Cultural Dispute Resolution: The Consequences of Conflicting Interpretations of Norms," *Willamette Journal of International Dispute Resolution* 10 (2002): 108–11. The court statement cited here is quoted in Renteln.

12. On "invented" or "edited" culture, see Eric Hobsbawm, *Nations and Nationalism since 1780: Programme, Myth, Reality* (New York: Cambridge University Press, 1990).

13. State v. Latif Al-Hussaini, 579 N.W.2d 561, 563, Neb. Ct. App. 1998.

14. Ibid.

15. That was an innovation from the traditional judicial position of not crossing national borders; earlier cases would ascertain, for example, the "whiteness" (often understood in cultural, not racial, terms) of Muslims, Hindus, and others in order to measure successful assimilation into American society. Congress had, in its first formal pronouncement on citizenship, restricted naturalization in 1790 to "white persons." This requirement for citizenship remained in force until 1952. Applicants from China, Japan, Burma, and the Philippines, as well as those of mixed-race background, failed in their efforts to become citizens. Mexicans and Armenians were classified as white. There were borderline cases as far as the courts were concerned, and in such cases the courts wavered. See, for example, *Ex Parte Mohriez*, 54 F. Supp. 941 (D. Mass. 1944) (granting an Arabian immigrant's petition because he was found to be a member of the white race). For a general discussion, see Ian F. Haney López, *White by Law: The Legal Constructions of Race* (New York: New York University Press, 1996).

16. Robert M. Cover, "*Nomos* and Narrative," *Harvard Law Review* 97 (1983): 11, 18, 23, 29.

17. Celia W. Dugger, "Rites of Anguish: A Special Report; Gender Ritual Is Unyielding in Africa," *New York Times*, 5 October 1996, A4, quoted in Susan Moller Okin, "Is Multiculturalism Bad for Women?" in *Is Multiculturalism Bad for Women?* ed. Cohen, Howard, and Nussbaum, 14. See also Elizabeth Heger Boyle, *Female Genital Cutting: Cultural Conflict in the Global Community* (Baltimore: Johns Hopkins University Press, 2002), chap. 5.

18. Although her name appears as Kasinga in the legal case materials, in her autobiography she spells her name "Kassindja." For the sake of simplicity, I retain the "legal"

spelling. See Fauziya Kassindja and Layli Miller Bashir, *Do They Hear You When You Cry?* (New York: Delacorte Press, 1998).

19. *In re* Kasinga, 21 I. & N. Dec. 357, BIA 1996.

20. The only exception was for surgery essential for the health of the patient, and then to be undertaken by a licensed physician.

21. Pub. L. No. 104–208, 110 Stat. 3009, 1997, cited and quoted in Carol M. Messito, "Regulating Rites: Legal Responses to Female Genital Mutilation in the West," *Buffalo Journal of Public Interest Law* 16 (1997–98): 33–77.

22. Boyle, *Female Genital Cutting*, 90.

23. Bronwyn Winter, "Women, the Law, and Cultural Relativism in France: The Case of Excision," *Signs: Journal of Women in Culture and Society* 19 (1994): 943.

24. Boyle, *Female Genital Cutting*, 83–110, and Messito, "Regulating Rites," 49–54. The term *female circumcision* is something of a misnomer, implying equivalence to male circumcision, and understates the profound impact for women's sexuality of most female genital mutilations. The male equivalent (sexually, not reproductively) would be, as a number of observers have suggested, "penidectomy," or the removal of all or most of the penis.

25. Quotations cited and case reported in Jane Maynard, "Re J (Child's Religious Upbringing and Circumcision)," *Family Court Reports* 1 (2000): 307–14.

26. Erving Goffman, *Relations in Public: Microstudies of the Public Order* (New York: Basic Books, 1971). The section that follows draws from my "New Frontiers: Territory, Social Spaces, and the State," *Sociological Forum* 12 (1997): 121–33.

27. Edward Alsworth Ross, *Social Control* (New York: Macmillan, 1908), cited in Goffman, *Relations in Public*, 6.

28. Goffman, *Relations in Public*, 6.

29. A lively academic debate has taken place on multiculturalism and the issue of conflicting cultural practices. See in particular Will Kymlicka, *Multicultural Citizenship: A Liberal Theory of Minority Rights* (Oxford: Oxford University Press, 1995). See also the discussion on the United Kingdom and French models below in chapter 10.

30. F. Dhondy, "Our Islamic Fifth Column," *City Limits*, vol. 11, no. 4 (2001). Phillips also said that multiculturalism was out of date and no longer useful, not least because it encouraged "separateness" between communities. He suggested said that there was an urgent need to "assert a core of Britishness" across society. See also "Britain 'Sleepwalking' to Segregation," *Guardian*, 19 September 2005.

31. Before the 1996 Act of Arbitration, Sharia courts were not officially allowed to operate in the United Kingdom. But a number of Sharia courts have been active in the UK for many years. According to statements of Muslim community leaders obtained by the London *Times*, the first Sharia court was established in Birmingham in 1982. Additional courts were established elsewhere in the country subsequently. The Arbitration Act of 1996 set out rules under which parties in a dispute were to be allowed to use "impartial" tribunals outside of the civil courts. The first Sharia courts under this Act were formally established in 2007, and their decisions are legally binding. The courts were initially allowed by the government to arbitrate on a range of business and financial disputes if both parties consented in advance to the Sharia court's decisions. The courts have since expanded into family law. Some allege that the Sharia courts have strayed into on criminal matters, which are still under the jurisdiction of the Civil Courts. See Neil Addison, "Foreword: Sharia Tribunals in Britain—Mediators or Arbitrators," in *Sharia Law or 'One*

Law for All'? ed. D. Green (London: CIVITAS, 2009); Murad Ahmed and Frances Gibb, "From Layton to Dewsbury, Sharia Courts Are Already Settling Disputes," *The Times*, 8 Febuary 2008; Fiona Barton and Alex McBride, "A Brutal Beating and Justice Meted Out in a Humble Back Street Cafe: How Sharia Law Already Operate in Britain," *Daily Mail*, 10 February 2008; Nick Tarry, "Religious Courts Already in Use," *BBC*, 7 February 2008; "Sharia Rulings 'Can Go to Court,' " *BBC* 2008; and Colin Brown, "Let Us Adopt Islamic Family Law to Curb Extremists, Muslims Tell Kelly," *The Independent*, 15 August 1996.

Chapter 9 · An Education

1. A study showed that, for example, a Christian citizen of France with an African background was two and a half times more likely to be called for a job interview than a similarly qualified Muslim citizen with the same ethnic background. See Claire Adida, David Laitin, and Marie-Ann Valfort, *Proceedings of the National Academy of Sciences*, November 22, 2010, www.pnas.org/content/early/2010/11/17/1015550107.

2. For evidence of this happening in the riots of the 1980s, see Doug Saunders, *How the Largest Migration in History is Reshaping Our World* (New York: Pantheon Books, 2010). For a more contemporary viewpoint, see Sylvia Poggiolo, "French Muslim Women Forge New Islam Activism," *National Public Radio*, 25 January 2008. Available on the Internet at www.npr.org/templates/story/story.php?storyId=18119226.

3. See Jonathan Laurence, *The Emancipation of Europe's Muslims: The State's Role in Minority Integration* (Princeton, NJ: Princeton University Press, 2012). The French scholar Jocelyne Cesari put it this way, following the 2005 French riots in the *banlieues*:

> It is ironic to note that the American media have had no qualms in using terms such as "intifada" or "jihad" to describe the recent riots, whereas both in France and throughout Europe, the emphasis has been placed primarily on social and economic conditions. Indeed, neither Islam nor religious concerns were motivating factors in the riots. The proof, as reported by Xavier Ternisien in the November 9, 2005 edition of *Le Monde*, is that attempts by the heads of the UOIF (Union of French Islamic Associations) to communicate with the young rioters and bring them back to reason and calm met with little success. ("Ethnicity, Islam, and Les Banlieues: Confusing the Issues," *Social Science Research Council, Forum on Civil Unrest in the French Suburbs*, 30 November 2005)

Though Cesari may in large part be correct, the rejection of the UOIF does not *ipso facto* negate the role of Islam as such, but rather of a particular "official" or establishment Islam.

4. See, for example, Christopher Caldwell, *Reflections on the Revolution in Europe: Immigration, Islam and the West* (New York: Doubleday, 2009); and Melanie Phillips, *Londonistan* (London: Encounter Books, 2006).

5. Tony Blair, *A Journey* (London: Hutchinson, 2010), 104.

6. For more on this discussion, see Hans-Peter Shavit and Yossi Blossfeld, *Persistent Inequality: Changing Educational Attainment in Thirteen Countries* (Boulder, CO: Westview, 1993); and also T. Fabian, "Persistent Inequality in Education Attainment and Its Institutional Context," *European Sociological Review* 24 (2008): 543–65.

7. Regarding the limited consideration of gender and national integration issues, see, for example, Patrick Simon's presentation, "Beyond Assimilation: The Second Generation in France," *Centre for Comparative Immigration Studies*, 18 January 2011. Available on the Internet at http://ccis.ucsd.edu/2011/01/patrick-simon-beyond-assimilation-the-second -generation-in-france/#.

8. These numbers are further explored in Yann Algan, Christian Dustmann, Albrecht Glitz, and Alan Manning, *The Economic Situation of First- and Second-Generation Immigrants in France, Germany and the United Kingdom*, CEP Discussion Paper No. 951, Centre for Economic Performance, October 2009. Although second-generation female immigrants from Muslim countries in both the UK and France made large gains over the first-generation women, they are doing better in terms of education and workforce participation in France than in Britain. Maghribi women in France have more years of full-time education and higher rates of employment in the aggregate, compared to Pakistani and Bangladeshi women in Britain.

9. Daniel Nilsson DeHanas, "Believing Citizens: Religion and Civic Engagement among London's Second Generation Youth" (Ph.D. diss., University of North Carolina at Chapel Hill, 2010).

10. I benefited from conversations with Jonathan Githens-Mazer, University of Exeter, regarding his research findings, in September 2011.

11. This topic is further explored in Zacharias Pieri, "Prohibiting Sins and Promoting Virtues in Contemporary Islam: The Case Study of Shari'a Zones in London and Lessons From Further Afield," unpublished paper, University of Exeter, 2012; and Michael Cooke, *Forbidding Wrong in Islam* (Cambridge: Cambridge University Press, 2003).

12. Abt SRBI conducted the survey for a multi-university and international research team, funded by a grant from the Minerva competition of the U.S. Secretary of Defense and administered by the Office of Naval Research. The survey was conducted in the period from June to August 2011 in France, Germany, the United Kingdom, Niger, Senegal, Nigeria, and Malaysia. The sample was n=2,800 completed interviews for an n=400 per country. David Jacobson was the director of the survey, and the survey instrument was developed in collaboration with the research team of the Minerva grant. The research team included in-country specialists and researchers. Abt SRBI provided advice regarding question order, wording, and content, as well as executing the surveys and quality control. Interviews were conducted in multiple languages (including that of immigrant populations in Europe) and were translated and back translated, using additional translators when discrepancies arose. The sample was representative of the population. The survey was conducted after strict independent human subjects review and with prior host country acknowledgement. Additional information is available on www.OfVirginsand Martyrs.com.

13. All the commissioned survey results reported in this book are significant at p<.000.

14. For a discussion of future Muslim population projections, see *The Future of the Global Muslim Population: Projections for 2010–2030*, Pew Research Center, 27 January 2011. It is available at http://pewforum.org/future-of-the-global-muslim-population-regional -europe.aspx.

15. Mehmood Naqshbandi, "Islam and Muslims in Britain: A Guide," *Muslims in Britain .org*, http://guide.muslimsinbritain.org/guide3.html#3.3.1.

16. *Future of the Global Muslim Population.*

17. Office for National Statistics (ONS), *Education: Ethnicity and Identity* (London: ONS, 2006), www.statistics.gov.uk/cci/nugget.asp?id=461. The ethnic group aggregate differences noted here date from 2004. The British education system is divided into a number of types of education, with the two main ones being the state sector and the public sector (which in Britain means private schools). The majority of schools belong to the state sector, with all of the schools under the state sector operating the same grading system as recommended by the government. This is also true of the public school system, although some public schools allow their students to sit European style exams that they regard as more rigorous. For the most part, the vast majority of students at the age of 16 must sit the General Certificate of Secondary Education (GCSE). It is a legal obligation for all young people to attend school until this age and take the GCSE exams. Between the age of 16 years and 18 years an increasing number of students progress to take Advance Level (A Level) qualifications, and it is these grades that allow students to apply to University. The basic way the grading system works in Britain at GCSE Level is that each student is awarded a grade from A* to G for each subject in which they take an exam. The A* grade is the best grade a student can achieve, with G denoting a fail. The government has set a target stating that they want more young people in Britain attaining at least 5 A*–C grades at GCSE. The importance of this is that in order to proceed to A Level and then on to university, 5 A*–C grades is the minimum expectation.

18. Office for National Statistics (ONS), *Education: Ethnicity and Identity.*

19. QED, *Muslim Graduates in the Labour Market,* A Seminar Report, 2005. See also http://qed-uk.org/050719.php. In 2004, people from Bangladeshi, black Caribbean, and Pakistani ethnic groups were less likely than white British people to have a degree (or equivalent qualification). Among men, those of Bangladeshis and black Caribbean origin were the least likely to have a degree—11% for each group. Among women, those of Bangladeshi and Pakistani origin were less likely to have a degree—5% and 10%, respectively. This would also seem to suggest that while Bangladeshi and Pakistani females outperform their male cohort at school, fewer females than males from these groups continue on to degree-level qualifications, although there is some recent evidence that the gap is narrowing. Angela Dale, Nusrat Shaheen, Virinder Kalra, and Edward Fieldhouse note in "Routes to Education and Employment for Young Pakistani and Bangladeshi Women in the UK," *Ethnic and Racial Studies* 25 (2002): 942–68, that although Bangladeshi and Pakistani men are out-graduating women at post-secondary levels of education, gender gaps in application and enrollment numbers are receding. By the 1999/2000 school year, Bangladeshi and Pakistani women represented 44% and 46%, respectively, of first-year UK domiciled degree-level undergraduates. This is an increase from 38% for both groups just five years prior. However, Pakistani and Bangladeshi women in Britain still lag behind their Maghribi counterparts in France, of whom 20–30% hold a university degree, according to the *Trajectoires et Origines* survey in 2008.

20. Z. Bunglawala, *Valuing Family, Valuing Work: British Muslim Women and the Labour Market* (London: London Development Agency and The Young Foundation, 2009), 4.

21. See Joanne Lindley, Angela Dale, and Shirley Dex, "Ethnic Differences in Women's Demographic Family Characteristics and Economic Activity Profiles, 1992 to 2002," *Labour Market Trends* 112 (2004): 153–65.

22. Bunglawala, *Valuing Family, Valuing Work.*

23. Office for National Statistics, *Focus on Ethnicity and Identity*, 2006, www.statistics .gov.uk/cci/nugget.asp?id=462.

24. Ibid.

25. The main economically inactive groups, as officially defined, are students, people looking after family and home, long-term sick and disabled, temporarily sick and disabled, retired people, and discouraged workers. The UK National Statistics website explains, "Economic inactivity is measured in the UK by the Labour Force Survey (LFS) and consists of people aged 16 and over without a job who have not sought work in the last four weeks and/or are not available to start work in the next two weeks." See www.statistics .gov.uk/hub/labour-market/people-not-in-work/economic-inactivity.

26. See Bunglawala, *Valuing Family, Valuing Work.*

27. See, for example, N. D. Tackey, J. Casbourne, J. Aston, H. Ritchie, A. Sinclair, C. Tyers, J. Hurstfield, R. Willison and R. Page, *Barriers to Employment for Pakistanis and Bangladeshis in Britain*, Institute for Employment Studies, commissioned by the UK Department for Work and Pensions, September 2006. See www.employment-studies.co.uk /pubs/summary.php?id=dwp360.

28. Ibid.

29. Avtar Brah, *Cartographies of Diaspora: Contesting Identities* (London: Routledge, 1996).

30. Response of Shagufta, 20-year-old female Pakistani Student quoted in D. Tyrer and A. Ahmad, *Muslim Women and Higher Education: Identities, Experiences and Prospects: A Summary Report* (Liverpool: Liverpool University and European Social Fund, 2006).

31. Lindley, Dale, and Dex, "Ethnic Differences."

32. In fact, the British Labour Force Survey, with data collected from 2000 to 2002, showed that less than 20% of Pakistani and Bangladeshi women who were without dependent children and who were 35 or over worked either full or part-time. This held true whether the women were single or married. Married females of White English, Black Caribbean, Black African, and Indian descent see less than half these levels of inactivity after having children, and they also return to the labor market full or part-time as children become more independent in much higher numbers—over 70% for White British, Black Caribbean, and Black African, and over 60% for Indian. These data are explored further in Lindley, Dale, and Dex, "Ethnic Differences."

33. Bunglawala, *Valuing Family, Valuing Work*, 46.

34. Nii Djan Tackey, Jo Casebourne, Jane Aston, Helen Ritchie, Alice Sinclair, Claire Tyers, Jennifer Hurstfield, Rebecca Willison, and Rosie Page, *Barriers to Employment for Pakistanis and Bangladeshis in Britain*, Department for Work and Pensions, Research Report No. 360, Leeds, 2006.

35. A report for the London Development Agency by the Young Foundation has argued that the "widespread perception that Muslim men and families do not let women work, or that they hold Muslim women back is a myth—or at least no longer true in twenty-first-century Britain." Another report suggested that real or perceived religious discrimination is a barrier to Muslim women becoming an active part of the British workforce. Women wanting to wear the hijab or niqab to work were viewed as a principle concern. See Bunglawala, *Valuing Family, Valuing Work.*

36. Sarah Cassidy, "Second Generation Ethnic Minorities Make 'Remarkable Progress' in Work," *The Independent*, 31 August 2006. The study examined data from the

General Household Survey and the Labour Force Survey for 34 consecutive years be-tween 1972 and 2005. For the original study, see: Yaojun Li and Anthony Heath, "Minor-ity Ethnic Men in British Labour Markets," *International Journal of Sociology and Social Policy* 28, no. 5/6 (2008): 231–44.

37. The finding is open to interpretation, but one possibility is that it reflects a com-bination of the pressures of patriarchy and discrimination. This set of data emerges as a result of the following question in the 2001 UK Census: "Over the last 12 months would you say your health has on the whole been Good, Fairly Good, Not Good." Across all reli-gions (and those with no religion), with the exception of Buddhists, women were far more likely to rate their health as "not good." This difference across the women and men was most noticeable in Muslim women (16%), Sikh women (14%), and Hindu women (11%). These rates were all 3 to 4 percentage points higher than their respective male counter-parts. The differences between males and females among Christians were minimal, and no difference existed between those who said they had no religious faith. Muslims had the highest rate of disability when factoring in age. Almost a quarter of Muslim females (24%) and one-fifth of Muslim men (21%) reported a disability. Office for National Statis-tics, *Focus on Religion: Health and Disability*, 2004, http://www.statistics.gov.uk/cci/nugget .asp?id=959.

38. French government estimate. See "Muslims in Europe: Country Guide," *BBC News*, 23 December 2005, available online at http://news.bbc.co.uk/2/hi/europe/4385768 .stm.

39. See Sonia Tebbakh, *Muslims in the EU: Cities Report, France*, Open Society Institute, EU Monitoring and Advocacy Program, 2007. http://www.soros.org/initiatives/home /articles_publications/publications/museucities_20080101/museucitiesfra_20080101 .pdf.

40. See Pew Report, *The Future of the Global Muslim Population: Projections for 2010 –2030*, 2011.

41. The French education system is divided in two main sectors: the state sector and several types of private schools. All public and private schools are operating according to the same grading system as recommended by the French government. For the most part, the vast majority of students at the age of 14 must take the General Certificate of Second-ary Education (GCSE). After this first step of secondary school, several choices of *lycée* (a second round of secondary school between the ages of 16 and 18) are possible: *lycée general* (the most prestigious), *lycée professionnel*, and *lycée technologique* (vocational schools). At the end of the second step of secondary school, students at the age of 17 or 18 must take the baccalaureate (school-leaving certificate), which is compulsory in order to apply to univer-sity. After baccalaureate, students can choose to attend university, preparatory schools (business schools, for instance), or college for further education.

42. See *Trajectories et Origines Survey Ined-INSEE*, 2008. http://teo.site.ined.fr/.

43. For those of Algerian descent, men's advantage is modest. Some 25% of the first-generation males have a university degree, compared to 22% of the women. The gap is similar for men and women in terms of GCSE: 18% and 13%, respectively. Among those without any educational certification, men are at 25% and women are at 30%. First-generation Moroccans and Tunisian show a similar disparity when it comes to gender, favoring men by about 5% in terms of a university degree, and 3% for a General Certifi-cate of Education. For first-generation immigrants from Portugal, Spain, Italy, and the

other European Union countries, the numbers are reversed: Women do much better than men in educational attainment.

44. See *Trajectories et Origines Survey*. In terms of those entering working-age without any qualifications, a much smaller proportion of women of Spanish and Italian descent are doing so in the second generation, compared to an increase in the proportion for men. However, for immigrants from other European countries, we see the reverse, with larger proportions of women entering working-age without qualifications than the first generation, and smaller proportions for men.

45. Ibid. The data accords with those of other surveys. See A. Dupray, S. Moullet, "Quelles discriminations à l'encontre des jeunes d'origine maghrébine à l'entrée du marché du travail en France," in M. Maruani, D. Meulders, R. Silvera, C. Sofer, et al., "Marché du Travail et Genre dans les Pays du Maghreb," *Brussels Economic Series*, Editions du DULBEA, 2004; A. Frikey, J. Murdoch, J. L. Primon, "Les Débuts dans la Vie Active des Jeunes Après des Études Supérieures," CEREQ, NEF, 2004; and R. Silberman and I. Fournier, "Les Enfants D'immigrés sur le Marché du Travail, les Mécanismes D'une Discrimination Sélective," *Formation Emploi* 65 (1999): 31–55.

46. See *Trajectories et Origines Survey*.

47. A suggestive (if controversial) German study suggests that the likely outcome for males falling behind, while having grown up in highly patriarchal environments—that is, where their social and economic status is in opposition to the patriarchal narrative and rhetoric—is more violently oriented males. See Dirk Baier, Christian Pfeiffer, Susann Rabold, Julia Simonson, Cathleen Kappes, *Kinder und Jugendliche in Deutschland: Gewalterfahrungen, Integration, Medienkonsum*, Forschungsbericht 109 (Kriminologisches Forschunginstitut Niedersachsen E.V., 2010). For an English news report, see DPA, "Study Claims Devout Youth More Prone to Violence," *Gulf Times*, 10 June 2010.

Chapter 10 · Islamist Tipping Points

1. Quoted in Olinka Koster, "British Soldier a 'Home Grown Terrorist' Extremist Website Claims," *Daily Mail*, 5 July 2006. See also Matthew Hickley, "First British Muslim Soldier Killed in 'War on Terror," *Daily Mail*, 4 July 2006.

2. Quoted in Koster, "British Soldier."

3. The data for the United Kingdom are available in Robin Simcox, Hannah Stuart, and Houriya Ahmed, *Islamist Terrorism: The British Connections* (London: Centre for Social Cohesion, 2011). The French data is difficult to get in a publicly available, collected form. Working with research assistants Leyla Arslan and Rafael Serrano, I examined the biographical data for approximately sixty terrorism-related convictions in both the UK and France in the 1990s through 2010. The data were collected from all available public information sources, relying primarily on data in *Islamist Terrorism: The British Connections* by the Centre for Social Cohesion and from French and British news reports and the research of Leyla Arslan and Rafael Serrano.

The data collected for the French case are available on www.OfVirginsandMartyrs.com. Individual converts to Islam were separated from the analysis—these cases warrant separate consideration given their unique circumstances and backgrounds.

4. In this section, I have benefited greatly from the writings of, and ongoing conversations with, Joanna Rozpedowski, from 2010 to 2012.

5. The literature is extensive indeed and growing constantly. Most of the academic arguments tend to favor, generally on normative grounds, the Anglo-American model. I note here some of the major writings: Talal Asad, *Formations of the Secular* (Stanford, CA: Stanford University Press, 2003); Seyla Benhabib, *Another Cosmopolitanism* (Oxford: Oxford University Press, 2006); Jürgen Habermas, *The Inclusion of the Other* (Cambridge: MIT Press, 1998); Martha Nussbaum, "Veiled Threats?" *New York Times*, 11 July 2010; John Rawls, *Political Liberalism* (New York: Columbia University Press, 2005); and Charles Taylor, *Modern Social Imaginaries* (Durham, NC: Duke University Press, 2004).

6. John R. Bowen, *Why the French Don't Like Headscarves* (Princeton, NJ: Princeton University Press, 2007), 15. Bowen cites a conversation with the French philosopher Blandine Kriegel for this description.

7. Joan Wallach Scott, *The Politics of the Veil* (Princeton, NJ: Princeton University Press, 2007).

8. Laura Barnett, *Freedom of Religion and Religious Symbols in the Public Sphere*, Library of Parliament (Ottawa, ON: Parliament of Canada, 2008), 21.

9. Alvin Rabushka and Kenneth A. Shepsle, *Politics in Plural Societies: A Theory of Democratic Instability* (Columbus, OH: Merrill, 1972).

10. Rawls, *Political Liberalism*, xxv.

11. See Jonathan Laurence, *The Emancipation of Europe's Muslims: The State's Role in Minority Integration* (Princeton, NJ: Princeton University Press, 2012).

12. Ernst H. Kantorowicz, *The King's Two Bodies: A Study in Mediaeval Political Theology* (Princeton, NJ: Princeton University Press, 1957).

13. See John Boli, "Human Rights or State Expansion? Cross-National Definitions of Constitutional Rights, 1870–1970," in *Global Human Rights*, ed. Ved P. Nanda, James Scarritt, and George W. Shepard Jr. (Boulder, CO: Westview Press, 1981), 173–93.

14. Seyla Benhabib, *The Claims of Culture: Equality and Diversity in the Global Era* (Princeton, NJ: Princeton University Press, 2002), 94.

15. Patrick Wintour, "David Cameron Tells Muslim Britain: Stop Tolerating Extremists," *Guardian*, 4 February 2011.

16. Interestingly, while there was a significant drop between the generations in the UK regarding support of the niqab, there was a slight increase in France between the generations.

17. While 59% of British Muslims strongly or somewhat agree their government is hostile, this is the case for only 51% of French Muslims. However, if we take just the category of "strongly agree" that their government is hostile, the French Muslims are 26% in the affirmative to the British Muslims' 20%. So the French responses are more bifurcated than the British but with a heavy weighting toward rejecting the notion that the French government is hostile, as reflected in the 40% "strongly disagree" figure.

18. See discussion in Omri Nasri, *Inside the Jihad: My Life with Al Qaeda* (New York: Basic Books, 2006); and Melanie Phillips, *Londonistan* (London: Encounter Books, 2006).

19. See data on www.OfVirginsandMartyrs.com and "Huit Présumés 'Islamo-gangsters' face à la justice," *LeMonde*, 3 January 2011.

20. See Alison Pargeter, *The New Frontiers of the Jihad: Radical Islam in Europe* (Philadelphia: University of Pennsylvania Press, 2008), 140–65.

21. Ibid., 151, quoted from "Inside the Breeding Ground of Fanatics," *Sunday Herald*, 17 July 2005.

22. Both the percentage of UK foreign-born and the Tribalism Index are significant to .000 as predictors of number of terrorist incidents on UK soil. An increase from 0 to 1 on the Tribalism Index means 4 more incidents of violence from nationals of that country, controlling for percentage of immigrant population to Britain that come from the country. An increase of one percent in immigrant population from a country implies one additional violent incident. These two variables have an R-squared of .27, so they explain 27% of the variance in UK Islamist violence.

23. Pargeter, *New Frontiers*, 77–97.

24. Ibid.

25. Bernard Godard and Sylvie Taussig, *Les Musulmans en France: Courants, Institutions, Communautés: Un état des Lieux* (Paris: Hachette, 2009), 223.

26. N.A., "Study Shows 'Demonization' of Muslims," *Guardian*, 14 November 2007.

27. Daniel Nilsson DeHanas, "Believing Citizens: Religion and Civic Engagement among London's Second Generation Youth" (Ph.D. diss., University of North Carolina at Chapel Hill, 2010).

28. What can be out of the ordinary in this instance in bridging different social worlds is that the struggle is not just one of "self-definition." It is also about the felt character of the self. The second generation finds itself, in many cases, navigating ideas of "self- ownership" vis-à-vis the notion of communal obligation. Ed Husain, who was an Islamist in his late teens and early twenties but then turned against Islamist ideology, later described the paradoxical experience, from a radical perspective: "In private I was a free thinker. Among Islamists I was a 'brother.' I was not to dispute our unquestioned perceptions: hatred of Jews, Hindus, Americans, gays, [and] the subordination of women. I still had two faces, two personalities. . . . I switched off my critical faculties and accepted the religious and political assumptions that were dominant [among the brothers]." Husain, *The Islamist: Why I Joined Radical Islam in Britain, What I Saw and Why I Left* (London: Penguin Books, 2007), 171.

29. Often, however, the actual knowledge of Islamic jurisprudence of individuals who think in these terms can actually be quite thin.

30. But the Tablighi are drawn into political give and take. A case in point is the controversy in London over the Mega Mosque, a Tablighi project planned as a mosque that would accommodate 12,000 worshippers. It has been bitterly opposed by, among others, residents in the area. The Tablighi had to engage in the politics that consequently developed. See Daniel Nilsson DeHanas and Zacharias P. Pieri, "Olympic Proportions: The Expanding Scalar Politics of the London 'Olympics Mega-Mosque' Controversy," *Sociology* 45, no. 5 (2011): 798–814.

31. Some scholars argue otherwise, and claim that such groups should be viewed as akin to Christian Democrats in Europe. See, for example, John Esposito, *The Future of Islam* (Oxford: Oxford University Press, 2010).

32. Jocelyne Cesari, "Muslim Identities in Europe: The Snare of Exceptionalism," in *Islam in Europe: Diversity, Identity, and Influence,* ed. Aziz Al-Azmeh and Effie Fokas (Cambridge: Cambridge University Press, 2007). I take the term "body symbolism" from Werner Schiffauer, "From Exile to Diaspora," in *Islam in Europe*, ed. Al-Azmeh and Fokas, 84.

Conclusion

1. On the German case, see Steffen Kröhnert and Reiner Klingholz, *Not Am Mann: Von Helden der Arbeit zur neuen Unterschicht?* (Berlin: Berlin-Institut für Bevolkerung und Entwicklung, 2010). On Russia, see BBC, "Privatization 'Raised Death Rate,'" *BBC News*, 15 January 2009, http://news.bbc.co.uk/2/hi/health/7828901.stm.

2. Ghanaians suggested to me, at once jokingly and seriously, that men were more likely than women to use the money for alcohol or harbor grandiose ideas of starting a multinational corporation in Dubai.

3. An article by a single woman asking rhetorically why she should marry when "men are falling apart" drew enormous attention and an offer materialized to turn the theme into a television series. See Kate Bollick, "What, Me Marry? In Today's Economy, Men Are Falling Apart. What That Means for Sex and Marriage," *Atlantic Monthly*, November 2011, 116–36.

4. Yaroslav Trofimov, "Brutal Attack in India Shows How Caste System Lives On," *Wall Street Journal*, 27 December 2007, A1.

5. Lydia Polgreen, "Rapes of Women Show Clash of Old and New India," *New York Times*, 26 March 2011.

6. Ibid. The India scholar Subrata Mitra of the University of Heidelberg suggested to me in this light the more prominent and celebrated role of women in the East in India: "The East is the home of the cult of the Goddess and the bhakti cult—strains of Hinduism which carry a different connotation of the feminine, seen as power (*shakti*) or piety and sublimation as in the cult of Krishna" (personal communication, March 28, 2011). See also Veena Das, *Life and Words: Violence and the Descent into the Ordinary* (Berkeley: University of California Press, 2007). I am grateful to Radu Carciumaru for bringing my attention to this book.

7. The phrase *cherchez la femme* is commonly attributed to Alexandre Dumas (père) in the 1854 novel *Les Mohicans de Paris*.

8. In the commissioned Abt SRBI survey, the respondents were asked how Sharia should fit into the legal system. Of the Muslim respondents in the UK, France, and Germany, 22% indicated they saw Sharia as a guide to moral behavior and it should not be enforceable law; 30% responded that Sharia should be the only source of law; 24% said that it should be the main source of law; and 11% said it should be one of many sources of law.

9. Tariq Ramadan, the prominent Muslim philosopher and grandson of the founder of the Muslim Brotherhood Hassan al-Banna, claims to have articulated such a civic Islam. But he is viewed with deep suspicion, especially in France. The writings by and on Tariq Ramadan are considerable. For his own work, see, e.g., *Western Muslims and the Future of Islam* (Oxford: Oxford University Press, 2004). For an overview of the debate on Ramadan, from a critical perspective, see Paul Berman, *The Flight of the Intellectuals* (New York: Melville House, 2010).

10. Ibn-Khaldun, *The Muqaddimah: An Introduction to History*, translated from Arabic by Franz Rosenthal (New York: Pantheon Books, 1958), 152.

11. Melissa Maerz, "Lara Logan Breaks Her Silence on '60 Minutes': 'They Raped Me with their Hands,'" *Los Angeles Times*, 2 May 2011.

12. David Ignatius, "How bin Laden Is Winning," *Washington Post*, 29 April 2012, A19.

13. Olivier Roy, "The New Islamists," *Foreign Policy*, 16 April 2012.

NOTABLE FIGURES

Muhammad (circa 560–632): Messenger of God, believers' hold, to whom the Qur'an was revealed.

Abd al-Rahman ibn Muhammad Ibn Khaldun (1332–1406): Muslim historian and sociologist regarded as one the most influential social historians of the medieval period. Developed the concept of *asabiyya* (social bonding and solidarity) and authored numerous books including the *Muqaddimah* and *Kitab al-Ibar*.

Muhammad ibn Abd al-Wahhab (1703–1792): Muslim reformer credited with founding Wahhabism and who later gained political support for his religious positions from Muhammad ibn Saud, considered the founder of the Saudi dynasty. His teachings are outlined in his book *Kitab al-Tawhid* (Book of Monotheism).

Ayatollah Ruhollah Khomeini (1902–1989): Leader of the Iranian revolution of 1979 that deposed the Shah of Iran.

Mawlana Sayyid Abu al-Ala Mawdudi (1903–1979): Founder of Muslim activist and political movement Jamaat-i-Islami, which spread a revivalist vision of Islam steeped in tradition, and a major figure in Pakistani politics.

Hassan al-Banna (1906–1949): Muslim reformer who founded the Muslim Brotherhood in 1929 in Egypt. A school teacher and imam, he was assassinated in 1949 by Egyptian authorities, who were wary of his political activities.

Sayyid Qutb (1906–1966): Activist and leader of the Muslim Brotherhood in Egypt. Regarded by many as being the key ideologue of the Muslim fundamentalist movement whose work still inspires extremist thought. Accused of attempting to overthrow the Egyptian state, he was executed by hanging.

Gamal Abdel Nasser (1918–1970): Led a military coup in Egypt in 1952 against King Farouk and was subsequently elected president. A major figure of Arab nationalism.

TERMS

Abaya: Arabic term for a loose, usually black, robe that covers a woman from head to toe; traditionally worn by some Muslim women.

Allah: Arabic term for God, usually associated with Islam.

Apostasy: Willful rejection or abandonment of one's religious beliefs or faith.

Balto: Narrow garment, usually all black, worn like a raincoat over clothing, sometimes worn with a belt.

Bid'a: A term indicating for Muslim scholars *innovation*, signifying the introduction of something new into the practice of Islam for which there is no precedent. The term in a religious context often has a negative connotation.

Burqa: Loose, all-encompassing garment, usually with veiled holes for the eyes, worn by some Muslim women.

Caliph (khalifa): Successors to the Prophet who led the Muslim community after the Prophet's death.

Caliphate (khilafat): The dominion and territory of the Caliph.

Companions of the Prophet, or **Sahaba:** Those who were close to the Prophet during his lifetime and therefore were considered historically significant figures.

Dar al-Islam (House of Islam): Territory and regions under Muslim rule, and where Muslims can freely practice their religion.

Da'wa (invitation or call): A term generally understood by Muslims to refer to teaching, preaching, and inviting to Islam.

Din: Term used in the Qur'an that has come to signify the notion of the path of divine direction and obligation.

Fatwa: Non-binding religious and legal opinion rendered by Muslim scholars who are regarded as having the appropriate status and training.

Fiqh: Islamic jurisprudence, a complement to Sharia Islamic Law, with evolving rulings or interpretations by Islamic jurists.

Fitna: Denotes periods of secession, upheaval, and chaos; sometimes referred to as civil war.

Fundamentalism: Idea commonly applied to religious traditions, including Islam, where the constant fundamentals of belief and practice are emphasized in response to changes in society and modern times.

Hadith: The sayings and actions of the Prophet Muhammad collected after the Prophet's death by Muslim scholars.

Hajj: The annual pilgrimage to the Ka'ba in Mecca during the last month of the Muslim calendar; it is one of the five pillars of Islam.

Halal: Term in the Qur'an that refers to that which is lawful or allowed; in particular, it is used to describe permitted forms of food and drink.

Harim: Living quarters for women in a traditional Muslim home.

Hijab: Head covering or modest clothing traditionally worn by Muslim women.

Hijra: The migration of the Prophet and his follower from Mecca to Medina in 622.

Ijma: Consensus of learned religious scholars and jurists at any given time; one of the foundations of Sunni legal theory and law.

Ijtihad, or Mujtahid: Concept of exercising rational independent judgment over legal or theological questions. One who practices ijtihad is called a mujtahid and must be knowledgeable on the sources for religious and legal issues.

Imam: A spiritual and religious leader. For Shias, a descendant of Muhammad, divinely appointed to guide Muslims.

Islamic Banking: Created to respond to the need for interest-free banking, these financial institutions lend money to borrowers and become partners sharing all associated risks and profit.

Islamist: Term generally used for Muslim individuals and groups seeking to enforce ideological views of Islam on political and social life of society.

Jahiliyya: Term used to describe the period of ignorance before the coming Islam.

Jihad: Term generally understood to mean struggle for just and divine order in society. Among some Muslims there is greater distinction given to the greater jihad, inner struggle, and the lesser jihad, war and defense, but there is variation in the interpretation of this term.

Jihadist: Literally, one who undertakes jihad in any of its forms, but generally understood as one who undertake violent or military action on behalf of Islam.

Jinn: Term in the Qur'an that refers to beings who are invisible and yet possess great power for good and evil.

Ka'ba: The most important sanctuary in Islam, a structure located in the center of the Great Mosque in Mecca.

Karbala: Pilgrimage location in Iraq for Shias and site of the martyrdom of the grandson of the Prophet, Husayn Ibn Ali, in the year 680.

Khawarij, or Kharijis: Early Muslim group that chose to leave the recognized Muslim community because of doctrinal disagreements with the Caliph. The group expressed their opposition through violence and militant means.

Kafir (*Kufr*): Term generally understood to mean unbeliever, apostate, or atheist, an individual accused of *kufr* is known as a *kafir*.

Madrasa: Muslim institution of legal and theological learning, also sometimes used to denote regular schools that provide religious training.

Majlis: Gathering of tribal elders for religious, scholarly, or political purposes.

Martyrdom: Term in the Qur'an that refers to those who die in the way of God and promises reward for their struggle and sacrifice.

Masjid, or **Mosque:** Place for prayer in Islam.

Mecca, or **Makkah:** Birthplace of the Prophet and site of the Ka'ba and the annual hajj.

Medina, or **al-Madina:** City in modern day Saudi Arabia to which the Prophet migrated in 622, an action known as the hijra.

Modernist Muslim Thought: Thought in Islam that seeks to address modernization and changes in society.

Mufti: Recognized Islamic authority of matters of law and practice.

Muhajir, or **Mujahidin:** Term first used to describe those who migrated with the Prophet to Medina but has grown to encompass more modern Muslim migrants and those who travel for the cause of jihad.

Mulla: Persian variation of the Arabic honorific for master, usually reserved for religious scholars.

Nikah: Term understood as the practice of marriage.

Niqab: Veil worn by some Muslim women in public, covering all of the face except for the eyes.

Orientalism: Western scholarship focus on the study of the Orient and the East; more broadly, a critique targeting Western scholarship on the claim that it is marked by simplified and prejudicial views of Arab and Islamic peoples and their culture.

Pesantren: Educational centers and boarding schools in Indonesia and Malaysia.

Pilgrimage: In Islam, the practice of the annual hajj to Mecca.

Post-colonial: Period immediately after independence from colonial powers.

Prayer: One of the five pillars of Islam, known as salat.

Purdah: The practice in which women are hidden from men or strangers by means of a screen of some kind, or in all-enveloping clothes.

Quraysh: The dominant tribe of Mecca on the emergence of Islam. It was the tribe to which the Prophet Muhammad belonged.

Ramadan: Ninth month of the Muslim calendar marking the period of fasting.

Salaf: The early Muslims of the first three eras, or generations: the Companions of the Prophet, Successors, and their successors.

Salafi: A follower of an Islamic movement that takes the *Salaf* of the period of early Islam as exemplary models. The *Salaf* are collectively referred to as the Companions of the Prophet, namely the members of the first three Muslim generations.

Salat: Understood as prayer or worship, the ritual prayer for Muslims, performed five times daily in a set form.

Sawm: The act of fasting (primarily during the month of Ramadan); Muslims abstain from food and drink and gambling and all sensuous pleasures from sunrise to sunset during Ramadan. One of the five pillars of Islam.

Schools of Islamic Law (madhhab): Process of systematizing and codifying Islamic law by successive generations of Muslim scholars.

Shah: Title primarily used for Persian rulers until recent times.

Shahada: The affirmation of faith in Islam, the first, and arguably the most important, of the five pillars of Islam.

Shahid: Term literally meaning witness but generally used to denote those who die while striving for the cause of Islam, or martyrs.

Sharia: Commonly understood as Islamic law, Sharia stems from the Qur'an and the sunnah, or practice of Muhammad, which in turn is based on God's word and on scholarly consensus and analogy.

Shaykh: Title of respect for the leader of a group or elder.

Shura: Qur'anic concept of consultation.

Sira: A life narrative, particularly applied to the life of the Prophet.

Sunnah: Refers to the practice of Prophet Muhammad, from his teaching and his exemplary acts. Sunnah is one component informing Sharia.

Sura: Term denoting a chapter in the Qur'an.

Tafsir: Explanation or interpretation of Qur'anic verses.

Tajwid: The art of Qur'anic recitation.

Takfir or Takfiri: In Islamic law, takfir refers to the practice of one Muslim declaring another Muslim an unbeliever or kafir, or an apostate.

Tawhid: Term meaning monotheism; it is the first part of the *Shahada*.

Ulama: Muslim religious scholars.

Ummah: Term used to denote the global Muslim community.

Wahhabism: A religious movement in Sunni Islam. It was founded in the eighteenth century by Muhammad ibn Abd al-Wahhab from what today is Saudi Arabia.

Zakat: Giving a portion of one's wealth based on a percentage of one's income as charity; one of the five pillars of Islam.

GROUPS/ORGANIZATIONS

Abbasids: Muslim dynasty that succeeded the Umayyad dynasty and ruled from approximately 750–1258. Founded and ruled from the capital city of Baghdad, it claimed power as the descendents of the Prophet Muhammad's uncle, al-Abbas.

Al Qaeda: Extremist organization founded by Abdullah Azzam and Osama bin Laden that has been responsible for numerous deadly terrorist attacks on both Muslims and non-Muslims.

Armed Islamic Group, or **GIA** (from the French, Groupe Islamique Armé): A militant Islamist group seeking to overthrow the Algerian government and to establish an Islamic state.

Hizb al-Tahrir, or **Hizb al-Tahrir al-Islami** (Islamic Liberation Party): Islamist organization that started in Jerusalem during the early 1950s as a political party aiming to establish an Islamic state.

Hizbullah: Shia Muslim group founded as a political party in Iran during the revolution that has spread to Lebanon and is designated a terrorist organization by the United States and other Western governments.

Islamic Salvation Front, or **FIS** (from the French, Front Islamique du Salut): Algerian Islamist political party established as an alternative to the failed economic and social policies in Algeria. When the party seemed to be on the brink of winning a victory in 1990, a coup instilled a military regime and disbanded the FIS. The Armed Islamic Group (GIA) emerged subsequently.

Muslim Brotherhood: Muslim reformist and Islamist movement and political party in Egypt, Jordan, and other Arab states, with other representatives across the world. One of the largest Islamist movements, it was founded in 1928 by Hassan al-Banna.

Muslim League: Originally founded in 1906 as the All-India Muslim League, which under the leadership of Muhammad Ali Jinnah advocated for the state of Pakistan and led the country through its early development.

Ottoman Empire: The last of the Muslim empires. It spread from Asia Minor beginning about 1300 and ending in 1923 with the establishment of the Republic of Turkey. At its height, in the sixteenth and seventeenth centuries, it controlled the territory Southeastern Europe, Southwestern Asia, and North Africa.

Tablighi Jamat: Muslim movement founded in India circa 1928 by Mawlana Muhammad Ilyas to teach and spread Islam in India and globally, with a spiritual, non-political focus